SHRINK

A CULTURAL HISTORY OF

SHRINK

PSYCHOANALYSIS IN AMERICA

LAWRENCE R. SAMUEL

University of Nebraska Press | Lincoln and London

Library of Congress Cataloging-in-Publication Data
Samuel, Lawrence R.
Shrink : a cultural history of psychoanalysis in
America / Lawrence R. Samuel.
p. cm.
Includes bibliographical references.
ISBN 978-0-8032-4476-4 (cloth : alk. paper)
1. Psychoanalysis—United States—History. I. Title.
BF173.S2793 2013
150.19'50973—dc23   2012038314

Set in Sabon Next LT Pro by Laura Wellington.
Designed by A. Shahan.

Canst thou not minister to a mind diseased,
Pluck from the memory a rooted sorrow,
Raze out the written troubles of the brain,
And with some sweet oblivious antidote
Cleanse the stuff'd bosom of that perilous stuff
Which weighs upon the heart?

MACBETH 5.3.43–48

CONTENTS

INTRODUCTION

Who in the world am I? Ah, that's the great puzzle!

ALICE, in Lewis Carroll's *Alice in Wonderland*

"Give your faves phone envy," reads a recent headline of an ad for T-
Mobile, an homage to the more anatomical concept originated by one
Sigmund Freud more than a century ago. Freud and his "systemized,
scientific working hypothesis about human behavior," as Gregory Zilboorg described psychoanalysis in 1949, are very much with us today in
one way or another as the T-Mobile ad suggests, deeply embedded in
the discourse of American popular and consumer culture. "Psychoanalysis and its ideas about the unconscious mind have spread to every nook
and cranny of the culture from Salinger to *South Park*, from Fellini to
foreign policy," wrote Patricia Cohen of the *New York Times*. Almost
sixty years after Zilboorg, the topic is seemingly everywhere, despite its
current relatively minor presence as a therapy.[1] Even as classic psychoanalysis—the psychological theory and method developed by Freud
based on the ideas that mental life functions on both conscious and
unconscious levels and that childhood events have a powerful influence
throughout life—became just a bit player on the nation's therapeutic
stage, its presence in American culture continued to grow to the point
where we now accept it as one of the seminal ways to explain human
nature. We've all been "shrunk," it could safely be said, whether or not
we have actually spent time on the couch.

Shrink: A Cultural History of Psychoanalysis in America tells how and
why this came to be, focusing not on the technical details of the field
but on the major role psychoanalysis has played in the United States
since it became a cultural phenomenon immediately after World War

I. The goal of this book is thus not to retrace the seemingly endless ideological debates within the field or outside of it, as many books have done very well, but rather to locate the trajectory of psychoanalysis within American cultural history for scholars, students, professionals, and general readers alike. As a cultural historian (rather than psychologist or scientist), my interest, and I believe that of many readers, resides principally in using incredibly rich subjects like psychoanalysis in order to get a better understanding of what makes America and Americans tick. While literally hundreds of books have been written about some aspect of psychoanalysis, it is difficult if not impossible to find an accessible, nontechnical history of the subject. As a descriptive narrative of the public image of and interest in psychoanalysis rather than an intellectual or institutional history, *Shrink* tracks the waxing and waning of the field, that is, whether it was trending up or down over the past ninety years. By offering insight into the popular discourse around psychoanalysis throughout its American career, we gain a very good idea of how Freud's ideas about and approaches to the treatment of mental and emotional illnesses were put in play, something I believe is much more valuable than another analytical, systematic treatise on the subject. What follows is thus largely an attempt to fill this Grand Canyon–sized gap in our literary landscape.

With a deep appreciation for Freud's contribution to our understanding of human behavior, I have tried nonetheless to tell a "fair and balanced" story through the accounts of both advocates and critics of psychoanalysis. Even its harshest critics acknowledge that psychoanalysis has a certain magic and amazing staying power, our curiosity still piqued as the debate over its legitimacy continues to simmer. My interest in writing this book sprang out of writing a previous one called *Freud on Madison Avenue*, in which I investigated the history of motivation research and subliminal advertising in America. Having caught the psychoanalytic bug (motivation research was based on Freudian and other psychological theories), I felt that a full study of the phenomenon in the United States was very much needed. Rather than follow the revisionist history vogue of proposing some new and shocking revelation to turn the field upside down, my intent is more to determine the degree to which psychoanalysis shaped our me-based, self-absorbed culture. Too many top-down histories of psychoanalysis by mental health experts have been written, I believe, and only a bottom-up approach from an outsider's perspective is able to capture the broader significance and implications of the field. And instead of relying on arcane, largely picked-over materials tucked away in musty boxes of archives, this story makes use of popular sources, as a cultural history should. If you are mostly interested in the intricacies of dream interpretation, the Oedipal conflict, or some other Freudian theory, there is no shortage of excellent books and information-filled websites to take you down these paths.

What in American culture fostered and favored our "primitivist" rush to Freud? With our love for all things modern, ambivalent feelings about sex, pronounced streak of individualism, and entitlement to happiness, it should hardly be surprising that psychoanalysis found an ideal climate in which to flourish here. Focused on the unconscious, psychoanalysis was "a new, virgin territory, an interior frontier," Philip Cushman, author of *Constructing the Self, Constructing America*, has observed; in effect, the method conveniently arrived soon after Frederick Jackson Turner's 1893 declaration that the nation's western frontier was officially closed.[2] The vivid reminder that we were animals, not machines, certainly had something to do with it, the theory's focus on our more primal nature a welcome relief from the overt rationalism, order, and efficiency of the times. The idea that we were the slaves of basic human drives like sex and hunger was controversial enough, but Freud's concept of the "death drive" (conceived in the context of the emotional wounding of soldiers in World War I) made psychoanalysis especially intriguing territory. Its primary promise—an inside peek into the dark and mysterious world of the mind, justified as an opportunity for personal growth and awareness—was simply too tantalizing a proposition for many Americans to resist, even though the method was never intended to be a therapy for the masses. The sheer danger of psychoanalysis—that one was possibly playing with things people could not and should not understand—was itself one of its key draws. Seductive as a forbidden fruit, psychoanalytic thought quickly became firmly embedded in the nation's cultural firmament, fast becoming an integral part of who we are as a people. Despite now accounting for only a fraction of today's therapy marketplace, psychoanalysis remains an essential and likely permanent strain in our DNA, and a valuable lens by which to view the American idea and experience.

Likewise, psychoanalysis was much transformed in America by Americans, the nation's social landscape significantly altering the trajectory of the field. Eli Zaretsky has noted the substantive difference between the way psychoanalytic theory and treatment was received in Europe versus the United States, a perfect example of the contrasting ways of the Old World with those of the new. Psychoanalysis "emerged *against* an older, traditional, patriarchal order" in Europe through World War II, he observed, while it "became a method of cure and self-improvement" in America because of a less rigid society. As well, with their can-do spirit, Americans firmly believed they could solve personal problems, preferably on their own but open to some help if necessary. While Freud's influence in the United States is undeniable, "the spirit of America has also infused psychoanalysis with an optimistic and pragmatic spirit that has in many ways transformed it," agreed Cushman. Americans, he believed, had reoriented the field toward personal improvement and productivity.[3] While marginalized in Europe, psychoanalysis was thus absorbed into the United States, largely limited to intellectuals and elites in the former but perfectly positioned to grow into a mass phenomenon in the latter. The fact that psychoanalysis did not have to confront and challenge a deeply rooted psychiatric community in America as it did in Europe also played a key role in its rapid development in the States, with medical schools receptive to new methods of and techniques in mental healing. "American psychoanalysis rode the wave of professionalization, scientism, and the growth of a mass culture characteristic of the second industrial revolution," Zaretsky concluded. The field benefitted from physicians' desire to put amateurs practicing quasi-psychological techniques like mesmerism, homeopathy, and various other "mind cures" out of business for good.[4]

The biggest factor reshaping European-style psychoanalysis was, without a doubt, American "ego psychology." Developed between the two world wars as "an investigation of unconscious defenses against instinctual drives," as Nathan G. Hale Jr. described it, ego psychology recognized that, through mechanisms of control such as morality and intelligence, individuals could and did sublimate (or at least postpone) aggressive behavior. Although it deviated from classic, conflict-oriented psychoanalysis, such an approach was perfect for the national temperament, accommodating the central mythology that Americans were an enlightened, superior, and even chosen people. As well, success and social acceptance relied on controlling instinctual drives, making ego psychology particularly appealing in the keep-up-with-the-Joneses 1950s.[5] After flourishing during the postwar years, ego psychology (like psychoanalysis itself) waned, a victim of competitive theories and modes of therapy.[6] That Freud's theories had taken a different turn in America with ego psychology was almost beside the point, the phenomenon itself bigger than its particular principles or philosophy. "The actual practice of analysis was less important than its cultural impact," Zaretsky declared, concisely expressing the most amazing part of the story.[7]

Because psychoanalysis (along with psychology—the scientific study of the human mind and mental states—and psychiatry, the medical specialty concerned with the diagnosis and treatment of disorders associated with mental or behavioral symptoms) is so thoroughly woven into our national quilt, telling its story means intersecting with a number of topics central to the American experience. Psychoanalysis has always had an uneasy relationship with science. Researchers trained in using systematic observation and experiments to study the physical world are often skeptical about the methods and claims of psychoanalysis. Religion too has bumped directly into the path of psychoanalysis, the devout viewing the upstart field as a worthy contender for the individual's mind, if not his or her soul. Education and business, on the other hand, have for the most part been allies with psychoanalysis, with large institutions interested in identifying perceived threats to the "norm." For those in the arts and literature, psychoanalysis opened up a whole new way to interpret texts, with the inner, darker recesses of the mind seen as a wellspring of creativity. Psychoanalysis redirected the trajectory of these and other dimensions of everyday life, reshaping American culture (and Americans) in the process and becoming a key signifier of our national identity. "Psychoanalysis permanently transformed the ways in which ordinary men and women throughout the world understand themselves and one another," Zaretsky noted, describing the method as "the first great theory and practice of 'personal life.'"[8]

Of course, the central component of psychoanalysis is identity, or the self, and so I will argue that it is no coincidence that psychoanalysis found a receptive home in the United States in the 1920s—the period during which the modern idea of the self was born. Psychoanalysis in America "was caught up in a process that emphasized personal empowerment, self-regulation, and individual charisma," Zaretsky thought, drawing on the nation's profound sense of self. Mental healing was a big part of this, the religious movements of the nineteenth century paving the way for subsequent philosophies promising some kind of spiritual or psychic betterment. The Boston-based Emmanuel Movement, advocating a psychological approach to religious healing, reached its apex of popularity shortly before Freud came to Clark University in 1909; the quasi-religious group consisted of both ministers and doctors offering its members a sort of proto-psychotherapy. The pump was thus very much primed for the appearance of Freud's writings around the turn of the century, with psychoanalysis viewed as the next (and, importantly, more scientific) generation of "mind cures."[9]

Throughout the rest of the twentieth century and into the twenty-first, psychoanalysis has run on a parallel course with the rise of the self, the field both shaping and reflecting the ascent of individualism in American society (for better and worse). As both a theory and therapy, psychoanalysis served as a primary catalyst for Americans to discover their inner selves in order to fully realize (or complete) their personal identities. The possibility to "know thyself" by exploring conflicts, feelings, and dreams became recognized as perhaps the ultimate achievement in Western and, especially, American culture. This was true whether one was actually in treatment or not, our psychological society encouraging, if not demanding, the formation of one's "true" self. From the early 1920s through the early 1960s, psychoanalysis helped to reprogram the American mind by shifting our orientation from civic interests to personal ones in all spheres of everyday life. Psychoanalysis in all its many forms has thus been a major factor in the development of the "cult of the self," undoubtedly one of the biggest stories over the past century. While discovering and expressing one's true identity has allowed many to find fulfillment and live rewarding lives, it is clear that we are now paying a heavy price for our wholesale rush to the self. Alienated from society, the American of the twentieth century became an "empty self," according to Cushman, more likely to find fulfillment in consumerism than anywhere else.[10]

As the original, purest, and most intense form of psychotherapy, psychoanalysis played a major role in seeding the rise of our me-based culture. "It's All About Me" is not just a funny phrase seen on t-shirts worn by Paris Hilton types; rather, it is an anthem for our times in which individualism—and its evil twin, narcissism—rule. "It was on the couch that we boomers learned to boom, that the Me Decade perfected its self-absorption, and that we grew into adults obsessed with childhood," Susan Cheever wrote in 1995 for *Harper's Bazaar*, having herself started therapy when she was eleven years old. "We turned to psychiatry for everything once provided by religion, community, and parents who knew what they were doing," she continued, seeing her parade of shrinks as "more like teachers than teachers, more like priests than priests, more like parents than parents."[11] Cheever's experience was emblematic of what Nancy Schnog described in 1997 as "inventing the psychological," a reorienting of the ways in which many Americans conceived their inner selves. "Since at least the 1920s middle-class Americans have been educated into understandings of self and psyche shaped by mainstream concepts of psychoanalytic thought," she wrote. Freud's core ideas—repression, resistance, the centrality of sexuality, the Oedipus complex, and transference—made the nation psychology minded, both figuratively and literally.[12]

Don't blame Freud for our me-first, egocentric, self-obsessed culture, however. A host of criteria—a certain type of personality, a particular kind of problem, a considerable amount of intelligence, and, perhaps most important, lots of time and money—was used to screen candidates for analysis by most practitioners, thereby limiting the number of people who qualified for treatment. The founder of psychoanalysis may have started it all with his theory and therapy centered on the self, but it was what followed that helped turn America into the shamelessly narcissistic society we are today. Although it was probably inevitable, I suggest that the transformation and expansion of America's psychiatric landscape beginning in the mid-1960s was an unfortunate development. These quicker, cheaper therapies were responsible for turning our interest in ourselves into an obsession. Psychoanalysis often did not work (the one-third "cured," one-third "improved," one-third "failed" rule was probably about right), but when it did, it worked wonders. Its practitioners argued that only an intensive course of therapy was able to resolve deep-seated neuroses buried in the unconscious. Over time, as their patients migrated to competitive treatments and psychotropic medication, psychoanalysts repeatedly made this point, but few listened. The appeal of so-called McTherapies and drugs (typically covered by health insurance) was not just powerful but irresistible. In his now classic *The Culture of Narcissism*, Christopher Lasch described the "therapeutic sensibility" that emerged in the 1970s, with "personal preoccupations" and "psychic self-improvement" the centerpiece of the awareness or consciousness movement that swept across the country. (Lasch echoed and expanded many of the themes in Tom Wolfe's equally iconic 1976 *New York Magazine* article "The 'Me' Decade and the Third Great Awakening.") The rash of new therapies (reaching into the hundreds) was a big part of what Lasch referred to as "the social invasion of the self," with the resulting "narcissistic personality of our time" a predictable and unfortunate consequence.[13]

Today we hardly notice the narcissism all around us, our reliance on life coaches, infinitely refillable prescriptions of antidepressants, the billion-dollar self-help business, and the relentless pursuit of meaning and purpose in life all reflective of a quick-fix approach to emotional well-being. Applying Band-Aids to those having serious wounds has done more damage than good, I believe; the covering up and superficial triage of traumas experienced in childhood or later in life has actually made us less content and secure people. Our expectations of happiness have risen in direct proportion to our inability to fulfill them, this existential two-ships-passing-in-the-night accounting for the generally sorry emotional state of affairs in the United States in the early twenty-first century. Look anywhere and everywhere—Facebook, blogs, Twitter, *American Idol*, Guitar Hero—and you will see not just a desire but a desperate need to be heard and valued. "Not only are there more narcissists than ever, but non-narcissistic people are seduced by the increasing emphasis on material wealth, physical appearance, celebrity worship, and attention seeking," observed Jean M. Twenge and W. Keith Campbell in their 2009 *The Narcissism Epidemic*. The two psychologists found that our obsession with ourselves has become a scourge in the thirty years since Wolfe and Lasch wrote about it.[14] Our "trading up" culture, not to mention pure, unadulterated greed, which not too long ago nearly crashed the entire economic system, are at their roots an urgent plea for some kind of recognition and respect. What we fail to see, and what Freud tried to teach us, this book shows, is that these values can only come from within, a lesson we still have not learned.

The rise of the cult of the self that began in the 1920s was a direct result of psychoanalysis linking itself to American popular culture (and vice versa), something that other historians have underappreciated. Psycho-analysis became a key trope in many avenues of popular culture, includ-ing literature, film, and art, and this alliance with the "creative class" became a primary form of social currency. More important, psycho-analysis entered the vernacular of popular discourse, part of our everyday conversation and way of looking at the world (especially other people). Psychoanalysis was soon no longer just a psychological theory or therapy but a kind of social tool, a huge leap in the field's status and significance. Although it remained largely a therapy that only the upper and upper middle class could afford, in terms of both money and time, the theory behind it trickled down from the American cultural elite—intellectuals, the wealthy, and celebrities—to the middlebrow. Psychoanalysis quickly became part of mass culture as its core ideas crossed social boundaries with reckless abandon, a national pastime rivaling baseball. "Freud's ideas pervade our culture to such an extent that often we use Freudian language—narcissism, sibling rivalry, ambivalence, neurosis—without even realizing it," said Peter Gay in a 1988 interview with *People Magazine*, the source alone suggesting the pervasiveness of Freud's theories.[15]

Although there have been many schools of psychoanalysis over the last century, this book focuses on Freudian analysis, the best-known and most controversial theory and treatment. Through a long and intense "conversation," the patient (while yes, lying on a couch) says whatever comes into his or her mind in Freudian analysis, with thoughts and feelings considered unacceptable in normal settings encouraged. As explained by British psychotherapist Philip Chandler, in a 2008 article in *Psychology Review*, thoughts and feelings of an aggressive or sexual nature are viewed as having their roots in childhood, that crucial time in our lives when we define the boundaries between ourselves and others and determine how to express emotions. Learning how to tolerate frustration, finding a proper balance between "I" and "we," understanding the impact of one's parents as an adult, dealing with depression and anger, and figuring out why one is attracted to the "wrong" boy or girl were and remain common themes in analysis, themes probably not much different from those that regularly surface in other forms of therapy.[16]

Naturally, it is incumbent upon a book called *Shrink* to take a long, hard look at shrinks (short for "headshrinkers," the somewhat derogatory slang term for psychologists, psychiatrists, and especially psychoanalysts) themselves, as without them we have no story at all. Although psychoanalysis was viewed with considerable suspicion in the academic world before World War II (the field was positively despised at universities both here and abroad, particularly in Vienna), subsequently, analysts began to be awarded an almost godlike status in the 1950s. The goateed analyst with notebook and pen in hand quickly became an iconic image in American popular culture. A vague European accent was icing on the cake, and something that allowed those who actually had it—Jewish refugees who had fled the Nazis in the 1930s and after—to charge more.[17] As doctors of the mind, psychoanalysts were assumed to have special, divinely ordained powers, able perhaps to read what was going on in one's dirty little mind. For those actually experiencing the couch, fifty-minute horizontal sessions were a chance to examine one's life and possibly retell it, a "voyage of inward discovery." The typical session with the typical analyst was an intense experience ("right-wing scholasticism," Susan Sontag called it)—the industry's unofficial motto was to "Think Yiddish, Act British." Once viewed as the secular equivalent to one's minister, priest, or rabbi, therapists are now considered more as an essential part of one's "team," an ally or coach with access to the pharmacological wonderland. That a good number of Americans still go on a collective freak-out every August when therapists typically take their holiday speaks to their enduring power and to the relevance of this book.

How did a once marginal, highly suspect treatment seed today's pervasive therapeutic culture? The arc of psychoanalysis, from the shock of the new to a mature body of knowledge, was without doubt a roller-coaster of highs and lows. With its founder being called everything from "the Columbus of the mind" to "a modern Plato," psychoanalysis began a rapid ascent in the 1920s, soon rivaling baseball as our Great National Pastime. A smart cocktail party of the 1920s would hardly be complete without the requisite psychoanalytic parlor tricks, with amateur shrinks explaining why one chewed gum (obviously oral fixation), guessing one's birth order, and decoding the most innocent slip of the tongue. Psychoanalysis and other forms of psychiatry became aligned with the self-help ("self-knowledge," at the time) movement in the 1930s and 1940s, thereby rounding off some of its sharp edges and broadening its appeal. By the 1950s, the strange and decidedly Jewish practice had become relatively mainstream, the taboos surrounding it (emotionality, vulnerability, sexuality) weakening. (Although Freud was a self-described "completely godless" Jew, Jewish thought—and analysts—pervaded the field he founded.[18]) From its prewar days as a bonbon among the wealthy and intellectual elite, psychoanalysis transformed itself into a populist therapy for a postwar middle class intimately familiar with the concept of repression. But with little need to keep one's id in check starting in the mid-1960s, psychoanalysis began its long slide that continued until the early 1990s. Psychoanalysis has since rebounded somewhat, its place now within the psychiatric community and society at large a relatively secure one.

Much of the power of psychoanalysis resided in its ability to embed itself in other fields in an almost parasitic manner. Between the wars, Nathan G. Hale Jr. wrote in his *The Rise and Crisis of Psychoanalysis in the United States*, "psychoanalysis functioned as an iconoclastic psychology of intellectual drives," informing modern views of education, social work, and criminology.[19] The impact of émigré analysts in the 1930s and 1940s cannot be overestimated as these hundreds of Europeans (many of whom came from Freud's inner circle or were students of those men and women) enlarged and complicated the field here in the United States. Propelled by three wars as GIs received treatment to heal their mental wounds, psychoanalysis found a happy home in military circles, viewed in its own way as American as apple pie. The notion that the human mind and thus life itself was rich with drama and hidden meanings was embraced by those in the arts and literature; Freud's concept of trauma came in especially handy for critical interpretation of texts going back to Shakespeare. By the time of Freud's death in 1939, the movement had passed the father of the field, as a steady stream of "neos" and "posts" (including his daughter) altered the trajectory of psychoanalysis. Psychoanalysis had by now entered the realm of political discourse, with the lowliest cub reporter weighing in on Hitler's failure as a young artist, Eisenhower's paternalism, Nixon's paranoia streak, Bill Clinton's self-destructive urge, and George W. Bush's need to make his father proud. Almost everything and anyone could be read through the lens of psychoanalysis, it seemed, something deeper and darker lurking underneath the surface.

Many historians and social critics too have plumbed the depths of psychoanalysis over the decades, knowing a good story when they see one. Hale's two-volume history of the subject is nothing less than a tour de force, and C. P. Oberndorf's 1953 *A History of Psychoanalysis in America* was as good as anything written about psychoanalysis up to that point. Paul Roazen's enormous body of work, spread out over more than three decades, is a small library of the field, as is the Psychiatry and the Humanities series published by Johns Hopkins and edited by Joseph H. Smith. Others, notably Peter Gay (focusing on the social impact of psychoanalysis), Philip Rieff (its cultural significance and our therapeutic ethos), Sherry Turkle and Elizabeth Roudinesco (Freud's "French Revolution"), Frederick Crews (a key player in the "Freud wars" of the 1980s and 1990s), Mari Jo Buhle (feminist theory), and Glen Gabbard and Kim Gabbard (portrayal in Hollywood films), have all made significant contributions to the history of the field.

John Burnham has understood the impact and influence of psychoanalysis on American culture perhaps more than anyone else; his writings in the 1970s offer what I believe to be the richest insights into the social dynamics of the field. In a chapter he contributed to *American Psychoanalysis: Origins and Development* in 1978, for example, Burnham saw the history of psychoanalysis in America as divided into two waves, the first coinciding with the flourishing of modernism during the first few decades of the twentieth century and the second with the rise (and subsequent splintering) of mass culture between the 1930s and 1970s.

(The Ohio State history professor did not predict a third wave in which both biotechnology and information technology would revolutionize virtually all aspects of society, including mental health.)[20] And in an article titled "From Avant-Garde to Specialism" published in the *Journal of the History of the Behavioral Sciences* the following year, Burnham showed how, after Freud's much-celebrated visit to Clark University in 1909, proponents of psychoanalysis actively sought to acquaint ordinary Americans with the man's ideas. Although psychoanalysis was attacked by the medical community, Greenwich Village bohemians "welcomed Freudianism along with feminism, socialism, and other isms," as he put it, this sparking interest in the field among the general public. Blessed by the avant-garde, early advocates of psychoanalysis spread the word to the mainstream in the 1920s, popularizing Freud's ideas while considerably diluting them in the process.[21]

By the 1930s, it was not artsy types living unconventional lifestyles but the intellectual elite who served as the principal sponsors of psychoanalysis, Burnham continued. Jewish analysts fleeing the Nazis (the latter considering the field to be a "Jewish science") helped turn the United States (and specifically New York City) into the world capital of psychoanalysis.[22] These refugees were instrumental in transforming the field from an already visible presence to one that was virtually impossible to miss. Permanently imprinted with these ethnic, physical, and linguistic markers, the "analyst" emerged as an identifiable, if not already iconic, figure during the Depression years. He (and, rarely, she) was considered to hold special powers that were even greater than those of the medical doctor. This actually made sense as all analysts at the time were medical doctors who had undertaken years more education and training.[23]

It was the Second World War that pushed psychoanalysis over the top, Burnham and other historians have shown. The method's ability to help heal mentally wounded soldiers was broadly recognized and greatly appreciated by both physicians and the general public. Although Freud's ideas were already well entrenched in the United States between the wars, as Ellen Herman has demonstrated, psychology in general was dramatically advanced during and after World War II, as behavioral scientists shaped political and social policy. "Enveloped in a climate of catastrophic global militarism and divisive national debate over the realization of racial and sexual equality," she wrote in her *The Romance of American Psychology*, "psychological experts shaped the direction and texture of public life deliberately, with results that were striking and unprecedented." The war represented a singular chance for psychologists to prove the practical worth of their theories and techniques, the atmosphere of conflict an invitation for them to work in or become advisers to government. From the war through the Vietnam era, Herman convincingly wrote, psychologists seized this opportunity, with the Cold War and the civil and gender rights movements providing the need for a better understanding of concepts such as the development of personality, formation of attitudes, and power of persuasion. Wielding a new kind of influence, academics and clinicians were thus instrumental in infusing a psychological mindset during the postwar years, with psychoanalysis a key part of this accelerated interest in and commitment to mental health.[24]

Now accepted by the medical establishment, psychoanalysis went on a phenomenal twenty-year run, its success buoyed by being perfect fodder for American popular culture. "Novels about mental illness (*Private Worlds*, *The Crack-Up*, *Brainstorm*, *Snake Pit*, and others) were frequent," Burnham noted, with Hollywood movies also jumping on the bandwagon (*Spellbound*, *All About Eve*, and *Splendor in the Grass*, to name a few). At least three children's books about Freud soon could be had and, more important, psychoanalytic theory showed up in Benjamin Spock's influential work. The psychic well-being of what would turn out to be the largest generation in history was believed by many to be hanging in the balance. "The public acceptance of psychoanalysis/psychiatry mushroomed in that brief moment of expansive optimism of the 1940s when many Americans really did believe that they could make the postwar social environment a significantly better place in which to live," Burnham observed. The country and the world would benefit from Freud's teachings. By the late 1960s, however, it was clear that the great run of psychoanalysis (and arguably the United States) was ending. The field was increasingly viewed as out of touch with the times.[25] In his 2009 *Psychoanalysis at the Margins*, Paul E. Stepansky charted what he termed the "near-demise" of psychoanalysis as a mental health profession.

The fracturing of the field over the past four decades resulted in what he believed to be "less a cohesive profession than a loose federation of psychoanalytic subcommunities."[26]

While the long-standing conflicts between American psychological science and psychoanalysis comprise a book unto itself, it is important to acknowledge this "war," which still rages at some level today.[27] Most psychologists ignored psychoanalysis when it first arrived in the United States, according to Gail A. Hornstein in her 1992 article for *American Psychologist*, "The Return of the Repressed," but that soon became impossible. "By the 1920s," she wrote, "psychoanalysis had so captured the public imagination that it threatened to eclipse experimental psychology entirely," marking the beginnings of what would be a nearly century-long feud. The source of the conflict was the thorny issue of science, specifically how it should be defined with regard to the study of the mind. Psychoanalysts wanted little or nothing to do with the scientific method that psychologists cared so much about, believing that the process itself and the results were enough for their upstart field to qualify as a legitimate science. Psychologists, already sensitive to claims that their own rather new field was less than a true science, compared to biology or even philosophy, found this absurd and began to attack the Freudians and their medical model with increasing intensity. Psychoanalysts defended themselves, (conveniently) pointing out that only those who had personally experienced the process were qualified to evaluate it. The notion that being psychoanalyzed instantly bestowed the title of scientist only made American psychologists that much more incensed for a couple of important reasons. One, it implied that science was subjective rather than objective, the latter requiring publicly verifiable data based on controlled variables, a bold proposition to say the least; and two, it suggested that psychologists were not scientists because they had not laid on the couch, this last point considered even more outrageous and insulting.[28]

Understandably, psychologists defended their field by employing even more stringent scientific standards to further distance themselves from what they generally saw as more of a foreign religion than anything else. In 1934, however, nearly everyone was shocked to learn that Edwin G.

Boring, a leading experimental psychologist at Harvard, had himself entered analysis. Boring explained to his colleagues that he was doing the unthinkable only for research purposes, but the truth was that he was depressed, anxious, and unable to work. After ten months (and 168 sessions at ten dollars apiece), Boring had had enough, his hopes for what he later described as "a new personality" dashed. Still looking five years later for some evidence that his treatment (with Hanns Sachs, who had been part of Freud's inner circle) may have been at least partially effective, Boring proposed to the *Journal of Abnormal and Social Psychology* that it publish the accounts of notable psychologists like himself who had ventured into enemy territory to be analyzed. Perhaps their stories could shed some light on his own disappointing experience, he thought, titling his own contribution, "Was This Analysis a Success?" His answer was, of course, no, his colleagues reporting equally dismal results in their attempts to explore the depths of their unconscious through free association.[29]

Spurred by the special issue of the journal (which quickly sold out), the battle lines between psychology and psychoanalysis were now clearly drawn. More popular than ever, psychoanalysis was viewed by most people as the same thing as psychology or, perhaps, the overarching discipline, when in fact it was the other way around. (I would venture to say that nine of ten Americans even today cannot tell psychoanalysis from psychiatry from psychology.) With two decades plus of criticism not working, psychologists took it upon themselves in the mid-1940s to determine which, if any, psychoanalytic concepts were scientifically valid, this smart move finally turning the tables in the mental health field. Over the next thirty years or so, virtually every psychoanalytic tenet was literally put to the test, with fairly predictable results. According to Hornstein, "Every shred of evidence seeming to support psychoanalysis was scrutinized for methodological flaws, whereas studies opposing the theory were flaunted as examples of good science." The ideological differences between the sister fields were deemed more important than what the findings actually revealed. "Research on psychoanalysis was invigorating because it gave psychologists a sense of mastery," Hornstein added. Freudian theory was now effectively co-opted and safely contained.[30]

Appropriated by mainstream psychology, psychoanalysis was, after a tumultuous half-century or so, no longer much of a threat, with B. F. Skinner's 1953 *Science and Human Behavior* delivering the heaviest blow. Introductory college textbooks did further damage, typically reducing psychoanalysis to a footnote in history or presenting the field's ideas as a stray offshoot of psychology. And while undeniably brilliant, Freud was more of a novelist than a scientist, students were taught, this marginalization still very much apparent in the psychological and psychiatric literature and within therapeutic culture. (Telling cognitive-behavioral therapists at parties that I was writing a book about psychoanalysis often produced anything from a mild look of skepticism to a hearty laugh.) In many ways, however, Freudian theory is at its cultural and professional zenith, with some of his concepts (such as self-perception) fully embraced by both the psychological community and laypeople. That psychoanalysis evolved into a much different thing over the course of the last four decades has gone a long way toward making it much less of the monster it appeared to be, as has the balkanization of the field over this same period of time. "As psychoanalysis became less threatening, psychologists were able to notice that the two fields actually shared many of the same basic assumptions," Hornstein concluded, these being "a commitment to psychic determinism, a belief in the cardinal importance of childhood experience, and an optimistic outlook about the possibility of change."[31]

With psychoanalysis less likely to be viewed as the enemy or an oddity, Freud and his ideas have over the past decade or so enjoyed a renaissance of sorts, made most apparent by a greater appreciation for his grand theory of the unconscious. While Freud did not invent the concept of the unconscious mind—philosophers, poets, and even some psychologists had earlier proposed there was a part of the brain in which we stored things that we were not aware of—it could fairly be said that he recognized its importance and significance as no one before and, arguably, no one since.[32] "Despite what pollsters would label as 'high negatives,' Freud's influence continues to permeate our secular society, with many of his ideas and symbolic terms acting as a Rosetta stone to explain jokes and everyday slips of the tongue, as well as providing provocative and profound insights into fashionable arts and literature," wrote

Suzanne Fields in her review of a massive retrospective of the man and his work at the Library of Congress in 1998.[33] Others were more to the point. "Without Freud, Woody Allen would be a schnook and Tony Soprano a thug," mused Jerry Adler in *Newsweek* in 2006, considering the man to be "our postmodern Plato, our secular St. Augustine."[34]

What is perhaps most amazing about America's love affair with psychoanalysis is thus its mere survival. Freud's theories have, somehow, withstood the torrent of criticism from all corners over the decades, not to mention the rise of Prozac Nation, the emergence of faster and cheaper therapies, and draconian policies of managed care. ("He's survived more assassination attempts than Rasputin," quipped Edward Dolnick, author of *Madness on the Couch*.)[35] "Freud bashers" of the "Freud wars" (notably Peter Medawar, Allen Esterson, and Frederick Crews) were hyperbolically critical of the theory and practice, seeing psychoanalysis as one of the biggest intellectual con games ever pulled off. Still, some critics of Freud were able to see the value of the discipline he created, a sign of its tremendous resiliency. In his 1985 *The Psychoanalytic Movement*, for example, Ernest Gellner scolded Freud for leading a self-righteous, secretive guild employing authoritarian (and doubtful) practices, while recognizing his theory of the unconscious and techniques of free association and transference as major contributions to the fields of psychology and psychiatry.[36]

More remarkably, Freud is posthumously getting the last laugh, as a small but dedicated cadre of scientists blesses his healing art. "It appears that Freud's broad brushstroke organization of the mind is destined to play a role similar to the one Darwin's theory of evolution served for molecular genetics—a template on which emerging details can be coherently arranged," wrote Mark Solms in a 2004 *Scientific American* article, "Freud Returns." A few leading neuroscientists have recently found that the father of psychoanalysis could have been, in some respects, a hundred years ahead of his time. Many of Freud's key concepts—the existence of an unconscious, repression, the pleasure principle, the libido, and that dreams have meaning—are being shown to be real functions of the brain, this perhaps the sweetest victory for psychoanalysis.[37]

Ironically, psychoanalysis has been in many ways a victim of its own success, paving the way for America's self-help movement that not coincidentally took off just as Freud was pronounced dead at the scene. Our line of therapeutic royalty of the past half-century—Dr. Spock, Dr. Joyce Brothers, Dr. Ruth, Dr. Phil—are Freud's progeny, the teary revelations and confessions on *Oprah* also a direct descendant of the "talking cure." On an even grander scale, our inner-directed culture, in which feelings and relations ("feminine" values, interestingly) are so highly prized, is rooted in psychoanalysis, as is the flipside of this—that we are a shamelessly self-centered, narcissistic people. Although psychoanalysis as a therapy is at a major competitive disadvantage to quicker-fix cures when time is money, its way of looking at the world and ability to see the entire landscape remains a compelling proposition. "Knowingly or not, we have absorbed the lessons of psychoanalysis," thought Jonathan Engel in his 2008 *American Therapy*. Freud's legacy is "firmly rooted in our everyday vernacular."[38]

Finally, it is important to make a distinction between psychoanalysis and psychodynamic or psychoanalytic psychotherapy. The latter, as Jonathan Shedler defined it, refers to a "range of treatments based on psychoanalytic concepts and methods that involve less frequent meetings and may be considered briefer than psychoanalysis proper." In psychoanalysis, patients typically have three to five sessions a week and lay on the couch, while in psychodynamic therapy they have just one or two sessions a week and sit face-to-face with the therapist. Much of the public (and some academics) is unaware of this distinction, something that has caused considerable misunderstanding about the field, past and present. Many people today are unaware that the field has been modernized, the (mostly valid) criticisms of psychoanalysis past still lingering. This is unfortunate, as psychodynamic therapy appears to offer longer-term gains than more popular (and affordable) cognitive-behavior therapy by focusing on the whole person rather than specific symptoms. Freud's body of work thus remains a valuable vehicle by which to relieve individuals' emotional suffering and improve their relationships, very much part of the mental health fabric of the twenty-first century. "Freud's legacy is not a specific theory but rather a sensibility," Shedler wrote in *Scientific American Mind* in 2010; his lasting contribution is "an appreciation of the depth and complexity of mental life and a recognition that we do not fully know ourselves."[39]

Because I believe that journalists serving on the front lines of the scene represent our most valuable resource in recovering unfiltered stories of psychoanalysis, *Shrink* relies primarily on period magazines and newspapers as its source material and secondarily on previous books written about aspects of the topic. From these hundreds of journalists' reports from the field, many of them obscure and largely forgotten but important firsthand accounts of psychoanalytic goings-on, we really do get the first draft of history. As a historian rather than a psychiatrist, I rely on my sources' use of psychological terms, notably "subconscious" and "unconscious" (Freud used only the latter, but the former was often referred to by later practitioners and laypeople alike). This book tells its story chronologically, showing that there have been six major eras of psychoanalysis since the end of World War I. The first chapter, "The New Psychology," shows how psychoanalysis exploded on the American scene in the 1920s, while chapter 2, "The Voodoo Religion," takes readers on the psychoanalytic roller coaster ride of the 1930s and 1940s, decades in which the ups and downs of the method tracked with those of the nation as a whole. The third chapter, "The Horizontal Hour," dives into the 1950s, when psychoanalysis hit its full stride in American culture, and chapter 4, "The Pernicious Influence," shows how psychoanalysis hit a major crossroads in America in the 1960s, its joyride of the postwar years over for good. Chapter 5, "The Impossible Profession," takes readers through the 1970s and 1980s, when psychoanalysis (and psychoanalysts) struggled to keep its sinking ship afloat, while the final chapter, "The Comeback Couch," explores events of the last twenty years, when psychoanalysis regained a good bit of the cultural currency it had lost the previous two decades. All indications are that psychoanalysis will continue to be a fascinating part of the cultural landscape, its exploration of the human condition to continue shaping and reshaping the American idea and experience.

SHRINK

CHAPTER 1: The New Psychology

> The unconscious is the larger circle which includes
> within itself the smaller circle of the conscious.
>
> SIGMUND FREUD, *Dream Psychology: Psychoanalysis
> for Beginners,* 1921

In May 1927 a wealthy New Yorker wrote a check for five thousand dollars and handed it to his psychoanalyst to personally give to Sigmund Freud in Vienna. The man felt that the treatment he received had been so valuable for him and his family that he wanted to do whatever he could to ensure that "the new psychology" would continue to thrive. "Those of us who have money owe it to the culture of the world to see that Freud is supplied with all necessary funds to continue his scientific investigations and educate those who will carry on psychoanalysis in the future," the anonymous donor said in 1927. He was just one of many satisfied customers of this new, very controversial form of psychiatry.[1]

While the rich man's act of generosity was unusual, it reflected the sheer passion that surrounded psychoanalysis in the 1920s as it took America by storm. "What can be more dramatic than to call up from the vasty deep of our submerged selves some hitherto forgotten and unpleasant incident of the past, now grown into a monster, and to be able to slay it with a password?" asked Thomas Masson in 1923, capturing much of the public's fascination with psychoanalysis.[2] By applying the ordinary methods of science—observation, recording, discovery, and hypotheses—to an individual's behavior, psychoanalysts set themselves off from the mystics (and, later, phrenologists) of the past who had also believed there was a realer reality than was readily apparent. In a way, however, psychoanalysis acted as a reminder of man's past, concerned

1

not with his civilized achievements but with his primitive needs, that is, sex and hunger. In an increasingly modern, complex age filled with more and more machines and bigger and bigger cities, psychoanalysis focused on the animal within, this "shock of the old" perhaps more shocking than any "shock of the new."

Psychoanalysis was also not completely new in that it was part of the secularization of Western culture that had been in play since the beginning of the Renaissance some five hundred years earlier. As science encroached upon religion, there was a gradual philosophical breaking away of the will of God as the idea that people created their own destiny gained currency. Similarly, there was the increased recognition that observable phenomena—accidents or germs, say—had a direct influence on one's physical health, meaning that demons or other evil forces were not the cause of sickness or death. Psychoanalysis showed the world that there were real and specific causes of poor mental health; the study of the mind was catching up to the other sciences, which had long ago begun to identify the physical laws of the universe. The theory that thoughts and emotions could affect the nervous and cellular structure of the body further established the legitimacy of psychoanalysis in the early twentieth century. That there was a direct link between the mind and the body proved to be as giant a step in the history of science as any.[3]

Talking Things Over

The man primarily responsible for the new psychology was of course the "father of psychoanalysis," Sigmund Freud. By the 1920s, Freud was, with the possible exception of Albert Einstein, the most famous scientist alive. "He has almost ceased to be a person," thought George Sylvester Viereck in 1925, viewing Freud as a "cultural force" akin to the larger-than-life Irish playwright George Bernard Shaw. Freud was also being compared to Columbus, the latter discovering a continent while looking for a passage to the East, the former discovering the unconscious while trying to find a new kind of treatment for mental illness.[4] Not since Kepler, with his laws of planetary motion, or Darwin, with his theory of evolution, had there been such a scientific discovery. Many believed that Freud's cracking of the psychic code was every bit as significant as any prior breakthrough in biology, chemistry, physics, or astronomy. Freud, in fact, saw his revelation that the "I" wasn't "master in its own house" as the third of mankind's three "great outrages against its naïve self-love"—the first being Copernicus's discovery that the earth was not the center of the universe and the second Darwin's research showing that humans had descended from animals and were thus not specially created by God.[5]

The belief that human history could now be divided into pre-Freud and post-Freud was almost universal by the 1920s, as intellectuals on all sides of the fence acknowledged the man's body of work. Freud's charting of the unconscious was "one of the most important practical contributions of science in modern times," James S. Van Tesslaar wrote in 1921. Psychology was just then beginning to "redeem the promise it had long held out of becoming a practical guide in the management of our everyday life."[6] In part because of Freud and his disciples (notably Carl Jung, Alfred Adler, Wilhelm Steckel, and Sandor Ferenczi in Europe, and Abraham A. Brill, James Putnam, Ernest Jones, William White, Smith Ely Jelliffe, and Morton Prince in the United States), the twentieth century was being called the "age of psychology," a new era in the evolution of mankind as the workings of the mind were explored. "We are already making wide use of the Freudian conceptions and in the course of time they will probably become, like the conception of evolution, a part of the mental equipment which every thinker takes for granted," predicted Joseph Wood Krutch in the *New York Times* in 1926.[7]

In some respects, the story of psychoanalysis was foreshadowed a century earlier when another Viennese physician, Franz Anton Mesmer, recast the concept of "vital force" as a new scientific term—magnetism. Because of his scandalous experiments, Mesmer (of "mesmerizing" fame) was expelled from the Austrian Empire but was happily received in 1778 in Paris where he founded a school and drew support from some other physicians. Bitter disputes between Mesmer and his disciples would eventually ensue, this too anticipating what would happen between Freud and his own followers as they attempted to turn concepts located within the realm of metaphysics into a science.[8]

A century after the Mesmer sensation, the public again became fascinated with scientific studies of the mind via Jean-Martin Charcot's treatment of hysteria through hypnosis. Attending Charcot's *cliniques* at La Salpêtrière Hospital in Paris around 1880 was Joseph Breuer, a visiting physician, who returned to Vienna and pursued his own experiments in the nascent field. One of Breuer's students took a particular interest in these experiments; what would become psychoanalysis, then, began in 1883 as discussions between Breuer and Freud, then a twenty-four-year-old doctor. The conversations revolved around some positive results obtained by "talking things over" with a woman with a severe case of hysteria, a process the patient described as "chimney sweeping." (Popularly known as the "talking cure," Freud himself famously described it as "psychical regression" in his landmark *A General Introduction to Psychoanalysis*.) Exposed to the "mechanism of hysteria," Freud soon devoted himself to the treatment of nervous diseases, separating himself from his masters by focusing on the causes of mental illness rather than its effects and seeing in the unconscious mind a vast resource to heal the sick. "It is a vase filled to overflowing, in which it is proper to seek and find the source of our emotive life, not only in disease, but also in a state of health," Freud said in 1923, believing that the unconscious was a reservoir for "all our repressed urges, our lapses, our errors, our distractions, our dreams." A doctor first and philosopher second, Freud was never content with just understanding and explaining mental illness; his primary aim from the very beginning was to find possible causes.[9]

In Paris in 1885, Freud did further work in the au courant areas of hypnosis and suggestion at the renowned La Salpêtrière Hospital. However, his mentors there, Charcot and Pierre Janet—pioneers in, if not the founders of, modern abnormal psychology—were less than enthusiastic about his unusual hypotheses. Years later, Janet, who had mentored Freud in Paris as a young man, claimed that his ex-student had stolen his ideas and was thus essentially a fraud. In the mid-1880s, Janet was working with hysterical patients at the city's largest mental institution in the area of traumatic memory, trying to find out whether recovery from the memory of a painful event buried in the subconscious could be found in dreams, somnambulism (sleepwalking), or automatic writing.[10] Some four decades later, Janet, perhaps Freud's harshest critic, told the story in his new book *Principles of Psychotherapy*:

At this time a foreign physician, Dr. S. Freud, of Vienna, came to Salpêtrière and became interested in these studies. . . . He changed, first of all, the terms that I was using; what I had called psychological analysis he called psychoanalysis; what I had called psychological system he called complex; he considered a repression what I considered a restriction of consciousness; what I referred to as a psychological dissociation, or as a moral fumigation, he baptized with the name of catharsis. But, above all, he transformed a clinical observation and a therapeutic treatment, with a definite and limited field of use, into an enormous system of medical philosophy—Pansexuality.[11]

It was not until 1893 that Freud outlined his ideas about "chimney sweeping" on paper, the beginning of what would be a literally voluminous body of work stretching out over the next four decades. (Freud's writings were introduced to the American public in 1907 when they were translated by A. A. Brill of New York University.) Freud gradually shaped his views until he was ready to present them publicly. His choice of occasion to do just that was bold if not reckless: a meeting of the Vienna Neurological Society, headed up by Richard von Krafft-Ebing, author of the notorious *Psychopathia Sexualis*. Freud read his paper to deafening silence, his distinguished audience unable even to respond to what they had heard. It would be years before Freud's early works would be published (and more years before reviewers would acknowledge them), and it would take roughly a half-century for the Viennese academic community to accept his views.[12]

With no hospital appointment, Freud used his own home to publicly promote his theories beginning in 1902. A small coterie of curious students regularly gathered there, eager to hear his every word. The field made a major leap forward when two men from Zurich with hospital appointments—Eugen Bleuler and Carl Jung—began to apply his theories, and another when Freud and Jung were invited to lecture and receive honorary doctorate degrees at Clark University in Massachusetts in 1909. (The president of Clark University, G. Stanley Hall, was such a devotee of Freud's that he was asked to write the preface to the English translation of his 1920 *A General Introduction to Psychoanalysis*.) This was the first real academic recognition of psychoanalysis, an achievement in which Freud took great pleasure, particularly given its source. "Even in prudish America one . . . could . . . discuss freely . . . all those things that are regarded as offensive in life," he later wrote, pleased to see his unorthodox views accepted as true science. Freud established the International Psychoanalytical Association the next year in Zurich and named Jung president, scorning the many Viennese nonbelievers. In his *The History of the Psychoanalytic Movement* published in the United States in 1917 (which was more of an autobiography), Freud made it clear he was proud to have "disturbed the world's sleep," the insomnia he caused still pervasive on a global level.[13]

That psychoanalysis could be recognized as an entirely new kind of psychology was largely a function of its original design. Psychoanalysis was conceived by Freud as both a way to treat "nervous disorders" and, more broadly, a method of research devoted to understanding how the unconscious influenced human behavior. Because of the latter, basically any human endeavor—art, architecture, literature, religion, law, politics, and so on—was open territory for psychoanalytic interpretation, something that occurred with regularity as the field infiltrated the nooks and crannies of American culture. Freud's concept of the libido—the energy force responsible for any kind of creation—was thus at work not only at the biological level but at the social level as well, responsible for nothing short of civilization as we knew it.[14]

The term *psychoanalysis* was first used by Freud around 1895, and it expanded beyond its original concept as his most famous pupils, Carl Jung and Alfred Adler, along with a number of British and American psychologists, notably Edward Kempf, entered the field. That there was an unconscious part of the self was without doubt the biggest factor in making psychoanalysis the "new psychology," its focus on instincts and emotions (versus intellect) further distancing it from standard thinking. Although Jung's belief in free will and a collective unconscious, and Adler's "individual psychology" (with its emphasis on "ego instincts"— our wish for power and security), would push the field in different directions, it was Freud's views of sexuality that elevated psychoanalysis from obscure academic theory to cultural phenomenon. And like the movies (which, interestingly, developed on a parallel course with the field), psychoanalysis was much concerned with conflict, specifically the clashes between desire and reality and individuality and authority. As a struggle with the self, Freud's concept of conflict had a decidedly dramatic quality made even more compelling because conscious conflicts—for example, concerning career choices, or whether to get married—were rooted in an unconscious one.[15] Bringing unconscious ideas, feelings, and impulses into consciousness was the desired goal of the psychoanalytic process, affirming the Socratic dictum "know thyself" and adding "accept thyself" and "be thyself" as essential rules to live by.[16]

The Spoiled Child of a Realistic Age

The "new psychology" that captured America's attention after World War I was in fact not the first time the field had been said to be reinvented. Around the turn of the twentieth century there had also been a new psychology movement, one that used experiments to determine the relationship between the physiological and the cerebral. The new psychology of the 1920s was significantly broader in scope, as the body of psychoanalytic literature continued to grow through the decade. "The problem of our psychoanalytic commentators and simplifiers is now upon us," sighed Ruth Hale in her 1922 review of no less than four new books on the subject.[17] Some believed that psychoanalysis was already becoming passé by the mid-twenties but the ever-marching parade of literature on the subject suggested otherwise. "Although it is held by many that the vogue of psychoanalysis is waning, there is no end to the making of books upon the general subject and its tendencies," observed E. N. Merrington in 1926, rejecting the idea that the practice would go the way of the Charleston (or, hopefully, Prohibition).[18]

Although the new psychology had been floating in the ether for over a decade in the United States after Freud's visit to Clark and the translation of his early works into English, it was not until the dust settled from the First World War that it crossed over into popular and consumer culture. "At the present time, the Freudian theories are showing extraordinary vitality," observed the American magazine *Current Opinion* in 1920, adding that, "One can hardly pick up a newspaper or a magazine without finding psychoanalytic terms." New words or phrases or existing ones with new meanings, such as "ambivalent attitudes," "suppressed desires," and "conflicts," were regularly popping up in ordinary conversations, now part of the American vernacular. Highbrows too were often speaking Freudianese, not surprisingly, as could be seen in recent critiques of modernist paintings and, more specifically, in Van Wyck Brooks's *The Ordeal of Mark Twain*, in which the author "psychoanalyzed" Clemens and his complex, so to speak, relationships with his wife and mother.[19]

Not only was psychoanalysis informing current literature and criticism but many could not resist hypothesizing how it might have been employed by writers long dead. "We cannot help but wonder what would have been the effect upon Charles Dickens if, before creating Copperfield and Pickwick, he could have taken a course in Freud, or how, in the light of repressions and displacements, Shakespeare would have dealt with the character of Hamlet," wrote Thomas L. Masson in a 1923 article called "Psychoanalysis Rampant" for the *New York Times*. Music too was subject to psychoanalytic interpretation now that the parlance of the trade was up for grabs. In 1924, a critic for the *New York Times* panned the Boston Symphony's performance of Igor Stravinsky's "Rites of Spring," making one reader feel the need to tell the editor that the reporter missed the psychological underpinnings of the piece. "Stravinsky tries to do the 'psychoanalytic,'" a reader from Franklin, Massachusetts, informed the editor and others who may have attended the performance, declaring that the composer's goal was "to draw the thing out of the unconscious." The newspaper's critic was obviously not the only one to misinterpret the deeper meaning of the composition as pure noise. "Any one who has followed the course of 'psychoanalysis' and the violent revulsions it has caused, will perhaps understand why certain patrons and patronesses, and certain musicians, were leaving the hall before the end of the piece," the letter writer continued. These people seemed unable to "face the fact that there is still a lot left in us that is not quite so nice as would appear from the outside."[20]

The fact that all kinds of people and institutions were embracing Freudian theory did indeed suggest that psychoanalysis was rampant. "Psychoanalysis is not only coloring our literature, but, as a natural result, is creeping into and influencing life in many other directions," Masson wrote, noting that businesses had begun to use the technique to select employees.[21] There seemed to be no limit to how psychoanalysis could and would be used as more Americans became fluent in its general concepts. When a Smith College student went missing in 1928, for instance, a Boston psychoanalyst, Lydiad H. Horton, was hired by the woman's parents to assist police and private detectives in finding her.[22]

The intellectual trickle-down of psychoanalysis became more like a flood as it entered the discourse of consumerism. "Psychology has stepped down from the university chair into the market place," observed the New York Times in 1926, adding that, "It has become the order of the day to 'psychologize' everything, from our wandering day dreams to the color of our shoes."[23] Now that psychoanalysis was firmly entrenched in the public domain, it appeared that Freud's ideas might very well assume Copernican or Darwinian stature. "Passing from the clinic . . . into the market place, [psychoanalysis] seems destined finally to be absorbed into the general thought of the world and to become one of the tools which the thinker unconsciously uses," wrote Joseph Wood Krutch that same year.[24]

Even if psychoanalysis was turning out to be one of the biggest ideas of the millennium, some boiled down the whole thing to one little word: sex. Writing for the Nation in 1922, Maxwell Bodenheim felt that psychoanalysis was becoming so popular because it justified Americans' "sensual admirations," meaning it made them feel less guilty about thinking about sex. Blessed by science, sex was now invading American culture with a vengeance, the once-discreet subject on full display for all to see. "Psychoanalysis is the spoiled child of a realistic age," declared Bodenheim, "and its boisterous manners should be corrected by a metaphysical spanking." It was true that recently published and seemingly psychoanalytically informed novels by authors such as Sherwood Anderson, Theodore Dreiser, and F. Scott Fitzgerald were describing sex in elaborate detail, for the times at least, while nonfiction books like What Every Girl Already Knows addressed the topic with a new kind of candor. As well, women's bodies, particularly their legs, had rather suddenly become quite visible, not just on stage in theaters but on the street, this too something that he believed psychoanalysis had sparked. "The pruderies and petty evasions of the Victorian Age are being wildly avenged," Bodenheim observed, the social taboos surrounding sexuality fading fast now that it was all a matter of primitive but perfectly natural, scientifically approved instincts.[25] More telling evidence that psychoanalysis was avenging the Victorian Age was the response one would get to saying things like, "I had the queerest dream last night!" among a group of friends. Knowing looks and laughter would inevitably follow, the amateur shrinks interpreting the dream as sexual, much like professional ones would likely do.[26]

Although many did not quite understand or approve of the new psychology movement in America in the 1920s, one man was singularly disturbed by it: Sigmund Freud. Freud was rather horrified that his writings, intended primarily (but not exclusively) for a medical audience, were now in general circulation and, perhaps inevitably, being misinterpreted. (His *Introductory Lectures on Psychoanalysis* and some other works were written for a wider audience.) Many of his key ideas, particularly sexual repression and the Oedipal complex, were commonly overgeneralized by laypeople and professionals alike, an unfortunate and possibly dangerous situation. (Adler's "inferiority complex" was also often mistakenly attributed to him.) Why would the public want to understand the details of psychoanalysis when they had no such desire to know how, say, insulin could be used to treat diabetes? Freud wondered. For some, the answer to that question was simple. "Not to understand the general doctrine of the new psychology is to remain ignorant of a body of scientific facts that are as valuable to the average man in his daily life as the established rules of hygiene," flatly stated Harvey O'Higgins in 1928, obviously a firm believer in the power of Freud.[27]

In fact, knowledge of Freudian theory was considered handy if not vital in the modern age. "The lawyer and the judge, the teacher and the merchant, the lover and the creative artist, can no longer successfully conduct the difficult business of living without acquiring at least the rudiments of psycho-analysis," Viereck ventured to say.[28] The psychoanalytic faithful insisted that familiarity with Freud's view of the human mental system was an absolute must for doctors wanting to help their patients avoid conflicts among their id, ego, and superegos. "Innumerable conflicts of this nature in educational, religious, political, and other fields keep man at variance with his neighbor and cause the development of inhibitions and symptoms and at times of devastating illnesses," thought Jelliffe, a leading psychoanalyst of the Freudian school in 1927.

Jelliffe advised his medical colleagues to be as well acquainted with the workings of the mind as those of the body. That doctors should look "inside" those they treated was, of course, not an entirely new idea. Hippocrates, the "father of medicine" and of oath fame, taught that physicians should also treat the "soul" of their patients, recognizing that tensions of the mind could cause trouble for the body. As more of its members became exposed to psychoanalytic principles, the medical community was starting to accept the possibility that all kinds of illnesses, including pneumonia, typhoid fever, and influenza, could be functions of a flawed thinking process, the body trying to compensate for a lack or loss of basic human needs (such as love). "The doctor can no longer ignore the double nature of his task," Jelliffe suggested. Medicine was a whole new enterprise now that the mind was fully in play.[29]

As psychological theory worked its way gradually into the mainstream, Americans gained a basic (perhaps too basic) understanding of not just Freudian theory but that of his student-turned-rival, Carl Jung. (Most laypeople lumped the two men together, despite Jung's having intently set out on his own "analytical psychology" course by the 1920s.) Many of the more informed were taken with Jung's four psychological types, a "personality paint box" by which one could gain valuable insights into oneself and others. "To meet oneself through the good offices of Jung's theory of types is to be like the motorist who, after driving a car for years without knowledge of its mechanism, suddenly comes upon one of these cut-away engines and begins to understand the hows and whys of motor transmission," wrote *The New Republic* in 1926, helping readers discover their own and others' personality type (introvert or extravert) and attitudinal subtype (observant, expectant, personal, or analytical). Besides gaining greater familiarity with one's own "engine," a working knowledge of Jung could improve one's marriage and build stronger relationships with parents or children, a useful tool for negotiating the trials and tribulations of everyday life. "The collector of types acquires a new conception of wholesome living, a new basis for the criticism and if necessary the reconstruction of his own life," the magazine concluded, a means to improve one's chances of success, both personally and professionally.[30]

Jungian personality types could be used for even more important things than building better personal relationships, some thought. In her

1924 *The Re-Creating of the Individual*, Beatrice Hinkle borrowed Jung's psychological types to analyze historical figures and even nations, an interesting and, she believed, useful application of psychoanalytic theory. Had people recognized that Teddy Roosevelt was the perfect extravert and Woodrow Wilson the quintessential introvert, for example, they could have anticipated many of their decisions and, perhaps, helped make the world a more peaceful place. Likewise, she suggested, it was important to know that Germany was an introvert and England an extravert, the Great War an almost inevitable consequence of two rivals with different personalities pursuing the same goal. (Hinkle viewed France as a mature introvert and the United States, with its "emotional idealism," "speculation with tomorrow," "general optimism," and "consideration of life as a game," an adolescent extravert.) Greater international understanding would be the natural outcome of this kind of insight, she argued, elevating psychoanalysis to a whole new level of importance.[31]

A. A. Brill, the New York University professor who had the weighty task of translating Freud's books from German into English, also liked to use historical figures to illustrate personality types of his own design. For Brill, George Washington, James Madison, Andrew Jackson, and Woodrow Wilson were all "schizoids," while Abraham Lincoln, Teddy Roosevelt, Warren G. Harding, and Benjamin Franklin were "syntonics." Schizoids, Brill explained at the 1924 American Psychiatric Association convention in Atlantic City (psychiatrists apparently liked the beach), were independent and at times confrontational, while syntonics were social and cooperative. While one could quibble with Brill's classifications (Did Teddy Roosevelt really have a "sunny disposition," as he attributed to syntonics?), the course of history was heavily determined by the personality types of a country's leaders, Brill seemed to be saying, an intriguing application of psychology not just circa mid-1920s but even today.[32]

The Hades of the Unconscious

Some wondered, however, if having a spoiled child of a realistic age was a good thing. "Can anyone who is not an expert in Psychology have anything of interest, let alone value, to say regarding a subject so eso-

teric as the term Psychoanalysis suggests?" asked Harvey Carson Grumbine in 1920, wondering if laypeople like himself were qualified to
express their opinion about the mysterious field. Because most patients
were in fact laypeople, Grumbine, an English professor at West Virginia University, felt that the average person should be better informed
about psychoanalysis, especially regarding the treatments he or she may
endure. Those with a "psychosis" (defined then as a mental illness resulting from a conflict between wish and fact) would probably want to
know that a psychoanalyst would advise the patient to gratify their
desire (usually sexual) or else find a substitute for it that was almost as
satisfying (in other words, to replace one instinctive craving for another).
At the very least, one should expect to be made aware of one's repressed
wishes, Grumbine told readers of *Scribner's*, making one think that the
professor had some personal familiarity with the ways of the couch and
was passing on the information as a kind of public service.[33]

Given the number of Americans who could possibly benefit from a
good chimney sweeping, the professor's tutorial in Psychoanalysis 101
was timely. In his 1921 *Fundamental Conceptions of Psychoanalysis*, Brill
made the rather startling statement that 80 percent of doctor visits were
actually psychological in nature, meaning that Americans' mental health
was a lot worse than generally believed. Fortunately, the new psychology
had brought mental illness into the open, Brill felt, with the insane, or
just slightly mad, no longer considered criminals or demonically possessed as they had been for centuries. To their credit, psychoanalysts had
indeed done a lot not only to classify the symptoms of psychic sickness
but also its causes, a process that had really just begun. Brill foresaw that
over the long term the incidence of nervous and mental diseases would
be reduced, much as smallpox and typhoid had been, with psychoanalysis eventually able to prevent psychoses and neuroses. Curing patients
with such diseases was a long way off, however. The time and money
required was simply too great for the average person with any of the
three recognized types of mental illness—manic depression, paranoia,
or dementia praecox (complete indifference to the outside world).[34]

Sandor Ferenczi, a renowned psychoanalyst from Budapest (who had
accompanied Freud on his visit to the United States in 1909), also found
Americans to be in dire need of psychoanalysis on his return trip sev-

enteen years later. After an eight-month lecture tour across the country, Ferenczi came to the conclusion that because life in America was so "strenuous," its citizens were naturally predisposed to developing neuroses. (The mechanization of everyday life was also popularly believed to be wreaking havoc with Americans' mental health.) Children especially could benefit from some serious therapy, Ferenczi thought. "A whole army of psycho-analysts alone would be necessary to treat all those so-called incorrigible children, whose ailing and failings constitute a grave danger for the coming generation," Ferenczi told the *New York Times* in 1927, thinking that "gradually substituting sanitariums for penitentiaries" was also a good idea.[35] With "nervousness" defined by psychoanalysts as the result of an attempt to reconcile instinctive amoral tendencies with moral ones, it seemed clear that America's considerable psychological problems were not going away anytime soon.[36]

The nation's medical community actively responded to the psychic epidemic that apparently was taking place in the twenties. By 1927, most large mental hospitals had physicians trained in psychoanalysis, and general hospitals, too, were adding analysts to their staffs. The largest hospital in the world, the Manhattan State Hospital, had a dedicated psychoanalytic clinic to treat its more than six thousand patients, as did Mount Sinai across town. A landmark of sorts was achieved in 1926 when an entire day of the American Psychiatric Association's three-day annual meeting was devoted to psychoanalysis, something repeated at the following year's get-together.[37] Still, as of 1927, there were no psychoanalytic clinics in New York or anywhere else in the United States for physicians to learn the technique. American doctors had to go to Europe for training.[38]

This would soon change as more and more Americans became interested in getting, as it was called in slang, "psyched." Although skeptics often saw psychoanalysis as either a dangerous fad or a complete bore (while admitting it was useful for the truly mad), many of those who tried out the couch found it to be a literally life-changing experience. The odd logic of psychoanalysis—such as the therapist's interest in what one remembered only because it stood in the way of what one did not remember—was intriguing, at the very least, as were its strange techniques designed to penetrate the unconscious. The heart and soul of psychoanalysis—dream interpretation—was especially captivating ("The dream is the torch with which [Freud] leads us through the Hades of the unconscious," Viereck poetically wrote).[39] Patients would typically be asked to write down the dreams they remembered in the morning and bring the results to their sessions. Analysts would ask patients to read certain words from their notes aloud and then say whatever else came into their mind, this method of free association considered not unlike translating a foreign language. Months of this would often go by without any major revelations until one day—voila!—a big breakthrough would be achieved, much to the patient's (and analyst's) delight. "I came away sometimes with a release of energy so great that as I walked down the street the air seemed clearer, the sky bluer, the whole world brighter," reported Lucian Cary, a journalist who described "How It Feels To Be Psychoanalyzed" for the *American Magazine* in 1925. Cary discovered, among other things, that he had an unconscious wish to fail ("It is rather astounding how far you go in gaining the attention of your family and friends by *failing* instead of *succeeding*," he remarked), a not uncommon kind of revelation for those taking the psychoanalytic plunge.[40]

With that kind of experience the literal talk of the town, it was not surprising that psychoanalysis got people's attention, to put it mildly. Other important contributions to medical science had recently been made—the discovery of insulin for the treatment of diabetes, the use of ultraviolet rays to destroy malignant growths, the recognition that certain vitamins were essential to the human diet, to name a few—but the development of psychotherapy was undoubtedly the most conspicuous. Like other forms of medicine used to treat a serious abnormality, psychotherapy was considered a radical procedure, with prolonged analysis of the patient's past history the prescribed method. Moving memories from the unconscious to the conscious (in order to ease the mental conflict and unify the mind—a process called "synthesis") was not an easy thing, after all, but offered the best chances of recovery. Patients unhappy with the Freudian approach occasionally switched to a Jungian or Adlerian one (and vice versa), often finding that a different analyst with a different method led to better results.[41]

The suspension of moral or any other kind of judgment—a defining characteristic of the new psychology—was one reason why psychoanalysis was all the rage. That psychoanalysts viewed their patients' mental disorders, especially phobias, as a kind of disease was itself quite shocking. Their jettisoning of the two mighty pillars of traditional Western thought—argument and reason—ran directly against the stream. Psychoanalysts in fact considered argument worse than useless, believing that trying to persuade patients that their fears were irrational only made them seem more real. Likewise, early psychoanalysts looked at phobias not as a form of madness but more like a toothache that could be cured by talking about it, this too constituting quite a radical break from the conventions of the past.[42]

In the classic model of psychoanalysis, as we all know from the movies, patients were told to lie on a couch (eyes sometimes closed, sometimes open), relax their muscles, and resist any attempt to filter their thoughts (a state of "passive reverie," one top analyst called it). The analyst sat out of sight of the patient, usually at the head of the couch (occasionally behind a nearby screen). After many sessions, the patient hopefully became well, sometimes understanding the cause of his or her symptoms and sometimes not. Ideally, it was the former, as that was believed to ensure a complete cure, while not knowing the source of the illness meant susceptibility to future attacks. Although it was rarely specified as such—more because of the morality of the times than patient confidentiality—homosexual thoughts were often the "illness" in question, a condition that seemed to have spread dramatically since the Great War. While analysis could resolve this conflict, one was much better off addressing these feelings in one's youth as they surfaced. "If individuals were encouraged to take tutors and schoolmasters into their confidence, to go to doctors and talk these things out early, they could be saved from a very great deal of serious mental suffering," wrote psychoanalyst William Brown in 1929, referring obliquely to homosexuality and how it could be cured.[43]

The sheer difficulty, even oppressiveness of psychoanalysis only added to its enigmatic reputation and, for some, appeal. One could not talk to others about what was discussed in therapy, lest this interfere with the process. (This usually was not a problem, given the kinds of revelations about oneself that surfaced.) Getting one's ego beat to a pulp also was no fun, the analyst often pointing out to patients that they were a lot more selfish and acquisitive than they thought. (Learning that everyone else was equally vile and rotten was quite satisfying, however, this in itself almost worth the considerable expense.) Vulnerabilities in particular were exposed in dream interpretation as one's darker side came through loud and clear. Seemingly every element in each dream was significant in some way and, as often as not, unflattering, turning the patient into a human punching bag. "You, the uninitiated, have not the least idea of all the things one brief vision may symbolize," said one woman who got "psyched." She was so disturbed by her analyst's interpretations that she actually woke herself up when she started to dream so she would not have to tell him about it. In fact, fearing that one might learn of yet another unsavory personality trait, "forgetting" what one had dreamt about occurred with unusual regularity. Still, "I do not regret the weeks of torture and anguish through which I have struggled," the reluctant dreamer made clear, expressing the typical takeaway from the painful-but-worth-it experience.[44]

Psychoanalysis was (and remains) quite a commitment for both the patient and the analyst. Sessions were typically one hour long, three to six days a week, with the whole process lasting maybe eight or nine months. Patients were advised not to make any important decisions during treatment, including whether to get married, get divorced, or start a new career. Even in the mid-1920s, the process was not cheap, with analysts charging anywhere from seven to thirty dollars an hour. At two hundred total hours, patients would fork out somewhere between fourteen hundred to six thousand dollars, and this in a time before health insurance, which now often covers at least a portion of mental health costs. Even dearer than the financial costs were the emotional costs, because the process was frequently a painful ordeal. Making admissions and giving up illusions about oneself as well as taking responsibility for one's actions were not easy things for American pioneers of psychoanalysis, especially when friends and family were not particularly sympathetic to the enterprise. Not only was success not guaranteed, there was widespread belief that analysis could and did lead to insanity and suicide, making one wonder why anyone would put herself or himself through this new thing imported from Europe.[45]

Illicit Emotion Plumbers

Despite these major concerns, more and more people were eager to put themselves through psychoanalysis, hoping it could be the cure for whatever ailed them. The steady oozing of psychoanalysis into the American zeitgeist and escalating interest in undergoing therapy in the 1920s also made more people want to try to be become an analyst. Just as intrigued about this new and increasingly popular branch of medicine as patients, some doctors decided to enter the field after reading some of the literature and developing some familiarity with dream interpretation. No real credentials were required to call oneself a psychoanalyst at the time, making it easy to start a practice and not too difficult to find clients. In 1926, one such medical doctor who had made the move over to psychoanalysis recalled that there was no shortage of patients to be had: "Thanks to the public craze concerning the subject, a professional analyst's time was pretty well filled," he remarked. Men were as likely to sign up for analysis as women, this doctor found, although women spent much more time in treatment. While things went relatively smoothly for this converted analyst for some time ("A very great deal of analytic practice is really no more than confidential consultation followed by sage counsel," he admitted in an article for the *New Republic* called "Confessions of an Ex-Psycho-Analyst"), trouble eventually arose in the area of transference. "All my analytic technique came to be subordinated or directed to one thing: to producing in my patient the utmost degree of admiration, fear, worship, love—call it what you will," he wrote, finding this new kind of power initially flattering but eventually quite disturbing. Feeling embarrassed and unprofessional about the relationships he had formed with some of his patients as they unconsciously redirected their feelings onto him, the doctor soon retreated back to traditional medicine (much to his wife's delight).[46]

Especially for those analysts who had been physicians during World War I, the psychotherapist's office was in a way like a military hospital, the goal being to piece people back together so they could return to the front. More insightful analysts looked to their work as a natural consequence of the social, economic, and political institutions in place that put undue pressure on many Americans' lives. The need to conform to social norms and achieve as much as one possibly could was believed to be just too much for some. These wise practitioners recognized that although some kind of issue during childhood was typically the primary cause of neuroses, it was the "system" that was more generally to blame for creating so many sick people. The reconstruction of society itself thus embodied the larger need. "Analysis of abnormal conditions, revision of values, reorganization round a clear-cut reasoned philosophy: this seems to me the treatment needed for a sick and nervous world, as well as for neurotic individuals," said one such practitioner in 1929. "We are busy curing individual madmen, but do not even know it when we go mad all together," echoed A. Clutton-Brock in the *New Republic*.[47]

Although some were calling themselves psychoanalysts to take advantage of the increasing demand, there were relatively few legitimate (that is, Freudian-trained) practitioners in the United States in the mid-1920s, with precious few of these women. One analyst who was both legitimate and a woman was Grace Potter, who practiced her trade in New York after studying first in Zurich and then in Vienna (where she herself was analyzed as part of her training). With her classical approach, Potter believed that most adults' problems—physical, social, and work-related—stemmed from an emotional conflict experienced in childhood (before the age of seven, to be exact). Because this conflict was too difficult and painful to resolve at the time, the child receded from and created a barrier around it, eventually denying that the thing ever happened. By adulthood, the "negated" experience was now a "repression," buried in the patient's unconscious in order to prevent any painful reminder of it. However, because "the wishes in the Unconscious clamor for freedom and pleasure," as Potter explained in 1925, repressions will likely cause major problems—unhappiness, loneliness, discord—at some point, while the sufferers remain unaware of their origin.[48]

Even problems of sight or hearing could be a result of some psychic conflict experienced as a child, Potter and her fellow Freudians maintained. By means of analysis, the patient would at last be able to extract the event from the powerful, unreasonable unconscious. "Only the *unconscious mind* through an understanding of the mechanism that has produced these mistakes, can undo them," Potter told readers of the *American Magazine*, adding that many physicians now believed there to be a direct link between the mind and the body. Cases in which people displayed extraordinary strength in emergencies demonstrated that the unconscious not only existed but, as a source of tremendous power, could and should be used in daily life. Reportedly, a number of people instantly recovered from serious illness during the San Francisco earthquake, providing additional evidence that the mental ruled over the physical.[49]

Unfortunately, for every Grace Potter there was at least one analyst who should have kept his or her previous day job. Even reputable psychologists seemed to get in over their heads when they stepped into psychoanalytic waters. "Persons suffering from morbid dread or any form of hysterical instability should not attempt to cure themselves by self-analysis," thought R. H. Hingley, psychologist at Edinburgh University and author of the 1922 *Psycho-analysis*, "but there are innumerable minor disabilities that may be removed or mitigated by self-examination in the light of the principles of psycho-analysis." Indeed, according to Hingley, there were a host of personality flaws that a proper understanding of psychoanalysis could self-cure, including "undue hesitation," "thoughtless impetuosity," and a "lack of independence" (or too much). And given the number of physical disorders that Hingley believed could have psychological origins—asthma, hay fever, sore throat, stammering, headache, backache, tender spine, weak heart, spasmodic sneezing, and, last not but least, hiccups—everyone could benefit by picking up a few psychoanalytic tips.[50] Such advice was similar to that which could be heard in the psychology clubs that mushroomed in the United States in the 1920s and were popular for the next three decades.

George Jean Nathan was especially peeved about the flood of incompetents into the field and that nobody seemed to be doing anything about it. Referring to psychoanalysis, Nathan wrote in 1927, "It is passing strange that the moral police of the country have thus far overlooked those chiropractors of the subconscious who begin to flourish in every community that boasts so much as a brick railroad station and a gilt movie parlor, and whose occult enterprises constitute what is undoubtedly one of the high-voltage engines of sinfulness amongst us." While Nathan conceded that there were a few competent Freudians offering their services, the majority (nineteen out of twenty, he estimated) composed "such a body of quacks and charlatans as has not been heard of since Christian Science first got under full steam." Nathan's basic complaint was that the legitimate science created by Freud, Jung, and Adler had by the mid-twenties devolved into a moneymaking scam run by "illicit emotion plumbers" pursuing "easy pickings." Doctors and dentists who had lost their licenses were now calling themselves psychoanalysts, he claimed, with a motley crew of other phonies ("fortune-tellers, osteopaths, phrenologists and Italian counts," Nathan specified) also hanging out their shingle.[51]

Much worse than their swindling was the real damage these con artists were leaving in their wake, Nathan continued. Told more often than not that their problem was a "suppressed libido," married women were promptly dispatched on "fleshly errands," convinced of the moral legitimacy of indulging their physical (and psychic) needs. Good marriages were being broken up by these scientifically justified peccadilloes, he seriously believed, a valid point, perhaps, given the skyrocketing divorce rate. While in actuality many things contributed to the popularity of psychoanalysis, Nathan blamed one thing in particular—women's clubs—for planting these seeds of destruction. Bored of orators lecturing for hours about hermeneutics, poetry, or some other highbrow, dry-as-a-bone subject, women of a certain age found psychoanalysis positively fascinating and, more importantly, titillating. "What they really wanted was a little hot stuff carefully and politely wrapped in a literary, philosophical, or scientific cloak," thought Nathan. Secretaries of these clubs, who booked speakers, were keenly aware of this changing interest and knew it would guarantee a packed (and paying) house. Not coincidentally, lecture bureaus were filled to the gills with psychoanalysts more than happy to "give a good dirty show under cover" to "the old girls," as Nathan described the situation. The analysts would typically begin their talk with some harmless theoretical stuff and then segue into the Oedipal and Electra complexes, at which point the women would start paying serious attention. It was the third act of the play that really warmed up the room, as the speaker got into things like sexual symbolism in dreams, the dangers of repression, and women's innate impulse to flee husband and home, "the girls now leaning so far forward in their seats that the ushers have to stand guard lest they fall out."[52]

Unsurprisingly, true professionals in the field were not very happy that psychoanalysis was becoming a bit of a running joke. "Psycho-therapy has too often been attempted by ... men of limited perspective, thin and didactic intellect, arrogant and supercilious personality," thought one analyst in 1929, convinced that his colleagues' egotism was the biggest problem in the field. As well, more practitioners with dubious credentials were flooding into the field, including people who had taken a twelve-lesson course in the subject and now felt ready to call themselves professionals and solicit clients.[53] Some observers of the scene were less concerned about the parade of frauds populating psychoanalysis, seeing it as a natural evolution of the field. "There were astrologers before there were astronomers; there was magic before medicine. There were bone-setters and blood-letters before there were surgeons; there were midwives before there were obstetricians, and there will be innumerable grades of honest and dishonest psychotherapists before there are enough qual-ified medical psychoanalysts," Jelliffe explained in 1929. While his argu-ment made a lot of sense, it did little to solve the problem.[54]

Freud was doing everything he could to solve the problem, however, intent on putting those misusing his ideas out of business. In 1925 (while recuperating from one of many surgeries for his jaw cancer at a moun-tain resort near Vienna), Freud became the chair of the International Psychoanalytical Association, with part of the New York–based organi-zation's mission being to "combat the fake psychoanalysis now said to be rampant in the United States," as the *New York Times* described it. Edward Bernays, the "father of public relations" (and Freud's double nephew), was, rather fittingly, leading this charge on the American front, his task to, in his uncle's own words, "disseminate the true character and value of psychoanalysis" via a publicity campaign. Freud was also hoping that his friends across the pond would create institutes similar to the ones in Vienna and Berlin, which would both treat Americans and train physicians to be psychoanalysts, another approach that might stem the tide of phony analysts.[55]

Besides doing what he could to try to get rid of the quacks in the field, Bernays (whose mother was Freud's sister and whose father was the brother of Freud's wife) occasionally used legitimate psychoanalytic principles to create public relations campaigns. Rather than cold, hard logic, it was suppressed desires that drove most consumer decisions,

Bernays argued. The unconscious played a pivotal role in which products one purchased (and did not purchase). It was the common longings of the masses—sex, hunger, safety—rather than their differences that served as the skeleton key of persuasion, Bernays (and, a generation later, Ernest Dichter) made clear. Reasoning with consumers was a strategy that had little or no chance of working given the emotional creatures that made up the human race.[56]

As Lisa Held discussed in a recent article in *Monitor on Psychology*, Bernays consulted with Brill, then New York's top psychoanalyst, to help create Lucky Strike's 1929 "Torches of Freedom" campaign in which women smoked cigarettes in public places, rather daringly. Cigarettes represented male power, Brill had told Bernays; as such, the visible smoking of them by women could help expand their rights. (The first such demonstration was led by a group of debutantes during that year's Easter Parade on Fifth Avenue, with the stunt reported by newspapers all around the world.) For a campaign for Beechnut Bacon, Bernays used Freudian group psychology by asking himself, Who influences what the public eats? The answer to the question was physicians, Bernays believed, proceeding to survey a sample of them, almost all of whom recommended a hearty breakfast over a light one. The results of the informal study were used in an ad campaign for Beechnut featuring bacon and eggs, as Bernays recalled in his 1928 book *Propaganda*, forever influencing the way Americans ate breakfast. "Who knew that Sigmund Freud, the father of psychoanalysis and critic of all things American, was an unwitting contributor to the rise of Western consumer culture?" Held asked, marveling that the irrational forces driving human behavior could be harnessed by Bernays to sell cigarettes and bacon.[57]

Religious leaders, most of whom already had major reservations about this new field that was offering a kind of alternative faith (in oneself), were especially distressed about fraudulent practitioners. One of the many American clergymen unhappy to see members of their flock being taken advantage of by psychoanalytic imposters was the Reverend Francis Potter of the West Side Unitarian Church in New York. "I know that other clergymen besides myself have recently been called upon by poor, pitiable, unnerved and nearly demented victims of quack psychoanalysis who are unscrupulously seizing upon the present craze as a means for exploiting their victims, financially and otherwise," Potter told his congregation one Sunday in 1925. Potter was outraged that physicians had to have ten or more years of education and preparation while an analyst could earn twenty-five dollars a pop with "ten days' reading of Freud and Jung." It was indeed odd that so many qualifications were required for treating the body when absolutely none were needed to treat, as the reverend nicely put it, "that more delicate organism, the human mind." Potter had no quarrel with his flock seeing a professional psychoanalyst (after first talking with their family physician and himself), but he was incensed by all the amateurs out there preying on weaker souls. "Freud is the Columbus who has discovered the unknown continent, but there are many sad derelicts in his wake floating on the sea of life who have found that leaky rowboats and poorly constructed rafts are not seaworthy craft," he poetically preached.[58] Another man of the cloth, the Reverend John MacNeill, pastor of the Tenth Presbyterian Church in Philadelphia, felt that incompetent psychoanalysts were just part of a bigger problem. "Every third person today is daft on the subject of psychoanalysis," he said in 1926, offering the sound advice that "if you want to get rid of them quickly ask them to spell the word."[59]

The circumstances surrounding Alexander Goldenweiser, a lecturer in psychoanalysis at the Rand School in New York, were providing religious leaders like Potter and MacNeill great fodder for their sermons. A heated battle between Goldenweiser and his wife, Anna, ensued in 1926 when she filed for separation after her husband allegedly abandoned her. Her affidavit also stated that her husband had "frequent love affairs with other women to whom he wrote and from whom he received epistles of love containing expressions of tenderness." Mr. Goldenweiser planned to marry his former secretary, his wife added, and had recently obtained a passport so that he could run off to Mexico with the woman. An arrest order was promptly issued for Mr. Goldenweiser, with New York's finest scouring the city for him before he crossed the border. Goldenweiser, who had been a professor of anthropology at Columbia University before becoming an analyst, had made a name for himself a few years earlier when he proclaimed that habits and hobbies were forms of neuroses or abnormal mental states that bordered on insanity. Given his own apparent habits and hobbies, perhaps inspired by the sexual freedoms to be found in psychoanalytic theory, if one looked for them, Goldenweiser might have taken a dose of his own medicine to avoid the trouble in which he found himself.[60]

What You Need Is Vienna!

The "illicit emotion plumbers" who populated psychoanalysis in the 1920s were without a doubt bad apples, but even perfectly respectable analysts were said to be doing real damage to people's lives. Psychoanalysis was often blamed for leading to the occasional suicide, an accusation that was not entirely ridiculous. In 1922, for example, a New York City woman, Mercy Rogers, was said to have killed herself after a full immersion in what her supervisor at work called "Freudianism." Rogers, who was thirty-one years old and the daughter of a retired Pittsburgh reverend, asphyxiated herself by gas at the Bronx apartment she shared with two other women where "several works on psychology and allied subjects" were later found, the *New York Times* reported. Friends said that Rogers had become increasingly interested in psychoanalysis over the course of several years to the point of obsession. The summer before her death she attended a course in psychology at Harvard during which she "devoured 102 different works on the subject," her supervisor told the medical examiner. Even if that was a gross exaggeration, it did appear that the woman had picked up some of Freud's ideas, which many justifiably considered gloomy. Rogers had become "an abysmal pessimist," her boss told the *Times*, convinced that a belief in the hereafter was simply a "projection of the ego" that had no scientific justification. Interestingly, physicians, asked for their opinion on the matter, agreed that psychoanalysis could very well have played a significant role in her decision to end her life. "The 'practice' of psycho-analysis by girls too ignorant to grasp its full meaning and not sufficiently learned to discriminate among its theories, ha[s] become so prevalent, an educational corrective [is] needed, since its devotees often derive only a dismal outlook on life from its teachings," the newspaper paraphrased one of the physicians' take on the unfortunate event.[61]

It was true that Freud was not what one would call in any way a cockeyed optimist. As Freudian theory went, how we adjusted to disappointment as reality smashed into our relentless pursuit of pleasure (sex and hunger, mostly) determined our relative mental health, obviously not the rosiest take on the meaning of life. His 1918 *Reflections on War and Death* was an especially depressing portrait of human affairs, proposing that civilization itself was doomed (some philosophers of the day, such as Anatole France, agreed). Because of the unconscious, "war cannot be abolished," Freud wrote in the book. He insisted that those who believed we would one day overcome such primitive instincts were naïve idealists. And in his *Group Psychology and the Analysis of the Ego*, published a few years later in America, Freud made the case that due to "the herd instinct" (a phrase coined by another cheery fellow, Nietzsche), humans were naturally predisposed to ambivalence and hostility even toward those we loved.[62] Freud believed that people were born "bad" and became "good" only because of social pressures (this completely opposite from Jean-Jacques Rousseau's proposition that we were born "good" but that life ultimately made us "bad"). In fact, we would all be cannibals if the act were not considered socially inappropriate in civilized parts of the world, Freud argued, this lovely tidbit proving his point that goodness was learned rather than innate, he felt.[63]

While the core of Freudian theory borrowed freely on the age-old conflict between the sacred and secular in all its permutations (flesh versus spirit, God versus Satan, heart versus head, and so on), the Austrian "packaged" it in such a way as to make it seem entirely new and modern. Freud effectively appropriated this basic duality from the "mystics," these being philosophers such as Arthur Schopenhauer and Eduard von Hartmann (who had quite a success in 1869 with his *Philosophy of the Unconscious* at age twenty-seven). Without experimental data on which to base their cases, however, the scientific community (nicknamed the "rationalists") widely mocked the mystics and their work. Even Emerson and his idea of the "double consciousness" or inner and outer self was subject to ridicule. It would be Sigmund Freud who finally gained the respect of the rationalists. His 1895 *Studies in Hysteria* (written with Breuer) marked the beginning of his venture into the unconscious mind. Soon Freud was digging deeper into his patients' unconscious by studying their daydreams and fantasies, and then even further by analyzing their dreams. "And there he found an access to the subconscious which has raised the whole study into the field of experimental science and opened it up to psychiatrists," O'Higgins observed, concluding of Freud, "that is his great indisputable achievement."[64]

To his many believers, Freud's achievements were nothing less than monumental, his body of work representing a paradigm shift in intellectual history. "Seldom, perhaps, has the personality of one man dominated an intellectual movement as has Freud's," thought Cornelia Stratton Parker in 1925, stating simply that the man was "the God of psychoanalysis." Some people, especially Freud's disciples in Vienna, thought that he might be God himself, with everything the man ever said or wrote 100 percent correct. By the mid-1920s, Freud was doing a lot more writing than talking, the old man using his energy to document his ideas in books that would survive him. Whether one thought he was 100 percent correct or 100 percent wrong, there was no doubt that his ideas had changed people's views—the post-Freud world was now a different place than the pre-Freud world. In particular, his theories regarding the unconscious, the importance of one's early years in later life, and, of course, sexuality had had a lasting impact, especially on other psychoanalysts following in his big footsteps.[65]

Although Freud was in person soft-spoken, academic, and not particularly charismatic, he was also immensely famous, certainly one of the most prominent people in the world. In fact, Freud had become such a celebrity by 1925 that movie mogul Samuel Goldwyn flew all the way to Vienna to meet with the great doctor in an attempt to persuade him to star in a feature film about himself. A couple of days earlier, Goldwyn had sent a telegram to Freud and, getting word about the forthcoming arrival of the G in MGM, the Viennese press became very excited. Unfortunately, the movie or even the meeting between the two famous men was not to be. "I do not intend to see Mr. Goldwyn," Freud tersely told the newspaper *Stunde*, rebuffing the man from Hollywood and his big plans for a boffo biopic.[66]

Just as some believed that the masses would find Freud to be a fascinating figure on the silver screen, there were those who thought that the man's theories were fast becoming old hat. Jung and Adler had already broken away to forge their own schools, after all, the former arguing that there was both a personal unconscious and collective unconscious and the latter more interested in what Andre Tridon of the *New York Call* termed "physiological accuracy" than Freud's "romantic vagueness." Adler had abandoned Freud's core idea—the unconscious—completely, in fact, believing that the nervous system presided over mental activity. (Even bolder perhaps was his claim that cures could sometimes be achieved in just a few hours via his brand of psychoanalysis.) Now an American, Edward J. Kempf, was stealing more of Freud's thunder. The clinical psychiatrist at St. Elizabeth's Hospital in Washington DC emphasized the role of biology in shaping an individual's personality. "With Kempf's advent [something he called Dynamic Mechanism] we witness the passing of the old psychoanalytic order," Tridon proclaimed in 1920: "the romance of psychoanalysis, with its slightly naughty connotation, is dead."[67]

In Vienna, however, a number of prominent analysts were keeping Freud's legacy very much alive as the man himself gradually receded from public view. For years, Freud had been a regular at the Wednesday night meetings of the International Psychoanalytic Association, but he no longer made appearances at the Pelikangasse, the headquarters of Vienna's Analytic Society. Any Wednesday night one could find Theodor Reik, Siegfried Bernfeld, Otto Rank, A. J. Storfer, Paul Schilder, Helene Deutsch, or Dorian Feigenbaum waxing poetic about neuroses, the psychology of religion, a particular phase of childhood, or any number of other topics related to psychoanalysis, the air thick with cigarette smoke. On another night at the Pelikangasse, Alfred Adler could be found holding court in front of a packed house, his school of individual psychology (with its focus on the *Minderwertigkeitsgefuhl*, or inferiority complex) a worthy challenger to the Freudians. Dr. Schilder's Saturday night class in psychiatry at the city's big hospital or Dr. Erwin Lazar's clinic for "difficult children" at the children's hospital were equally popular, making Vienna the literal go-to city for the emotionally troubled as well as for students from across Europe and the United States. (Many of those who went to Vienna to get psychoanalyzed were known to return as amateur shrinks, eager to "help" friends and strangers alike with their newly acquired intellectual skills.) Analysts themselves frequently made a pilgrimage to Vienna to be analyzed, returning home with some new techniques to try out on their patients.[68] Given Vienna's well-deserved reputation as the world capital of psychology, Parker satirically imagined an American ad campaign to attract even more tourists to the city:

> Do you feel that distressed sensation on waking? On staying awake? Does it pursue you during the day? Does it increase at the thought of what has passed through your mind during sleep? What you need is Vienna! There, at from one-fifth to one-half the price of what it costs you in New York, Chicago, or Boston, you can find RELIEF! Be Psychoanalyzed in Vienna![69]

Although the Viennese had for decades largely treated their famous native son as persona non grata, the tide was beginning to turn for Freud and psychoanalysis in the city by the late twenties, at least from a legal standpoint. Rather amazingly, Austrian courts began accepting psychoanalysts' reports as sufficient reason for breaking legal contracts, a sign of the growing status of the field on its home turf. The first such case was in 1927 when one Richard Gauber, a star of the Vienna Opera, refused to return to the company after a two-month stint with the Berlin Opera. Not only was he psychologically unable to travel, Gauber claimed, but "he was able to act and sing much better before a German than an Austrian audience as the latter affected him mentally," the *New York Times* reported. As proof of his condition, Gauber handed over to the court a report written by none other than Sigmund Freud that said as much, and his contract with the Vienna Opera was promptly annulled. Not mentioned in Freud's report was the fact that the Berlin Opera paid Gauber much more money than did his recent employer, making those in the European entertainment business nervous that entertainers could now break their contracts with a note from their analyst. "Theater directors now fear that psychoanalytic treatment will be often used by capricious stars," noted the *Times*, quite a reasonable concern given how many stars both in Europe and the United States were starting to seek therapy.[70]

Another case in Vienna in which the legend actually appeared in court took place that same year when Newton Murphy of San Francisco sued Theodore Reik, one of Freud's star pupils. Murphy had arrived in Vienna planning to be treated by Freud but the seventy-one-year-old ailing man passed on the case to Reik, who did not hold a medical degree.

After several weeks of treatment by Reik, Murphy claimed he was in worse shape than before and blamed it all on Reik's not being a physician. The affair ended up in a Viennese court with Murphy, who was a doctor himself, suing for damages and, more importantly, trying to set a precedent that psychoanalysts had to be physicians (an issue that was also being hotly debated in the United States). Murphy went all out to try to win the case, bringing in as an expert witness the eminent Professor Wagner-Jauregg of the University of Vienna, who had long been an opponent of Freud and of psychoanalysis in general (despite having nominated Freud for the Nobel Prize in Medicine-Physiology a number of times). The professor, who won the Nobel Prize in 1927, testified that psychoanalysis was a dangerous thing when practiced by someone who was not a physician and named thirty-one doctors and professors of medicine who agreed. Before a packed house of the city's leading psychoanalysts and physicians, Freud then took the stand in Reik's defense, telling the court that a medical degree was not necessary "in cases where my treatment can effect good." Although it was thirty-two against one, Reik won the day, his star witness persuading the court that his brand of medicine was as good as any other.[71]

Out to Conquer the World

While Freud had achieved legendary status by the 1920s, he was of course hardly without his critics. Condemnation of Freud's ideas arrived in two general waves: moral outrage and shock, followed by denunciation of his methods. The first wave often involved religion, sex, or both, with psychoanalysis perceived as a serious threat to traditional ways. "It is out to conquer the world," opined George Matheson Cullen in 1921, the physician turned monk convinced that psychoanalysis was "striving to set the seal of its interpretation upon religion and morals, history, mythology and folk-lore."[72] It was true that many psychoanalysts looked to religion as the root cause of neuroses that appeared later in life, and thought society in general would be better off without it. Common psychoanalytic theory held that boys taught by religious parents that sex was sinful often had "perversions" as adults, especially among those with fundamentalist backgrounds. "It is extremely dangerous in our American civilization for a parent to put a morbid stigma on sex in any child's mind," said one analyst in 1928, "since the social and religious tabu is already so heavy."[73]

Some critics, however, saw religion and psychoanalysis as being in the same basic business—the curing of souls. This contingent went so far as to suggest that Christian ministers should become conversant with the latter's methods in order to treat distressed members of their congregation. Quite a few ministers were indeed taking courses in the subject at colleges or clinics, finding it useful in their counseling. Talk therapy was also sometimes referred to as a "scientific confessional," and Jesuits believed that the first years of a child's life determined his or her future as an adult; psychoanalysis and Catholicism seemingly had more in common than some would admit. Finally, many if not most psychoanalysts were familiar with the teachings of the church, some even helping patients achieve harmony, peace of mind, and confidence by linking the treatment to their faith in God. Given these connections, could religion and psychoanalysis get along happily together, each instilling in individuals a healthier relationship with oneself and with others?[74]

Certainly not, according to the masters of the game. Freud was quite specific about religious beliefs, seeing them as nothing more than a psychological phenomenon, as he made clear in his *Psychopathology of Everyday Life*:

> I believe that a large proportion of the mythological conception of the world which reaches far into the most modern religions is *nothing but psychology projected into the outer world*.... We venture to explain in this way the myths of paradise and the fall of man, of God, of good and evil, of immortality and the like, i.e., to transform *metaphysics* into *metapsychology*.[75]

Freud's rival, Carl Jung, was in his early work even more dismissive about religion, defining God as "a mere psychological function of an irrational nature." (He later came to see religion in a much more positive light.) There was little question that the central themes of religion fell outside the boundaries of science and, specifically, the scientific method, the very idea of "faith" inconsistent with that of "proof." Religion and psychoanalysis appeared to be strange bedfellows or out-and-out enemies, forcing individuals to choose which side of the ideological fence to inhabit.[76]

The cultural divide between psychoanalysis and religion was abundantly clear for some, with the new psychology already displacing traditional ways of life. Writing for *Harper's* in 1922, C. A. Bennett marked the rise of psychoanalysis by comparing what might happen to a teenager who got caught doing a bad thing like mistreating a stray dog. In the past, the boy would perhaps be sent by his parents to the local priest, who would talk about the evilness of such a thing and the need for self-control. Natural impulses were bad, the priest would explain, a function of our original sin. But now, Bennett proposed, a little tongue in cheek, this same boy who did the same thing might be sent to a psychoanalyst, who would analyze his dreams to uncover the underlying reasons for his actions. The boy could then be told he suffered from the "Gadarene complex," this being "an epiphenomenal derivative of the herd-instinct." Most important, the boy would learn he was not really to blame given that he was merely a victim of "maladjustment." Natural impulses were not bad, in other words, but simply natural impulses, and describing them as sinful would only lead to bigger problems down the road.[77]

The fact that most of the pioneers of psychoanalysis were Jewish did not stop many rabbis from thinking that, when it came to religion, shrinks did not know what they were talking about. "All admire Freud, the psychoanalyst, but that is no reason why we should respect his theology," Rabbi Nathan Krass told his congregation at Temple Emanu-El in New York in 1928 after reading *The Future of an Illusion*. In his new book, Freud argued that religion was an illusion and would eventually become extinct, a casualty of science. Krass considered Freud a layperson when it came to religion, and thus was not overly concerned that he would soon be out of work. "He analyzes religion as one who has studied anthropology," the rabbi said in his sermon (titled "Psychoanalyzing a Psychoanalyst"), reassuring his fellow Jews that "what I feel is as real as what I see out of a window."[78]

Even many of Freud's disciples in Europe who found their beliefs in psychoanalysis and God not mutually exclusive were disappointed to read the seventy-two-year-old man's new book. Most concerning to them was that by driving a wedge between science and religion, real damage to the field was likely to occur, playing right into the critics' hands. Besides his supposition that religion was a form of madness, Freud maintained that priests were fighting a losing battle by appealing to individuals' moral instincts. Neither of these ideas was particularly well received by true believers. However, superstitions such as religion were slowing the further advance of science, Freud felt, and it was time that we decided which path to follow. "Mankind must renounce all illusions to allow intellectual development," he told a reporter after his contentious book was published, explaining that "science is a walking stick to support a progressive world."[79]

Of course, not just the religious but other scientists, physicians, and psychologists tried to poke holes in Freud's theories. Perhaps because psychoanalysis presented a threat to their livelihood (why undergo a medical procedure when one could just talk it out?), physicians aggressively defended their turf against this new upstart. "Psychoanalysis is a pseudoscience like palmistry, graphology, and phrenology," claimed Samuel A. Tannenbaum, a New York physician who had actually used Freud's theories in his practice for ten years but by 1922 had come to believe they were baloney, a common accusation.[80] In an article published in the *Journal of the American Medical Association* around the same time, physician Frederick Peterson dismissed psychoanalysis as just a passing fad. "The theories of Freud and Jung are to psychology what cubism is to art—new, sensational, and rather interesting," he wrote. But psychoanalysis, he argued, like the works of Picasso, Braque, and Gris, was destined for the dustbin of history. "Let them take their place in our historical medical museum along with all the other curiosities which for centuries have accumulated," Peterson proposed, seeing Freud's and Jung's theories as having little or no lasting value.[81]

By blazing his own trail (and leaving them in the dust), Freud had in particular angered academic psychologists who believed that he went well beyond the accepted scientific boundaries of the field. With its heavy sexual orientation, psychoanalysis had too narrow a viewpoint, these critics also pointed out, something they felt had been borne out during the Great War. Treatment of soldiers who had returned from the war with "shell shock" showed that neuroses could develop from experiences that were clearly not sexual in nature, this supposedly contradicting Freud's theories.[82] Many if not most psychoanalysts (or psychotherapists, as some were beginning to call themselves) now believed there were a handful of instincts as important as the sexual one, with impulses such as self-preservation and self-assertion also driving thought and behavior.[83]

Attacks on Freud and psychoanalysis as a whole came from all directions. It "possesses all that moral authority and intellectual finality which we associate with a particular pattern of hats or whiskers," sniped Gilbert K. Chesterton in 1923, who, like Peterson, considered psychoanalysis simply a current fashion. Most people had not learned to use the conscious part of their mind much less their subconscious part, Chesterton remarked, making psychoanalysis "a nonsensical nuisance and nothing else." Psychoanalysis reminded Chesterton of what he believed was the last big intellectual fashion—Marxism—but instead of everything being economic, everything was now sexual. With even Marxists in Russia no longer subscribing to Marxism as it was originally conceived, "it was time for another monomania to appear."[84]

Clive Bell, a prominent British art critic (and brother-in-law of Virginia Woolf), was especially bothered by Freud's take on artists (and patrons of art). The artist was "one who is urged on by his instinctive needs, which are too clamorous," Freud had written in *Introductory Lectures on Psycho-Analysis*, these needs being "honor, power, riches, fame, and the love of women." Because such gratifications were beyond the typical artist, however, he "turns away from reality and transfers all his interest, and all his libido too, on to the creations of his wishes in the life of fantasy." For Bell, such a theory was pure rubbish. "Art has nothing to do with dreams," he insisted. "The artist is not one who dreams more vividly, but who is a good deal wider awake than most people." In conceiving Cordelia for his *King Lear*, for example, Shakespeare was not concerned with his dreams (nor hers), but rather with solving an artistic problem. Bell went so far as to meet with a "roomful of psychoanalysts" to explain Freud's misinterpretation of artists' motives but it was to little avail. When Bell presented Cezanne's repeated reliance on apples to illustrate the artist's quest to solve a particular problem, the analysts instantly "broke into titters," apparently seeing something very different in the significance of the fruit.[85]

Perhaps the most earnest criticism came from those who actually found some value in the process. "Possibly no science—or pseudo-science—offers more attractive possibilities to the seeker for truth than psychoanalysis," thought Edna Yost in 1928. Yost suggested that "the opportunity to reveal one's soul, to strip it naked before another, is a delightful temptation to the ego." However, having a number of friends who over the past decade had been or still were in analysis, Yost was convinced that this promise was going largely unfilled. Yost's problem with what she called "psychoparalysis" was larger than the usual complaint by the field's opponents. Yost berated the so-called Freudians who gave their male patients permission to sleep with their friends' wives, with the "repressed" men only too happy to follow their doctor's orders. After seeing her friends become dependent on therapy and their therapists, Yost wrote in the *Forum*, "I lack confidence in psychoanalysis because it gives one a false sense of freedom."[86]

Even worse, the psychoanalyzed seemed to have frozen personalities, a result of having achieved the much-desired discovery of their "real self" and then, afraid of mucking up the works, suffering "dry-rot." The methodology of psychoanalysis was the source of the problem, Yost argued. Its inherent introspective orientation was unnatural, lacked spontaneity, and was, most of all, "clingy." "Analyzed people cannot, or at least they do not often, get away from it," she had concluded. The tag or label assigned to them by their analyst—for example, "inferiority complex" or "sex repression"—was now firmly attached to their identity.[87] Other critics were disturbed simply by all the baring of souls going on. It was true that individuals' inner psyches had never before been so exposed and, for some, this was a line that just should not have been crossed. "Psychiatry ... has lit a lamp, and with its mental x-rays is pursuing her investigations, not only into the nature of love, but into the nature of everything and everybody else around her," wrote Mary Day Winn for *The North American Review* in 1928, arguing that the secrets of the soul should remain secrets. The fact that some psychiatrists had of late started to use a machine that measured one's heartbeat (supposedly revealing emotions should speech or facial expression fail) did not help matters, such an intrusion representing an even more unwarranted peek into our unconsciouses.[88]

Touching on all kinds of emotional issues—privacy, health, religion, sex, and, last but not least, the meaning of life—it was simply difficult to feel ambivalent about psychoanalysis, with Americans' attitudes about it tipping one way or another. "Probably no subject—unless it be religion—is provocative of such violent and contradictory opinion to-day, as the subject of psychoanalysis," stated an anonymous writer for *Century* magazine in 1929. The author concluded that younger, more liberal thinkers were inclined to support it but that older, more conservative Americans wished it would just go away. Even among those who had undergone treatment, psychoanalysis was proving to be a polarizing force. The cured typically claimed that their whole lives had been made over, while the uncured usually considered it an absolute waste of time and money.[89] The passion surrounding psychoanalysis was pushing the field into new directions, and the highly charged topic was well on its way to becoming a permanent fixture of the American experience. "We may be said to be living in a psychoanalytic age," wrote Joseph Jastrow in 1929, "for there has been insinuated into our outlook a Freudian temper."[90]

There was no doubt that Freudianism had by the end of the 1920s stretched well beyond psychoanalysis, elevated to a way of approaching life and moving through it. Jastrow saw psychoanalysis not unlike Prohibition, however, a noble experiment that was likely to fail in practice. Rather incredibly, some obscure research into hysteria had, over the course of a generation, "converted the human scene into a neurotic clinic," as Jastrow described it, but he believed this Freudian temper posed a menace to society. Perfectly normal people—"the lay mind"—were being tempted to have the contents of their unconscious exposed when they were better left undisturbed, a state of affairs perhaps equivalent to a surgeon slicing into a body to make sure everything inside was working right. Women were especially at risk, compelled to be "psyched" because it was a sign of emancipation but, ironically, put in an inferior position to the analyst, who was almost always male. As well, glibly using terms like "repression," "complexes," "sublimation," and "wish fulfillment," as many were, was dangerous stuff. The man or woman on the street had little or no idea what they really meant. To Jastrow, Freud's popularity seemed mostly due to its being lumped together with other liberations of the day—jazz and sex, in particular—this troika of hedonism comprising an "anti-repressionistic carnival."[91] The controversies surrounding psychoanalysis were just beginning, however, with a new chapter in its fascinating history about to be written.

CHAPTER 2: The Voodoo Religion

> This suicide is the result of too much psychoanalysis promoted and enforced by a cruel wife.
>
> Note found by the body of HAROLD L. SIPPY, a Chicago physician, in 1945

In August 1949, Leopold Kleiner, a Manhattan architect and designer, made quite a name for himself by announcing that homes for extroverts should be designed differently than those for introverts. Before becoming an architect, Kleiner had studied with Freud, an occasion providing the likely basis for Kleiner's psychoanalyzing all his clients before putting pencil to paper. Kleiner believed that because the "psycho-potential" of individuals varied, people would not be comfortable in certain surroundings, hence the need for what he called "psychodesigning." "Unless the places in which people live and work are designed to conform with their psychological make-up," he argued, "they will be unhappy." Extroverts required neutral environments that did not steal attention from themselves, for example, while introverts needed rooms with vibrant hues. Emotional states and even climate too played a role in one's "psychopotential," said Kleiner. "For a nervous extrovert living in New York, I would advise rooms done in gray, beige or tans," he advised. The introduction of loud colors could send a high-strung Gothamite over the edge.[1]

The advent of "psychodesigning" suggested how deeply psychoanalysis had seeped into the national consciousness by midcentury. Psychoanalysis was now almost everywhere you looked, an indelible part of the American scene. The path that psychoanalysis would take to get to this place was not an easy one, as the field faced its most strident criticism to date. The 1930s and early 1940s were very challenging years for psychoanalysis in America, the honeymoon of the 1920s clearly over. But just as the war would help bring the nation out of its Great Depression and revive the American economy, so would the international crisis give new life to psychoanalysis, paving the way for even greater glory days ahead.

A False Trail

The Great Crash of 1929 may have turned the American economy upside down but it did little to make people forget about psychoanalysis. Even if fewer people could afford it, psychoanalysis seemed to become an even louder part of the American conversation, woven into popular culture and ordinary discourse. A 1931 editorial for the *New York Times* made it crystal clear how thoroughly psychoanalysis had infiltrated everyday life in America:

> Since Freud populated such words as complex and fixation, the lingo of psychoanalysis, if not a deep understanding of it, has become as commonplace as measles. The stage has bloomed with mother-love gone Freudian, with father-fixations, with secret thoughts of characters spoken out as asides for a sage audience to analyze. Books have run riot on the dark trails of the subconscious. And the lowliest clerk can explain that his fussy office manager is simply suffering from an inferiority complex.[2]

To an increasing number of people, this kudzulike spreading of psychoanalysis across the American landscape was not a particularly good thing. About a year later, the same newspaper published another editorial titled "Down with the Unconscious," in which the editor criticized Americans' love of analyzing themselves:

> Many people of normal intelligence, eager to improve themselves in their contacts with others, have been inclined to embrace mental therapy as a sure remedy for personality defects. Delving into their own and their friends' unconsciouses, they have become too aware of mental processes. Young persons are particularly likely to enjoy self-analysis. Keeping up with the psychoanalytic literature and lectures, they seek within themselves for the symptoms discussed. Like

the man reading the medical book, they can find evidence of all the distortions and complexes in the psychoanalyst's calendar.[3]

Readers of newspapers also believed the nation's "complex and fixation" with psychoanalysis had gone too far, and that Americans were the worse for it. In his 1932 letter to the *Times*, for example, Frederick W. Brown of New York City made the case that

> psychoanalysis ... has, because of its very nature and purpose, served as a facile tool in the hands of the charlatans and quacks, who reap their harvest at the expense of inadequate personalities seeking a richer and fuller life. It has been popularized and exploited until we find in our literature, on the stage and in many of our social relationships a morbid sex interest and philosophy of self-gratification permeating the thought and activities of those forces which once served not only as a means of recreation but as a source of inspiration.[4]

A full-fledged backlash against psychoanalysis seemed to be in play in the early 1930s, its association with the now-suspect wealthy elite certainly a contributing factor for its fall from grace. Psychoanalysis rather famously had not helped Stanley McCormick, the mentally incompetent multimillionaire heir of International Harvester who lived in a huge mansion in Montecito, California, a real-life Charles Foster Kane. When in 1930 his doctors fired Edward J. Kempf, the noted psychoanalyst from New York, and hired a traditional psychiatrist, the fifty-six-year-old son of Cyrus ("The Harvester King") McCormick reportedly took a decided turn for the better. The new course of treatment even restored harmonious relations between McCormick and his wife, as well as those with his brother and sister, quite an achievement. McCormick had inherited a $50-million fortune from his father, making the $250,000 a year he spent on living costs (which included his own orchestra and motion picture theater) relative chicken feed.[5]

Increasingly seen as an excess of the 1920s, something Americans could and should no longer afford, psychoanalysis became the subject of intense scrutiny within the psychiatric community. More experts were coming out of the woodwork to critique aspects of psychoanalysis or dismiss it entirely, its philosophy of life built around sex pathology considered less than scientific and, perhaps worse, immoral. Adolf Meyer, a well-known psychiatrist at Johns Hopkins, for example, did not believe psychoanalysis should be completely thrown out, but thought it was being overused and that its effects were overstated. Noting that psychoanalysis was but one of many methods of treating mental disorders, in a 1932 lecture at the New York Academy of Medicine, Meyer stated, "I prefer to keep to our broad psychobiological principle of considering the whole of man . . . rather than the elusive subconscious."[6]

Meyer's treatment of choice was the new science of "psychobiology," an early attempt to unite the two basic entities of medicine, the physical and the mental, into an integrated whole, an approach that foreshadowed the direction psychiatry would take in the decades to come with psychotropics.[7] George H. Kirby, president of the American Psychiatric Association, endorsed Meyer's approach, thinking that psychobiology represented the greatest promise for future developments in his field. Psychoanalysis was invaluable, particularly as a method of investigation and research into mental ills, Kirby told his colleagues in 1934, but its applications in actual practice were limited, meaning psychiatrists had also to look to the human body to explain human behavior.[8]

Kirby's bigger problem with psychoanalysis was with those practitioners he called "parlor psychologists," primarily lecturers and writers who "disguise the pill of serious facts with a spicy coating of sensationalism . . . [as] a remunerative way of entertaining suburban ladies." The field indeed remained heavily populated with lay analysts and psychologists with a smattering of psychoanalytic knowledge. Anyone and everyone who took a course in the subject could instantly become a psycho-entrepreneur, knowing a good moneymaker when he or she saw one. It was not just those wanting to make a quick buck off psychoanalysis that posed a threat to the field, he thought; those smart enough to know better were also not treating the subject with the respect it deserved. "In certain circles of the intelligentsia, psychoanalysis is treated as a pastime or playing," Kirby complained to his fellow psychiatrists, urging them to do what they could to have the toy put away so that the field could be recognized as bona fide science.[9]

Greater interest in psychobiology among psychiatrists all over the country did not bode well for traditional psychoanalysis. Milton Harrington, psychiatrist at the Great Meadow Prison in Comstock, New York, for example, believed that biology played a crucial role in human behavior, pulling no punches when it came to Freudian theories at the 1932 joint meeting of the American Psychiatric Association and American Psychoanalytic Association in Philadelphia. "The psychoanalysts and others who follow Freud are following a false trail," he insisted. Faulty mechanisms of the body, not suppressed desires, were responsible for mental abnormalities. Harrington went much further than Meyer in looking to biology for the answers to psychiatric questions, with many parts of the human body—sense organs, nervous system, muscles, glands—factors in the way people acted. Another psychiatrist at the convention, David Slight, of Montreal, backed up Harrington, proposing that it was a specific biological condition—too much fat in the blood— that caused melancholia. After Slight and his associates changed the fatty diet of a group of suicidal patients to a starchier one, a couple of them reportedly returned to "normal mentality," just the kind of finding that was leading psychiatrists to take a closer look at the goings-on below the neck. Could potatoes and rice, rather than years of intensive psychotherapy, be the optimal cure for emotional problems?[10]

With psychoanalysis on the ropes, it did not help when A. A. Brill, the country's top psychoanalyst, decided to give a paper called "Lincoln as a Humorist" at the American Psychiatric Association's 1931 convention in Toronto. Lincoln and other famous figures from the past had already been posthumously psychoanalyzed but Brill took psychohistory to a new level with his reading of the Great Emancipator. Lincoln was, according to Brill, a "schizoid manic personality," suffering from what we would today call bipolar disorder. Brill stopped short of calling Lincoln insane, a good decision in retrospect given the ruckus he caused with his already contentious diagnosis. "Two contrasting natures struggled within him," Brill argued, Lincoln's dark side inherited from his brute of a father and his light side derived from his cheerful, affectionate mother. The president's habit of telling the occasional dirty joke was an outlet for his "sexually aggressive" personality, Brill added, this too something that definitely did not endear him or psychoanalysis in general to those already suspicious of the field.[11]

One man particularly irked by Brill's "necroanalysis" was another notable psychiatrist, Jacob Moreno, previously of Vienna. Psychoanalysis simply had not developed to the point where such claims could be made, Moreno countered. Because everything we knew about Lincoln was based on second-hand stories, he considered Brill's theory to be highly specious. Had Lincoln been psychoanalyzed and his case documented for posterity, Brill would be perfectly justified in drawing his own conclusions, but because the rail-splitter from Illinois died some thirty years before Breuer and Freud's *Studies In Hysteria*, Brill was way out of bounds. L. Pierce Clark, a consulting neurologist for the Manhattan State Hospital, also thought Brill did not know what he was talking about. Could a man who understood constitutional law so thoroughly and relate to the American people so well really be schizoid? Clark wondered. Such traits were not at all consistent with someone who failed to accept reality, a classic sign of the condition. Clark's complaint may in fact have been rooted in his rivalry with Brill, as he had been working on a psychoanalytic study of Lincoln's personality for the past five years, which he planned to publish as a forthcoming book, *The Spirit of Lincoln*.[12]

Others too were peeved by Brill's paper. William L. Love, a state senator from New York, was so angry to hear the sixteenth president labeled as a "schizoid manic personality" that he formally censored Brill in that state's legislature. Any attack on the man who freed the slaves—even a psychological one—was an unpatriotic act, Love believed. Love, who happened to be a physician, was not done with Brill and his ilk, soon telling a group of New York City Masons that he planned to introduce a bill at the next session of the legislature to ban the practice of psychoanalysis in the state altogether. Psychoanalysis was "akin to hypnotism" and had "an unhealthy effect on many persons, especially neurotic women," Love said to the lodge members. In fact, Love's other job as a medical doctor may have shaped his attempt to get rid of those whom he later called "pseudo psychiatrists and bootlegging psychologists." Furthermore, Love somehow had cause to believe that a woman whose body had recently washed up on a Long Island beach was a "victim of psychoanalysis," reason enough to at least launch a thorough investigation of the field.[13]

Attacked by everyone from innovative psychiatrists to overzealous politicians, the stock of psychoanalysis seemed to be falling as fast as those on Wall Street in the early thirties. Noted psychiatrists like Frederick Peterson were zeroing in on psychoanalysis, the field a relatively easy target given the impossibility of proving that it actually worked. And when Peterson talked, people listened. Peterson had impeccable credentials, including twenty-five years as professor of psychiatry at Columbia, past presidency of the New York State Commission in Lunacy and that state's Neurological Society, and author or coauthor of many books, including the widely read *Nervous and Mental Diseases*. Peterson had problems with a number of branches of psychology (Watson's behaviorism was "magnificent nonsense," endocrinologists were "chasing a rainbow," and personality study was "futile," he maintained), but he took special aim at psychoanalysis. "Psychoanalysis is, from my point of view, a voodoo religion characterized by obscene rites and human sacrifices," he said in 1932, not at all the science its adherents claimed it to be. It would be one thing if psychoanalysts limited their practice to the chronically insane, as that could do little harm and perhaps help a bit, but applying it to the normal or near normal was playing with fire.[14]

Francis Gerty, head of Chicago's psychopathic hospital, was almost as vituperative. He cautioned that normal people undergoing psychoanalysis, not because of emotional issues but to improve themselves or fix minor character flaws, were putting themselves at great risk. The process of transference, for example, in which patients often ended up revering (or falling in love with) their analyst, was particularly problematic. "Unless you strike a psychoanalyst of the most sterling character and ability, you are apt to come out of it worse off than when you started," he believed. The substitution of someone else's ideas for one's own was surely a mistake in most cases, and nothing short of disaster awaited those who put themselves in the hands of the wrong analyst, Gerty warned. This possibility alone presented a good reason for those of "normal mentality" to avoid psychoanalysis like the plague.[15] Less scathing but equally passionate critiques of psychoanalysis floated in the ether. Some of a certain age believed that psychoanalysis was taking much of the beauty and mystery out of love, for example, the word once considered sacred and used only when deep feelings were involved. "Then psychoanalysis became the rage and people began to dig down into the raw bones of love," observed Margaret Widdener, a Pulitzer Prize–winning poet, in 1932. The parsing of romance in the talking cure made it lose all of its magic.[16]

Along with the attacks on genuine psychoanalysis in the early 1930s was the continual effort to try to get rid of the fake variety. One of the more interesting cases in this matter involved a Mrs. Mayer, the head of a school in New York City that taught psychology and psychoanalysis, and a Miss Lillian Frey of Beechhurst, Queens. Frey (who had once been a patient of Adolph Lorenz, the famous Viennese "bloodless surgeon") suffered from paralysis of the right leg and went to Mayer for a course of "dream work." After failing to cure her leg, Mayer explained to Frey that she was not "philosophically ready" to be healed, perhaps not surprisingly raising some questions about the kind of therapy she was receiving. Frey had not only paid Mayer $3,200 for the treatment and other psychoanalytic services but had not gotten back a loan of an additional $2,500, meaning that Frey was out $5,700 and still had a bum leg. Frey promptly filed a complaint with the state's deputy attorney general, Sol Ullman, and the case landed in court, a rare instance in which a practitioner of psychoanalysis was prosecuted. Ullman was interested in the case not as a damage suit but rather as one that could help determine who could practice medicine, the real legal issue at stake. "There are many people in this city who have been gypped by fake psychoanalysts," said Ullman. It was now time, the state decided, to try to nip this kind of thing in the bud.[17]

An Egregious Failure

It was not all bad news for psychoanalysis in the early 1930s, however, as supporters of the field promoted its philosophy and found new ways to apply its ideas. Despite the Depression, an Institute for Psychoanalysis opened in Chicago in 1932, the second of its kind in the country and the sixth in the world. Heading up the Institute was Franz Alexander who had previously been with the Berlin Psychoanalytic Institute, the pioneer in the field that had opened its doors in 1920. Alexander had given a series of lectures at the University of Chicago a couple of years earlier, likely seeing the Second City as a good place to spread the seeds of psychoanalysis in America. The associate director of the institute was

Karen Horney who had worked with Alexander in Berlin, with five top-notch associates doing the heavy clinical lifting. "For the intelligent public today it is becoming as neutral to consult a psychoanalyst concerning a psychosis or a neurosis as it is to go to an ophthalmologist in case of eye trouble," said Alexander in announcing the institute's purpose; his colleagues agreed that the time was ripe to take the field to the next level.[18]

Part of the reason Alexander and his team were gung-ho on psychoanalysis was that they believed Americans were in sort of a group funk. Just a couple months after his appointment, Alexander gave a talk at the Illinois Society for Mental Hygiene, using his outsider perspective to assess America's rather poor mental health. While the economic mess was not helping matters one bit, it was the machine age that was most responsible for the nation's collective emotional woes, he thought. "Man has not yet learned to use his own invention, the machine, in utilizing the free time and free energies which the machine makes possible," said Alexander. Other conference speakers agreed that Americans had largely failed to adapt to their new, more mechanistic kind of environment. Rabbi Solomon B. Freehof, for example, blamed consumerism for the country's psychic problems, another pitfall of the machine age. "We have been misled into worshiping new objects," the rabbi stated, arguing that the temporary fruitlessness of our horn of plenty had left a distinct feeling of emptiness in many.[19]

Official institutions dedicated to psychoanalysis obviously helped push the agenda of the field, but it was through people or organizations having little or no real connection to psychiatry that its power could be felt. The tentacles of psychoanalysis were indeed reaching into some unlikely places, as the public looked to the practice as a way to solve a variety of problems. "Sooner or later motordom is going to be psychoanalyzed, or 'psyched,'" thought the *Washington Post* in 1933, reporting that the state of Connecticut was working with the psychology department at Yale to see if psychoanalysis could help distinguish good drivers from bad ones. The state's department of motor vehicles envisioned asking drivers a set of one hundred questions that would shed light on their judgment and "mental capabilities," a kind of psychological equivalent to the traffic-law test already being used. Getting unfit drivers off the road was the ultimate goal of the program, an application of psychoanalytic theory that Freud certainly never imagined.[20]

Amateur psychoanalysis also seemed to be on the rise in the early thirties as those with a bent for the field applied it to their own professions. Luther Z. Rosser, an Atlanta judge, for example, was using psychoanalytic principles to try to keep couples considering divorce together. Rosser would take unhappy couples into his chambers and dole out advice such as "Never crush the pride of your marriage partner"—one of his seven rules for a successful marriage.[21] Thankfully, perhaps, judges in domestic relations courts with less aptitude for psychoanalysis were increasingly referring cases of marital discord to professional analysts. With less social stigma attached to divorce and with more women becoming economically independent, separations were continuing to rise in the early thirties, a windfall for psychiatrists and psychoanalysts. So much of this kind of business was in fact coming shrinks' way that leaders of the field felt the need to provide guidelines for analysts to follow. "The only position which the psychoanalyst can assume in these matrimonial tangles is to bring to consciousness those unconscious factors which produce social discord," C. P. Oberndorf told members of the American Neurological Association. Oberndorf insisted that it was "not the function of the psychoanalyst to assume the role of guide either in keeping the couple together or in advising separation." Psychoanalysts were scientists, in other words, not marriage counselors. It was their job to provide objective facts versus subjective advice.[22]

Whether one was in favor of psychoanalysis or not, the field was continuing to pop up in all kinds of settings, increasingly viewed as a part of the American Way of Life. The trajectory of psychoanalysis up to this point was nothing short of remarkable, progressing from revolutionary theory (or work of a modern Antichrist, depending on your view) to legitimate, accredited medical specialty within the all-mighty American Psychiatric Association. Over the course of forty years, the public's general sentiment toward psychoanalysis had changed from hate to skepticism to tolerance to approval, its path cleared by the cultural transition from Victorianism to modernity. "The result of this scientific apotheosis is that Freudian psychoanalysis has invaded almost every conceivable field of human thought and conduct, and is, at present, attempting to impose its dicta of authoritative interpretation on almost every known discipline," thought W. Beran Wolfe in 1935. Wolfe was convinced that everything from anthropology to zoology had "all succumbed in some degree to the magical blandishments of the Viennese sage and his many disciples." Like other critics, Wolfe thought that given its past success and future intentions, it was high time for psychoanalysis to provide a kind of audit or performance review. "Society now has the right to demand that the Freudians render an account of their services to medicine and to society," he proposed. The public had a right to know whether this working hypothesis about human behavior had achieved all it had been credited with. Wolfe believed that if such a thing were demanded, psychoanalysis would not be seen as a miracle of the age, but as "an egregious failure," something which had fallen well short of its mighty promises.[23]

First and foremost of Wolfe's issues with psychoanalysis was that there was no proof at all that a "brave new morality" had been produced to replace our puritanical sex complexes. By applying their unique insight into human behavior only to the occasional individual versus society at large, psychoanalysts were, in a way, "traitors," having turned their backs on a common, greater good. Indeed, if the Freudians were right in their grand assumptions, doling out their doctrine to just those few with a few thousand dollars to spare was unforgivable, their avarice almost a crime against humanity. As well, psychoanalysis was now as dated as the Victorian age from which it sprang, the horsehair sofa in Freud's office an apt metaphor for the field. "The magic of the psychoanalytic couch, the fascination of dream interpretation, the excitement of the quest for phallic symbols—all these have waned in a world beset with the more urgent problems of work, crime, food, transportation, peace, leisure, social and international cooperation," Wolfe concluded. Freud and his followers were simply unequipped to take on these larger challenges in harsher, crueler times.[24]

Although psychoanalysts have been (and continue to be) deservedly criticized for treating only wealthy patients who could afford long-term therapy, and ignoring those who could not (especially those in mental hospitals), there were limited attempts to make possible "psychoanalysis for the poor." In 1936, for example, Paul Schilder of Bellevue Hospital in

New York psychoanalyzed a group of fifty-one patients classroom-style, focusing on censored thought and dream interpretation. This first documented case of "mass psychoanalysis" had mixed results, according to Schilder, with eleven "cured," sixteen "improved," and twenty-four "unrelieved." This "new application of Freudianism," as the *New York Times* called it, was cause for some excitement among Depression-era psychiatrists, the possibility of a New Deal for the mentally ill something that could significantly broaden the applications of the field.[25]

Most psychoanalysts, however, were not ready to make their services available to the impoverished. Such patients tended to be severely disturbed and thus were considered less intelligent than the field's bread-and-butter clients—the hysterics, worriers, and obsessed of the moneyed class. ("Stupid patients are not good subjects," went one of the general tenets of the field.) Because they were out of touch with reality, and thus typically lacked the poise or willingness to cooperate with the analyst to have their unconscious modified through deep self-knowledge (a Catch-22, of course), psychotics were also considered poor candidates for analysis. Older people too were deemed bad patients, most psychoanalysts agreed, with little hope of dramatically changing the ways of someone as young as forty. (Keep in mind that the average life span of Americans in 1935 was sixty-two years.) One thus generally had to be young and smart and have time and money to have an analyst dig past the consciousness—"the deceptive architectural front of a vast unknown structure," one writer called it—the prime purpose of psychoanalysis. The average "sitting" in the mid-1930s cost about ten dollars, with 250 to 270 sessions a year quite typical. With eighteen months to two years of treatment, one was looking at five thousand to six thousand dollars, and this in some mighty hard economic times.[26]

For those who did not have that kind of money lying around, there was a much cheaper lesson in psychoanalysis readily available. For just two dollars, one could pick up John Anders's *Prescription for Marriage*, a good example of how works of fiction were, for better or worse, being used to learn principles of the field. In the 1933 novel, the protagonist, Dr. Karl Porter (note the quasi-German or Austrian name) makes the psychoanalytic rounds of New York society, his specialty wealthy, emotionally troubled women. He is a master of the game, of course, recognized as an expert in the field and justifiably confident in his abilities to cure even the most neurotic dilettante. But then a beautiful but disturbed woman comes along, sent to Porter by her husband to be saved from imminent nervous breakdown or worse, who throws the happily married analyst for a loop. Porter does indeed rescue the damsel in distress but at great cost to himself, the dramatic finale possibly "of singular import to those theoretically interested in the workings of psychoanalysis," the *New York Times* opined in its review.[27]

An even cheaper psychoanalytic primer was *Interpreting Your Dreams*, a booklet sold by the *Los Angeles Times* in the late 1930s that could be had for just fifteen cents. "Dreams often tell their story in parables, or in poetic and figurative style," explained a 1936 ad for the forty-page, illustrated booklet, the stories "like a cipher or code to be understood only with the aid of a key." Psychoanalysis was that key, the ad continued, revealing through dreams "our wishes, loves, and hates, delusions of grandeur, [and] longings to escape from reality." As an everyman's guide to the goings-on within the unconscious, *Interpreting Your Dreams* showed how far psychoanalysis had penetrated pop culture: the desire to know how one's mind (or other's minds) really worked was now considered a perfectly normal and ordinary pursuit.[28]

Spellbound

Even Hollywood directors were known to use a kind of pop psychoanalysis when it worked to their advantage. Archie Mayo, a big-time director in the early thirties, prided himself on his ability to decipher stars' "complexes," using this information to get along with some notoriously temperamental people. As a self-proclaimed "scientific student of character," Mayo recognized that discovering the weaknesses of actors could come in quite handy on the set when things got a bit tense. "You have to reach Barbara's brain through her heart [and] after that there is no trouble whatever," explained Mayo in 1932, speaking of his directorial approach with Barbara Stanwyck on the film *Illicit*. "When I psyched Cagney I found he had been raised in an atmosphere of conflict," added the amateur shrink, using this juicy psychoanalytic tidbit to get the best out of the pugnacious star. Mayo had "psyched" quite a few leading stars of the day, in fact, figuring out that Constance Bennett's Achilles heel was her hair and that John Barrymore was a sucker for "embellishment." Mayo was currently lurking about the set of his new movie in order to analyze Kay Francis, with whom he had not yet worked, claiming that he had failed only·once to determine a leading man's or lady's "queer complex." Of Ted Lewis, Mayo exclaimed, "He was a band-master!" Even his impressive psychoanalytic abilities had not been sufficient to reign in the egomaniac, and Mayo had walked off the picture.[29]

Psychoanalysis also worked its way into the movies themselves, of course, a perfect device to achieve instant, intense melodrama. A guilt obsession was the focus of *The Eternal Mask*, for example, a 1936 film imported from Switzerland that played in New York at the Filmarte on West Fifty-Second Street ("a full half-mile and several intelligence quotients removed from the standard staples of the Times Square movie houses," Frank S. Nugent of the *New York Times* observed). In the film (based on the novel by Leo Lapaire), Dr. Dumartin, a staff member of a Basel hospital, gives an experimental meningitis serum he developed as a last resort to a dying patient, against the administration's orders. When the patient dies, Dumartin loses his mind and attempts suicide, unable to cope with the accusatory glances from his colleagues, the nurses, and the other patients. His life saved but identity lost, the remainder of the movie is "a record of the dream-world meanderings of a disordered brain" as Dumartin "roams through the misty, confused labyrinths of his own mind, seeing phantoms, fighting specters, [and] hearing oracular voices," as Nugent described the action. Almost inevitably, Dumartin's serum is proved to be effective after all, all the more reason for him to regain his sanity so that it can be given to the world.[30]

Emotions also ran high in *Blind Alley*, a 1939 film directed by King Vidor, which "graft[ed] Dr. Freud's facile theory of dream symbols on a typical Columbia [Pictures] melodrama," as the *New York Times* reviewed it. In the movie, a gangster who has a recurring nightmare (a theme that would be revived in *The Sopranos*) breaks in on the lakeside retreat of Dr. Shelby, an eminent psychoanalyst. Naturally, Shelby "psyches" the killer, discovering that his bad dream (and desire to murder people) is the result of an Oedipus complex. "You wouldn't believe how exciting terms like 'subconscious' . . . can be, until you see Dr. Shelby at work," the reviewer enthused, the infusion of psychoanalysis into a crime drama a nice formula, as writers of the hit HBO show *The Sopranos* also found some six decades later.[31]

It was the Broadway play *Lady in the Dark* that claimed first prize for most psychoanalytic entertainment produced to date. In the 1941 hit written by Moss Hart and with music by Kurt Weill and Ira Gershwin, the English actor Gertrude Lawrence played a magazine editor who relates her dreams to a psychoanalyst that then materialize on a number of revolving stages. In the first dream, Lawrence's character becomes the "Girl of the Moment," selected by the president of the United States to be on the new two-cent stamp. Things turn a bit darker in the next dream, as her character transforms into a bride at the altar with three potential grooms from whom to choose. After a few more somnambulant expeditions, she returns to reality and realizes that the advertising manager down the hall whom she thought was Mr. Wrong is actually Mr. Right, her inner conflict neatly resolved.[32]

For Donald Ogden Stewart, arts critic for the *New York Times*, *Lady in the Dark* was more than a random exercise in psychoanalysis. "Having just arrived in New York on a brief vacation from Hollywood, I am only too happy to rush into print with the announcement of a Trend," he wrote, the trend being "definitely toward psychiatry." Stewart first became aware of the trend when he worked with Ernest Lubitsch on the script for the film *That Uncertain Feeling* in which Merle Oberon's character is psychoanalyzed to resolve her troubled marriage (to husband Melvyn Douglas). Now, after seeing *Lady in the Dark*, Stewart was convinced that "psychoanalysis has definitely arrived," and it would be Hollywood's new obsession. "We may soon expect a series of pictures which open with a beautiful young lady reclining on a couch in an analyst's office," Stewart half-joked, the shrink naturally saying, "Hmmmm," or perhaps, "I see . . ." Stewart believed these movies could be more than just entertainment, capable of decreasing marital unhappiness by delivering a kind of vicarious psychoanalysis to the world. "Before long, we may expect that psychoanalysis will penetrate not only the humblest homes of our own country but also, say, the igloos of the possibly maladjusted Eskimos," he suggested tongue-in-cheek. "The natives of all other countries . . . [will] receive the educational benefits of this latest motion-picture Trend."[33]

Stewart's prediction that Hollywood would look to the couch was right on, with a film version of *Lady in the Dark* soon in the works. "Psychiatric drama need no longer be looked upon with fearfulness through the eyes of the cameras," wrote Nelson B. Bell of the *Washington Post* in his review of the 1944 movie. Bell concluded that cinema was a better vehicle to capture "the gossamer stuff of which dreams, retrospections, and secret longings are made" than the stage. As in the show, the protagonist, now played by Ginger Rogers, consults a psychoanalyst on the advice of her physician, leading viewers on the whirlwind ride through her various psychoses, inhibitions, phobias, and complexes. "It is the picturization of the results of his psychoanalysis that provides the picture's unprecedentedly broad sweep of moods, emotions and romantic complications, ranging from childhood to maturity," thought Bell. The visualization of her dreams and images of her unconscious were "out of this world," quite literally.[34]

If *Lady in the Dark* helped to further popularize psychoanalysis, *Spellbound* made it positively glamorous. Filmmakers were increasingly looking to what Bell called "the science of the mental specialists" for inspiration, but it took Alfred Hitchcock to turn it into Hollywood magic. With a script by Ben Hecht, working from Francis Beeding's 1928 novel, *The House of Dr. Edwardes*, the 1945 movie's rather familiar cops-and-robbers theme became truly spellbinding when presented in the context of psychiatry. Add Gregory Peck, Ingrid Bergman, a great supporting cast, and a surreal dream sequence created by Salvador Dali to the mix and Hitchcock ended up with a film that pleased critics and audiences alike. "No judicious picturegoer should allow himself to be frightened away from *Spellbound* by the announcement that it is a 'drama of psychoanalysis,'" wrote Bell, who considered the film a lot more entertaining than your typical angst-ridden therapy session.[35] Mae Tinee of the *Chicago Tribune* was equally enthusiastic. "Don't expect a serious, somber excursion into the realms of psychoanalysis or you may be disappointed," she wrote. The film is instead "a superior, slick and engrossing melodrama." "Take a bow!" Tinee told Mr. Hitchcock.[36]

With pro-Freudian sympathies strong from the role psychoanalysts had played during the war and the popularity of *Spellbound* (it was nominated for five Academy Awards, including Best Picture), the U.S.

Army produced *Let There Be Light*, a 1946 documentary about the contributions made by military psychiatrists. (William Menninger, who had
served as chief consultant in neuropsychiatry for the army's surgeon
general during the war, sponsored the film.)[37] Directed by John Huston
(sixteen years before he would direct his biography of Freud), the film
was perhaps "the most impressive piece of psychiatric propaganda ever
made," thought Glen Gabbard and Kim Gabbard in their *The Psychiatrist
in the Movies*. This was quite a statement given that few people had the
chance to see it for thirty-five years. *Let There Be Light* followed a group
of servicemen over the course of a couple of months of therapy in a
Long Island hospital, the veterans having made remarkable progress by
the end of the film. Intended to help men who had been psychically
wounded during the war to get jobs upon their return by showing
employers that recovery was indeed possible, the film ended up sitting
on the army's shelf for decades, reportedly because several patients had
declined to sign release forms. Some believed that the real reason to
keep *Let There Be Light* in the dark was that it would deter people from
joining the army. Given what the men must have gone through to require
the kind of intensive treatment they received in the film, this may have
been a reasonable argument. (The film was finally released in 1981.)[38]

Perhaps even more surreal than the circumstances surrounding *Let
There Be Light* (but not Dali's dream sequence in *Spellbound*) was a radio
program, *Rhyme and Reason*, which debuted in 1949 on WNEW in New
York. In each fifteen-minute show, Nandor Fodor, a real psychoanalyst,
played four songs and then analyzed the lyrics to "uncover negative and
positive psychological attitudes and implications," a sort of psychoanalytic
Name That Tune. In the first show, for example, Fodor decoded the lyrics
of "Alexander's Ragtime Band," "Oh, Daddy," "Homework," and "I Wonder Who's Kissing Her Now," no doubt surprising listeners with the
hidden meanings of the tunes. Judging by how popular psychoanalysis
was becoming, was a television talk show in which the host "psyched"
his guests in the works?[39]

Rebel Without a Cause

The emergence of psychoanalysis as a staple of American pop culture
belied what was actually going on in the field as other therapies made

serious inroads within psychiatry. The successful use of shock therapy by the Psychiatric Institute at the Illinois Research and Educational Hospital of Chicago in 1936 (using not electricity but rather insulin and Metrazol) was a serious blow to psychoanalysis in America, offering physicians the kind of spoonful of medicine they much preferred. Greer Williams of *Forum and Century* believed that as a result of shock therapy (which had been developed in Europe), a full-fledged "anti-Freud movement" was in the works, his "sex psychology" fast falling out of favor in psychiatric clinics across the country. Schizophrenia was a chemical imbalance that could be cured by drugs, more clinical psychiatrists were concluding. Manic-depression too was now being treated by these drugs, with hospitalization stays dropping dramatically after the shock treatment. (Hardcore Freudians would not be swayed, arguing that it was fear of death during the shock experience that freed the patient from his or her conflict or complex.) With a good number of the roughly half a million patients at the nation's five hundred or so mental institutions suffering from either schizophrenia or manic-depression, it appeared that shock treatment was at the very least a viable alternative to psychoanalysis.[40]

Others were determined to bring Freudianism down and, perhaps, even Sigmund Freud himself. In 1936, Odette Pannetier, a French journalist, received a rare audience with Freud, the sick, eighty-year-old man now seeing very few visitors. Pannetier went to quite some lengths to get her appointment in Vienna, going to the renowned Parisian psychiatrist Dr. Benjamin Logre with the sole purpose of receiving a letter of introduction that would at least improve the odds. "Madame Dubois," as Pannetier called herself, had certainly done her homework, convincing Logre that she was the victim of an idée fixe and had dreamt of committing suicide. (She even broke one of his knickknacks for pure effect.) Letter in hand, Pannetier flew to Vienna but was passed off by Freud to Paul Ferden, to whom she described her intense fear of dogs, assorted other phobias, and compulsive behavior. "I want to see Freud because he is the only man who can cure me," she told Ferden, at which point the doctor, seeing he had a truly interesting case on his hands, agreed to take her to Herr Professor (for a hefty fee of three hundred shillings). Pannetier successfully pulled off her stunt, with Freud agreeing to take on "Madame Dubois" as a patient for one hundred shillings a day (this no doubt his real incentive).[41]

Another European journalist, Gert V. Gontard, was also set on exposing psychoanalysis as a shell game. In his 1940 *In Defense of Love*, Gontard argued that it was time to psychoanalyze psychoanalysis, highly suspect of the aims of those foisting it on the American people. "Not even the God-for-saken corners of nowhere have been spared a member of [the] psychoanalytical network," he bellowed, viewing shrinks as a virtual fifth column who had infiltrated the United States for evil intent. Analysts were turning manly American men into effeminate boys, Gontard thought, a particularly dangerous thing as a world war was percolating. Europeans had planted aspects of their culture within our borders to maintain the integrity of their own, he felt; psychoanalysis was in effect a Trojan horse, something which was making us a politically, militarily, and socially weaker nation.[42] Growing anti-German (and likely anti-Jewish) sentiment certainly played a role in these new attacks against psychoanalysis; the field was now heavily populated if not dominated by émigrés with accents that sounded a lot like those of Nazis. Of course, these mostly Jewish émigrés were fleeing the Nazis, making Gontard's claim rather absurd.

Still, some back home agreed with Gontard's argument that psychoanalysis was a European invader that should be sent packing. More psychologists were saying that psychoanalysis was not only often unsuccessful but was occasionally harmful, and the field was rapidly losing its status as what the *Chicago Tribune* called in 1941 the "fashionable refuge of neurotics for the past decade." Dorothy Hazeltine Yates of San Jose State College, for example, had come to the conclusion that, based on her research, Freudian psychoanalysis was simply inconsistent with American values and should go back to Europe where it would be more at home. "The European attitude toward sex is different from that in this country," she told attendees at that year's American Psychological Association convention. The loose morals of the Old World, she argued, were in stark contrast with Americans' respect for "romance, honor, and privacy" in the bedroom.[43]

One prominent psychoanalyst, Karen Horney, thought the field was as American as apple pie. Horney's contributions to the field are difficult to overestimate. While many psychoanalysts were writing books on the subject, Horney was one of the few to successfully cross over to a general audience, making the field's basic concepts relevant to nonprofessionals. (Her explanation of why girls went "boy crazy," for example, was just the kind of thing that captured the public's and media's imagination.)[44] A big part of Horney's mission was to "eliminate the debatable elements" of Freud's theories, as she stated in her 1939 *New Ways in Psychoanalysis*, her "pruning" something that the forty-year-old field very much needed. Horney took swipes at a number of Freud's ideas, including his concepts regarding sublimation, aggression, frustration, masochism, and destructive instinct, but it was her rejection of his libido theory that pushed the field furthest into a different trajectory.[45] What made Horney different, as Lionel Trilling pointed out in 1942, was her ability to extend psychoanalysis to a philosophy of human nature and society, making her as much a cultural critic as clinical physician. Best of all to lay readers, Horney was a lot more optimistic than Freud, rejecting much of the gloominess and cynicism that pervaded his oeuvre. Horney (like Erich Fromm) believed that humans were ultimately "free" and "good," concepts grounded more in eighteenth-century liberalism than Freudian theory. Horney thus brought a distinctly American and populist sensibility to psychoanalysis, her rejection of Freud's biological determinism quite attractive to a nation wanting to have faith in the future.[46]

While Karen Horney did a lot in the 1930s and early 1940s to keep psychoanalysis afloat, some felt that an even more populist approach was needed for it to be fully embraced by Americans. Alan Gregg, director for the medical sciences at the Rockefeller Foundation, for example, saw big things ahead for the field if it could be better packaged to the American consumer. Psychoanalysis needed a better "hook" than sex, for one thing, he told the Institute for Psychoanalysis at its tenth annual meeting at the Palmer House in Chicago in 1942. The principal repression of the Victorian era was a bit old hat a half-century later, he argued. "Certainly sex cannot be the proper instrument for the explanation of psychoanalysis," Gregg suggested to his colleagues, apparently ready to throw Freud's central theory of the libido out the window because it no longer played very well in more sexually liberal times. Gregg had other interesting ideas regarding how to make psychoanalysis new and improved. "To popularize the science to the multitudes we should find some other media, perhaps the theater, the movie, or the novel," he recommended, adding that some kind of slogan would be another effective way to get more Americans to try out the couch.[47]

Gregg was no doubt delighted to see Robert Lindner's widely read *Rebel Without a Cause* on the shelves a couple of years later. As a complete, nonfictional transcript of one man's treatment, the book was the closest serious brush with psychoanalysis that many Americans had ever had, revealing the amazing possibilities of the technique. (The 1955 movie starring James Dean took its title but none of its story from the book.) Lindner, a psychologist at a penitentiary in Lewisburg, Pennsylvania, secretly recorded the forty-six sessions held with his patient, Harold, a twenty-one-year-old serving hard time for an unspecified crime, who blinked his eyes constantly. Lindner used hypnosis to treat Harold, the technique experiencing somewhat of a revival during the war years (especially at the Menninger Clinic in Topeka, Kansas). To figure out why Harold kept blinking, Lindner brought his patient back to an age of six to eight months, at which point he revealed his trauma—being terrified of a "wolf" (probably Rin-Tin-Tin) while sitting in his mother's lap at the movies and, the next morning, waking to see his "wolfish" father threaten her. Harold's psychosis was rooted in Oedipal jealousy, Lindner naturally concluded, his blinking cured by the hypnoanalytic experience. Traditional Freudians took issue with Lindner's approach (questioning especially his ability to take Harold literally back to the cradle), but *Rebel Without a Cause* helped to demystify psychoanalysis at a time when more Americans were beginning to wonder if they had neuroses that could and should be cured.[48]

The Present Emergency

The timing of the publication of *Rebel Without a Cause* could not have been better as Americans looked to psychoanalysis as a weapon to help win the war both abroad and at home. World War II brought many of the concerns about psychoanalysis into the open. The controversial techniques of the field were now being applied not just to wealthy people with emotional troubles but also to wounded soldiers. Given the virulent attacks on the method during the Depression years, concerns about psychoanalysis being used on wholesome, red-blooded Americans ran high. When psychoanalyst William Menninger was appointed as neuropsychiatry consultant in the army's Office of the Surgeon General in 1943, for example, both military brass and civvies went ballistic, so to speak, arguing that a "real" psychiatrist would have been a better choice. Not many psychoanalysts served in the Army Medical Corps; the few who did acted more as advisers than practicing shrinks. However, the senior consultants in psychiatry in the Office of the Air Surgeon, the Office of the Ground Surgeon, and the Office of the Surgeon General were all analytically trained and spread their methods through the military machine. When dogfaces showed no worse for the wear after being exposed to the psychoanalytic principles of releasing emotional tension (standard analysis was impossible because of the time required), many skeptics changed their tune; the field was increasingly embraced or at least tolerated by the mainstream psychiatric community. Even more important, hundreds of young military doctors became interested in psychoanalysis, and the nation's training institutes were flooded with applications from these same men and women after the war.[49]

The typical psychoanalytic session for the wartime patient was clearly a much different affair than what civilians on the home front would receive. Wartime patients (typically soldiers) were first sedated and then prompted to recall the incident that led to their illness, thereby reliving the painful, repressed event. After the patient fully awoke, the analyst revealed what he had heard, this process believed to be a cathartic and healing experience. Wartime psychoanalysis went beyond these compressed, drug-induced "sittings." The theoretical framework of the field was used in the army's guidelines for diagnosing psychiatric illnesses and, more broadly, teaching enlistees how they could maintain good mental health.[50]

"Shell shock" was nothing new to the psychiatry community, of course. The condition was initially believed to be a result of concussion during the previous world war, but that diagnosis was quickly rejected when it was learned that many of its sufferers had never been even close to the front lines. Psychiatrists of the day explained that rather than simple fear, shell shock was a subconscious attempt to escape from danger, the opposing fears of death and being considered a coward creating a (sometimes literally) paralyzing state. The next generation of analysts was toying with different theories about soldiers' breakdowns, however, one of them being that they were caused by "separation anxiety," a wartime and particularly intense version of homesickness. Through psychoanalysis, British physician Roland D. Fairbairn found that men with neuroses caused or triggered by the war had effectively fled back home to the safety and comfort of their families, the subconscious taking over when events within the conscious were too overwhelming. As in the last war, men with this condition often forgot their names or which regiment they were part of, in more serious cases deserting or even killing themselves as a way out of the hostile world in which they found themselves.[51]

Struggling to figure out how best to treat psychologically wounded vets, analysts also mixed and matched psychoanalysis with other treatments, sometimes coming up with interesting combinations. "Hypnoanalysis" was one such hybrid developed during the war, in which the suggestion of hypnosis was blended with the insights gleaned from psychoanalysis. Created by Merton M. Gill and Margaret Brennan at the Menninger Clinic, hypnoanalysis was a kind of extreme form of hypnosis, getting to the roots of a patient's anxiety by delving deep into his unconscious. "It might prove to be useful in dealing with a large number of cases whose hysteria and other neurotic disturbances are related to the present emergency," thought the *Washington Post* in 1943. Wartime analysts were eager for new approaches to chase away the demons of their battle-scarred GI patients.[52]

Other important events in the field took place on the home front as psychoanalysis, now officially authorized by the military and thus the United States government, gained traction. In 1944, for example, Columbia University established a psychoanalytic and psychosomatic clinic in its school of medicine, the first of its kind in the country. The creation of the clinic was in part a response to the medical community's decades-long hostility to psychoanalysis. This hostility may have been deserved given analysts' refusal to treat patients for free if necessary (a violation of the Hippocratic oath). Physicians were also angry at psychoanalysts for not sharing progress reports on patients they had referred, a practice considered business as usual in all other fields of medicine. The conflicting theories of the various schools of psychoanalysis were another thorn in the side for doctors, with the lack of solid, factual case histories to verify either success or failure yet another. With an academically grounded teaching clinic, however, a new generation of psychoanalysts could perhaps be produced who understood and, hopefully, catered to physicians' concerns. Such clinics could reform the field, many believed, a means of turning the bastard child into a truly legitimate branch of medicine.[53]

The gains psychoanalysis had made during the war continued after peace was declared. The field was now on a roll, credited with helping heroic Americans who had sacrificed their lives to preserve democracy and freedom. Recast as a patriotic cause, psychoanalysis became somewhat of a cause célèbre within the society crowd immediately after the war. In late 1945, for example, the New York Psychoanalytic Institute organized a campaign committee to raise three hundred thousand dollars to finance a three-year program to help veterans and others "affected by neuroses," who needed treatment but could not afford it. Six hundred swells attended the kickoff dinner at the Waldorf-Astoria, urged by campaign chair and interior decorator deluxe Dorothy Draper to give what they could to help create a service center within the institute to care for emotionally disturbed veterans as well as for less well-off civilians. As a direct result of "the present emergency," money would also go toward expanding the training of qualified physicians to help cope with the increasing demand for psychoanalysis. The institute had in fact recently constructed a brand new building on the city's Upper East Side, and its leaders expected it to soon be filled with people requiring its services. They would be proved right, as postwar Americans took to psychoanalysis almost as much as they did to this new thing called television.[54]

One kind of treatment the institute would no doubt be using was group psychotherapy, something which had been employed during the war for men who had broken down under the strains of combat. The technique had been carried over into outpatient work in veterans hospitals, with both psychoanalysts and psychiatrists finding it to be effective in giving veterans confidence and reintegrating them into civilian life. "Soldiers live, wait, feel, hope, fear, and fight in groups," Martin Grotjahn of Chicago's Institute for Psychoanalysis told the American Psychiatric Association at its 1946 annual meeting in that city. His research showed that psychic improvement was also more often produced in a group setting. Over a period of two months, Grotjahn had led twelve group sessions, each one composed of twenty-five enlisted men awaiting disability discharge, describing the typical proceedings as a "glorified bull session." Prodded by Grotjahn to express their afflictions emotionally rather than intellectually, the men made progress toward adjusting to their new lives, taking comfort in knowing that their buddies were going through a similar difficult process.[55]

The Line of Battle

A different kind of battle was meanwhile being waged in psychoanalysis itself as soldiers on opposing sides of the field took aim at each other. The skirmish between religion and psychoanalysis was fast becoming a war, with leaders of Catholicism delivering the biggest blasts. "It has become fashionable in Catholic circles to take pot shots at Freudianism and psychoanalysis," wrote psychologist Harry McNeill in 1947, in an article for *Commonweal*, trying to bridge the gap between the two schools of thought. Very few Catholics had actually been analyzed to date, McNeill pointed out, or were familiar with recent literature in the field. If they had been, they would know that the term "absolution" was popping up quite a bit in newer psychoanalytic works, something to which Catholics could indeed relate. Likewise, Freudians could learn a lot by becoming familiar with certain Catholic doctrines and practices, McNeill argued, concepts like neuroticism and repression not all that different from ideas addressed in the religion. "Whatever their similarities and differences, it is high time that Catholics and Freudians got together and swapped some of their trade secrets," he concluded. Surely this was an opportunity for the two enemies to join forces in their mutual and noble mission to save people's souls.[56]

Other Catholics fluent in psychoanalysis cautioned that, because of their fundamental differences, the two belief systems were not quite ready to jump into bed together. For the Reverend Victor White, for example, the idea that confession was an ancient form of psychiatry or, conversely, that psychiatry was a secular corruption of confession was absurd, as he made clear in his own article in *Commonweal* a year later. While psychoanalysts and Catholics were united in their effort to combat evil, the kind of evil each was concerned with were poles apart, he argued, neurosis being a much different kettle of fish than sin. White's opinion was that, while psychoanalysis and Catholicism were not mutually exclusive, it would be difficult if not impossible to bring the couch into confession or get confession to lie down on the couch.[57]

The row between psychoanalysis and Christianity had a long and complex history. Although Freud's focus on "pansexuality" had immediately made psychoanalysis suspect at best among "moralists," as Gregory Zilboorg, one of America's leading psychoanalysts of the 1930s and 1940s, called the faithful, it was his 1927 *The Future of an Illusion* that really alienated the field from those with religious inclinations (including many psychoanalysts). "The line of battle was drawn almost spontaneously," wrote Zilboorg in "Psychoanalysis and Religion," a 1949 article in *The Atlantic Monthly*, arguing that, if anything, the conflict had become only more intense over the past twenty or so years. If recent publicity was any judge, the uneasy truce that had existed between the world wars appeared to now be hand-to-hand combat. This was a situation Zilboorg considered unfortunate given that the Catholic priests he knew had no real quarrel with psychoanalysis, seeing it as a threat neither to their faith or vocation. As a "healing art" with the basic goal of making people better, psychoanalysis could indeed serve both God and man, Zilboorg believed, assuring Catholics that, "it threatens religion no more than the heliocentric theory or Newtonian physics threatened religion."[58]

Such voices of reason were in the minority. Not one but two major salvos were directed at psychoanalysis in 1947, each an attempt to persuade Americans, especially Catholics, to steer clear of all things Freudian. The first was a sermon on "Psychoanalysis and Confession" delivered by Fulton J. Sheen at St. Patrick's Cathedral in New York in which the monsignor attacked the "particular type of psychoanalysis called Freudianism." Freud was based on "materialism, hedonism, infantilism, and eroticism," he told his audience, all these values contrary to Catholicism. As the title of his talk suggested, Sheen was particularly interested in pointing out the differences between psychoanalysis and confession, the former having "no norms or standards" while the latter was "the key to happiness of the modern world."[59] Although he did not attack psychiatry or even psychology in general, many Catholic patients interpreted

Sheen's sermon as a directive to avoid any kind of treatment for mental health, which some no doubt decided to do. As well, Frank J. Curran, the chief psychiatrist at St. Vincent's Hospital in New York, resigned as a result of the matter, believing the church had sent a message that good Catholics like him should find a different kind of job.[60]

Sheen's Sunday sermon created a firestorm of controversy. A. A. Brill was quick to respond to the monsignor's statements, calling them not just "false views" but "foolishly untrue." After reading what Sheen had said, Brill had considered offering a thousand dollars to a Catholic charity of Sheen's choice if he could substantiate his statements, but he was preempted by the New York Psychoanalytic Institute when it officially responded via a letter published in the *New York Herald Tribune*. (The *New York Times* would not accept it.) Brill took the opportunity to do his own comparison of confession and psychoanalysis, his view being that the former was simply conscious thoughts while the latter was, through its technique of free association, rooted in the richer, deeper unconscious. "Psychoanalysts believe our conscious life is very small, very unimportant in comparison with our unconscious life and we try to bring the unconscious to the surface," he told a group of eighty rabbis at the Central Synagogue in New York. Brill branded Sheen's comments as not the kind that should come from someone claiming to be a "guardian of the soul." "We have just scratched the surface of the human soul," Brill added, the gloves now off in the ideological brawl.[61]

The effects of Sheen's sermon continued to ripple. Four eminent Catholic psychiatrists, including Curran, issued a statement at the 1947 convention of the Advancement of Psychiatry, defending the field against Sheen's attack.[62] Lawrence S. Kubie, chairman of the public education committee of the New York Psychoanalytic Institute (and professor of psychiatry and mental hygiene at Yale's School of Medicine), was the next to jump into the fray, declaring that Sheen had ignored requests from the psychoanalytic community to clarify his views on the matter via a "friendly private discussion." Echoing Brill's response, Kubie issued a statement that people had a right to expect "greater honesty and greater humility from anyone who pretends to represent the search for the good life"—tough words indeed, especially when directed to one of America's leading men of faith.[63] "The quarrel between Monsignor Sheen and the psychoanalysts reminds us of a jurisdictional dispute between the A.F. of L. and the C.I.O.," thought *The Nation*, the stakes being which organization would have access to Catholics' deepest secrets.[64]

The other assault on psychoanalysis that year came from writer and society figure Clare Booth Luce, who described her conversion to Catholicism in a three-part series of articles for *McCall's*. (Sheen had played a major role in Luce's conversion and, apparently, her decision to turn her back on psychoanalysis.) Luce's psychoanalyst was "a soul quack," she declared. The man had led her into "the godless and atavistic underbrush of Freudianism." (Her analyst was actually considered one of the best in the country, a pupil of a pupil of Freud.) Luce did not stop at Freud, blaming two other great thinkers of Jewish origin—Marx and Einstein— for America's spiritual failings. "We Christian innocents have been duped into our present godless condition by the unholy triumvirate of Communism, Psychoanalysis, and Relativity," Fanny Sedgwick Colby summarized Luce's argument in *The American Scholar*; these three ideological witches were "the result of the messianic impulse of the religiously frustrated Jewish ego." Colby thought both Sheen's and Luce's diatribes against psychoanalysis were not only ridiculous but "socially dangerous" in the impact they could have on Americans' collective well-being, the fact that all three men were Jewish hardly a coincidence.[65]

Not surprisingly, Jewish leaders were generally on the other side of the fence when it came to psychoanalysis. Joshua Loth Liebman's *Peace of Mind* made quite the splash with its message that a synthesis of religion and psychiatry could help resolve people's problems, an idea with which many readers resonated. Liebman, a rabbi from Boston, received thousands of supportive letters after his book was published in 1946, leading him to propose the establishment of fellowships through which young rabbis could study psychiatry and psychoanalysis in order to be better equipped to counsel members of their congregations. Sadly, Liebman died just a year after he asked rabbinical leaders to support his rather radical idea, ending what could have been a very interesting story.[66]

Are You Considering Psychoanalysis?

The heated clash between Catholicism and psychoanalysis did little to slow down the field from taking America by storm after the war. Horney's more democratic, optimistic, and pragmatic variety of psycho-analysis was in particular continuing to find a receptive audience, ide-ally suited to Americans' progressive orientation. A new book she edited in 1946, *Are You Considering Psychoanalysis?*, focused on the neu-roses that were likely to occur by undue concentration on the self, spe-cifically aggression, submission, and withdrawal. Improvement was possible for those willing and strong enough to reconfigure their atti-tudes and habits based on reality, her no-nonsense approach a reasonable and appealing concept even for those not psychoanalytically inclined. Coming face-to-face with this kind of thinking could thus turn the unhappy, disorganized person into a more content and even perhaps self-actualized one, Horney argued, just the right recipe for success that Americans now wanted to hear.[67]

Dreams especially were becoming a hot topic of conversation as Americans began to look inward after the war. "Because of the increasing influence of psychoanalysis many a man today believes that his dreams are important, that for him they hold meaning," observed Lucy Green-baum in 1946. What Freud had called "the royal road to man's uncon-scious" was no longer considered mere flights of fancy. Dreams were also appearing more and more in novels, Broadway plays, and movies, an ideal device with which to reveal a character's secret desires or worst fears, as *Spellbound* vividly showed. Most contemporary psychoanalysts were staying relatively true to Freud's view of dreams as vital clues to an individual's conflicts, seeing them as a way for repressions to escape while one's guard was down. "Much of what has been forbidden to him in reality, he will dream out at night," opined Zilboorg. The real-life repressions of increasingly conformist America were perhaps making dreams a more important venting mechanism.[68]

Americans counted on psychoanalysis for much more than explaining dreams. In postwar America, psychoanalysis could be a useful tool for determining the mental fitness of leaders in all kinds of fields, some thought, a way to ensure that those in positions of responsibility were of literal sound mind. Harold D. Lasswell, a professor at Yale's law school, urged in 1946 that business executives, labor leaders, and public officials all undergo psychoanalytic testing, with anyone making important deci-sions required to be psychoanalyzed. Lasswell told five hundred members and patrons of the Association for the Advancement of Psychoanalysis that they possessed "a refined scientific instrument for answering the question of who can be trusted with power." He argued that this instrument could be of considerable value in any number of situations where high-level decision making was involved. Through such testing, the procedures of collective bargaining could be improved as could congressional hearings, the professor said to the certainly pleased group; psychoanalysis represented a means of weeding out bad apples and their "non-rational" thinking that typically led to trouble.[69]

As Lasswell's proposal suggested, there was little doubt that the war had made psychoanalysis, and psychiatry in general, more acceptable and that the taboos surrounding mental health had been reduced significantly. "The increasing consciousness since the war of the frailty of human adjustment has . . . to a large extent broken down the obstacle that prevented men from going to psychoanalysts, whom they regarded as doctors for the insane," declared George S. Stevenson of the National Committee for Mental Hygiene. The mere fact that there was a national committee for mental health was itself a sign of the times. While the shame (and, ironically, the status) associated with going to a shrink was waning, two other issues hindering the "middle-classing" of psychoanalysis were not: time and money. Because psychoanalysis was, according to Stevenson, "the most detailed, intense, and unrestricted talking-it-over that we know of," the majority of Americans still could not afford the treatment, severely limiting the field's growth potential. Many experts in the field recognized this, with some determined to do something about it. Now in business for a decade and a half, the Institute for Psychoanalysis in Chicago was leading the way in creating a briefer (and thus cheaper) kind of psychoanalysis that was still within the spirit of Freud. Since 1938, in fact, Franz Alexander and his colleagues at the institute were experimenting with such a therapy, completing five hundred case studies and reporting the findings in a 1946 book, *Psychoanalytic Therapy, Principles, and Application.*[70]

The results? "In many instances, the analysts found that it was not necessary to recall all the events that contributed to a patient's neurotic reactions, and that they were able to sift out all the secondary and marginal causes of his emotional difficulties," wrote Stevenson, in his review of the book. Such a conclusion signaled quite a breakthrough if the approach could be replicated on a mass scale. Rather than drill down to the very core of a patient's conflict, in other words, the Chicago group concluded that a less intensive, more practical therapeutic approach was warranted for some individuals. As Stevenson summed it up, "Psychoanalytic theory and experience may indicate that the patient is better left undisturbed with his peculiar sensitivities and behavior and that the effort be focused on shaping his life situation, his work, his home, his friends, so that he can live more satisfactorily with himself." There was no real need for radical change. The authors defended their tweaking of classic Freudianism, correctly noting that the man himself consistently revised his own theories and techniques to make his discovery more effective (and scientific). Freud's pupils and their pupils had also traveled down some roads not paved by Herr Doktor, the entire Freudian tradition in fact one of experimentation. Science was, after all, all about testing new ideas and trying to prove new hypotheses, making the institute's bold venture something of which Sigmund Freud would likely have been proud.[71]

Any true Freudian was in fact happy to see the emergence of this more flexible approach to treatment. Some analysts deviated from the field's golden rules of regular, almost daily sessions and maintaining a passive attitude in which one did not interfere with the patient's everyday life. A new breed of "experimentalists" was changing the frequency of sittings, alternately increasing and decreasing them as a way to provoke emotional reactions and thereby speed up the therapeutic process. Interrupting treatment would also lessen patients' dependence on therapy, these analysts believed, a problem that had plagued the field since its beginnings. Even more radical, the experimentalists were taking an active interest in their patients' outside lives, encouraging or discouraging them to do certain things in order to more quickly overcome their neuroses. Although perfectly obvious to us now, the realization or recognition that patients were unique individuals (or "highly diversified human material," as Franz Alexander rather clinically put it), and that different kinds of psychoanalytic approaches were thus called for, was considered quite the bold idea in a field known for its rigidity and conservatism.[72]

The Cult of Contentment

The remaking of psychoanalysis was just what the doctor ordered, so to speak, to spark a renaissance of the field and bring it more into the mainstream fold. Although certainly less sensational than in the 1920s when it made its official debut on the American scene, the field of psychoanalysis was by the late 1940s no longer the "voodoo religion" many had believed it to be, as the taboos surrounding it fell and as new techniques were developed. "Never before has psychoanalysis been so much a matter of general discussion," thought William Menninger, who with his brother, Karl, ran the famous Menninger Clinic in Topeka. During the war, Menninger was fully aware that the use of psychoanalysis by the military to treat battle neuroses made Americans all the more familiar with its principles. Still, Menninger believed, most of the public remained confused about the workings of psychoanalysis, an aura of mystery continuing to hover over it (part of the reason he had sponsored *Let There Be Light*). Menninger felt the need to debunk the myths surrounding psychoanalysis and provide direct, honest answers to its many critics, doing just that in a 1947 article, "An Analysis of Psychoanalysis," which appeared in the Sunday magazine section of the *New York Times*. In the article, Menninger took on no less than eight major criticisms of the field, doing his best to explain how each—its obsession with sex, overly theoretical orientation, amorality, complexity, high cost, internal divisiveness, lack of scientific substantiation, and, last but not least, tendency to attract quacks like bees to honey—was more fantasy than fact.[73]

A better way for the layman to understand psychoanalysis, Menninger continued, was to focus on the three basic elements of the field—that it was (1) an investigative procedure by which repressed material in a troubled human mind can be uncovered; (2) a body of theory and knowledge developed over many years; and (3) a way for an individual to understand her or his inner conflicts and, ultimately, to be freed from them. "Psychiatry is generally and readily accepted; why is there suspicion of and resistance to psychoanalysis?" he asked, answering his own question by explaining that the subject was inherently fraught with anxiety, something of which Freud himself was quite aware. The notion that the ego was not "master in its own house" was understandably frightening to many, and the prospect of a powerful unconscious dictating one's behavior was not an easy thing to take. But by exploring one's own unconscious, an individual struggling in the dark could gradually come into the light and, eventually, be able to "put his house in order as he wishes," this the real value of the treatment.[74]

With momentum going in their favor, psychoanalysts recognized that the time was ripe to get their own house in order. The field was in fact enjoying a postwar boom all its own. "The psychoanalysts who are assembled in New York this week for the annual meeting of the American Psychiatric Association have reason to congratulate themselves on the flourishing state of their profession," reported the *New Republic* in 1947. With as yet no legal controls over psychoanalysis, however, some practitioners with truly odd theories were able to treat patients as they liked, a situation that was not helping the field win its continuing battle to be recognized as a legitimate science. Perhaps the oddest theory of all was Wilhelm Reich's proclaimed discovery of "orgone," whose name derived from the orgasm. For Reich, a once esteemed analyst from Vienna who arrived in New York in 1939, after spending a couple of years in Sweden and Norway, the sexual orgasm was cosmic energy, and thus represented a force by which to cure everything from neuroses to cancer. Even Freud's view of sexuality did not do justice to the importance of the orgasm, Reich, who had studied with the man, maintained. Quite a bit more than a clever trick devised by Mother Nature to ensure that the species survived, the orgasm was for Reich the body's energy regulator, chiefly responsible for one's emotional and physical health. Society's general antisexual attitude and morality had created a world of "orgastic cripples," he suggested, accounting for why so many of us were sick in the mind, body, or both. At Freud's urging, Reich had been kicked out of the International Psychoanalytical Association in 1934 but, a dozen years later, had found a rather receptive audience in America with his orgone-based analysis. In fact, only one scientific journal, *Psychosomatic Medicine*, had openly criticized Reich and his orgone, that publication calling his theory "a surrealistic creation."[75] The Food and Drug Administration was less pleased about Reich's claims, and had him arrested for fraud.[76]

Thankfully, space does not permit a full discussion of how Reich applied his theory of the orgone to cure people (suffice it to say it involved a six-sided, metal-and-wood box into which the patient climbed).[77] The more important point was that it was long overdue that a license be required to call oneself a psychoanalyst, something that druggists, plumbers, and even hairdressers had to have in order to practice their own trade in most states. Because Freudians, Jungians, and Adlerians (not to mention the dozens of other schools that had spun off over the last half-century) defined things so differently, making the standards adopted by the American Psychoanalytic Association in 1938 legal requirements seemed to make the most sense in order to bring more credibility to the field.[78]

"Psychoquacks," as Norman and Amelia Lobsenz of the *Los Angeles Times* called them, were indeed still doing quite the business, the pair estimating phony psychiatry to be in 1947 a "billion-dollar racket." Going by a variety of titles like "psychological consultant," "emotional counselor," and "personality adjuster," some twenty-five thousand full-time quacks were estimated to be plying their trade, a "psychologic [*sic*] underworld" that posed real danger to the American public. "They have hitched their rickety wagons to the star of a constantly changing science, and trade on its conflicting theories," wrote the Lobsenzes. Lamentably, the frauds' pseudoscientific gibberish made a lot of sense to those looking for solutions to their problems at an affordable price. Holding degrees like "Doctor of Metaphysics" from mail-order companies such as the College of Universal Truth in Chicago or the Indiana Physio-Therapy Institute, psychoquacks were indeed "magna cum baloney," as the couple quipped. Because services like "auto-hypnosis" were not really medicine, most states had a tough time prosecuting quacks because they were not breaking any specific law, a frustrating situation. Various proposals to make things more difficult for the charlatans were in the works but, for the moment, psychoquackery remained a lucrative field.[79]

Fortunately, legitimate psychoanalysis seemed every bit as popular as psychoquackery. Reviewing a flurry of recently published books on the subject, Frederick Wertham of the *New Republic* observed in 1948, "The fashion this season prescribes psychoanalysis." Wertham was sure that ordinary Americans' interest in reading about psychopathology was "an important social phenomenon," but he could not quite figure out its deeper significance. "What does it mean?" he asked, wondering if the public read the books purely as entertainment or for some kind of search for truth. Because they straddled the line of serious scholarship and cocktail party fodder, Wertham raised a good question. All of the books—Charles Berg's *Deep Analysis* ("Freud without frills," Wertheim thought), Emil Ludwig's *Doctor Freud* (an unauthorized, critical biography), Walker Puner's *Freud: His Life and His Mind* (another biography), *Freud: On War, Sex and Neurosis* (writings by the man himself, edited by Sander Katz), an updated version of Harry Stack Sullivan's *Conceptions of Modern Psychiatry* ("a discursive dissertation composed of affected platitudes and pseudo-erudite pronouncements," he sniffed) and, finally, Eric Berne's *The Mind in Action* (a layman's guide to psychoanalysis, which had been selected by the Non-Fiction Book Club)—offered principles of the field that could be used for either fun or profit. Wertham's takeaway was that the genre of psychoanalytic literature was evidence of a "cult of contentment" among postwar Americans as we shifted our attention from national and global problems to our individual selves, a keen observation of the recent cultural sea change from public concerns to private interests.[80]

Recognizing that psychoanalysis was in the process of being elevated from psychiatric treatment to social movement, leaders of the field proposed new measures to lessen the confusion concerning its aims and techniques. In 1948, Lawrence Kubie, the Yale professor, suggested that carefully controlled, long-term research of psychoanalysis would go a long way in that regard, a research institute of psychotherapy the ideal scenario. Kubie and a few colleagues discussed the matter at the New School for Social Research in New York, trying to figure out how to end the "passionate and disorderly" attacks on psychoanalysis once and for all. One member of the group, Sidney G. Margolin, associate psychiatrist at Mount Sinai, likened psychoanalysts to atomic physicists, each occupation beginning to view their respective sciences "in terms of the overall organization, structure and goals of society." Another member, Robert Waelder of the Philadelphia Psychoanalytic Institute, had a more political view of the problems facing the field. With the left having a natural bias toward mending Americans' neuroses through social change, and the right tending to explain things in biological terms, psychoanalysis was stuck in the middle, holding little political power.[81]

As in the past, it would be personal stories about psychoanalysis that represented the real power of the field. Following in the long tradition of journalists revealing their own experiences with psychoanalysis, Lucy Freeman of the *New York Times* told her story in 1949 (later extending her thoughts on the subject into a book). For Freeman, visiting an analyst was not the lark it was for other writers mostly looking for a good story that would sell magazines or newspapers. After going to fifty-nine(!) medical doctors for a sinus condition, the sixtieth one suggested she see a psychoanalyst. The rationale for this unusual suggestion was the notion, in place since the very beginning of the field, that there was a link between the nose and emotions (and women's sexuality, Freud's once good friend Wilhelm Fleiss famously believed). Desperate (she also suffered from major insomnia and indigestion), Freeman took the plunge, in search of the "truth," whatever that may turn out to be. "I was being helped to open the door on my inner self and take a look, even if the sight was painful, in order that I might become free," Freeman wrote. Her goal was to discover "what I was really like inside." Freeman's sessions were, as they were for most, turbulent and painful ones, as she peeled back the layers of her past, revealed her fears, and confronted things for the first time. For Freeman, the "truth" resided in the all-too-common recognition that she was unloved by her parents as a child, the rest of her life yielding a constant and relentless pursuit of acceptance and approval. Over time, Freeman's health improved and, after a year of analysis, she was completely better. "It was a way of punishing myself for feeling I was no good," she said of her maladies, deciding to continue on with psychoanalysis for a still greater understanding of herself.[82]

Lucy Freeman's story pointed the way to the future of the field as more Americans decided to search for their own personal truth through psychoanalysis. As midcentury approached, and as more and different kinds of Americans chose to seek psychoanalytic help, the potential of the field seemed nearly limitless. "Psychoanalysis may be likened to the latest act in the drama of scientific development that began some 400 years ago with the dawn of the modern era," wrote Franz Alexander in 1949. That act was to become only more dramatic in the 1950s.[83] With the most dynamic and exciting period of psychoanalysis waiting just around the corner, the field was poised to take America and Americans to places they could not imagine.

CHAPTER 3: The Horizontal Hour

> Its deliberations will, I'm sure, advance and improve
> our knowledge, methods, and skills for the betterment
> of the nation's mental health.
>
> PRESIDENT EISENHOWER, speaking of psychoanaly-
> sis, in a message of greeting to the annual meeting of
> the American Psychoanalytic Association in 1956

In April 1950, at the Henry Hudson Hotel in New York, Harold Kelman, president of the American Institute for Psychoanalysis, made a rather bold statement before a group of his colleagues. Psychoanalysis was not just a treatment for distressed individuals, Kelman proposed, but something that could help human beings achieve world peace—perhaps the ultimate contribution to society. "Sick people do sick things, and war is a sign of sickness," he said, as the moderator in a discussion on "Psychoanalysis and Moral Values." Kelman insisted that the field's ability to alter individuals' irrational behavior was more important than ever as the Cold War heated up. By undermining distorted values, psychoanalysis could help a person find "a hierarchy of genuine moral ideals which would have obligating powers for his life as an individual and in his relatedness to the group in which he lives," Kelman stated. Thus, maturation and insight attained at the individual level could become the foundation for keeping the superpowers from blowing each other up.[1]

Kelman's talk reflected the growing role of psychoanalysis in the country as "the American century" unfolded. Given new energy during World War II, psychoanalysis was clearly in the ascent, its presence across American society beginning to surpass that of the 1920s when the field established itself as one of the key markers of modernity. Over the course of the 1950s, psychoanalysis would assume a new identity that mirrored the rise of the middle class to become an integral part of the American Way of Life. The desire to understand oneself at the deepest level possible had now become a permanent feature of our national ethos.

The Psychoanalytic Joyride

One did not have to be an expert to recognize that, like the American economy, psychoanalysis was recovering nicely from its prewar doldrums. Although one might think there were many more, given the field's prominence, there were around five hundred psychoanalysts in the United States at midcentury. Except for the émigré analysts who had been trained in Europe, all of them were graduates of one of the nation's handful of authorized institutes. More than seven hundred students were in training to become analysts, a figure that would more than double the number of those currently in practice. As in World War II, American casualties with psychiatric problems in Korea were high, creating even greater demand for physicians with psychoanalytic training.[2] Psychoanalysis was also benefiting from the rise of psychosomatic medicine, the official recognition within the medical community that there was a direct connection between emotional tensions and illnesses such as peptic ulcer, hypertension, colitis, coronary heart disease, asthma, migraine, hay fever, and many others. While this may have been obvious to the ancient Greeks and Romans, the acknowledgment that the mind and body were symbiotically linked was quite the breakthrough for Western physicians, and something that further brought psychoanalysis into the medical fold.[3]

With demand for shrinks greater than supply, as psychoanalysis increasingly became seen as psychiatric medicine, the status of having one was also continuing to grow. Finding oneself by identifying goals and carving out a place in society, as Karen Horney described the purpose of psychoanalytic therapy, was becoming not just more accepted but more admired; it signaled a kind of intelligence that others did not possess. In certain circles, in fact, being or having been in analysis was considered as desirable as having a graduate degree, evidence that one had engaged in serious study (in this case of oneself). More than that, having been extensively analyzed gave a person a set of intellectual skills and vocabulary that one could (and, more often than not, did) use in all kinds of situations.[4]

With the good came some bad. The "baggage" that came with the typical psychoanalytic experience (if there is such a thing) was a necessary evil for both the patient and his or her circle. Direct quotes from one's analyst not infrequently popped up in ordinary conversations, for example, startling other people with the from-left-field jargon. More disturbingly, friends and family of the analyzed could not help but occasionally feel that they were part of his or her therapy, not a particularly good foundation for a relationship. Spouses often found themselves jealous of their partner's analyst, justifiably feeling that they were playing second fiddle when it came to mutual problem solving and decision making. Some psychoanalysts in fact firmly believed that a marriage consisting of an analyzed and an unanalyzed was a bad pairing, the couple like an unmatched set of silverware. As well, dependency on psychiatric aid remained a problem for some, particularly if the patient was unable to act decisively without first consulting his or her therapist. The fact that humans had done reasonably well for thousands of years before the three wise men—Freud, Adler, and Jung—spread their theories was proof that psychoanalysis was not necessary for survival, a far cry from the food and shelter on Maslow's bottom rung of needs. One would not know this from walking into an analyst's waiting room, however. "Appointment books are crowded with the names of men and women who consume countless hours of doctors' time with matters formerly resolved by simpler methods," observed Dorothy Ferman in the *Nation* in 1950. What she ironically called "the psychoanalytical joy ride" was showing no signs of slowing down.[5]

Although Ferman's indirect experience with the couch was a nightmare (she and her husband were divorced after he had seen three analysts over the course of seven years), others' personal stories of psychoanalysis no doubt pushed some to take the ride. John Knight's 1950 *The Story of My Psychoanalysis* was a not-very-pretty account of the "psychogenic forces" that led a young man to the couch, his authoritarian father, overprotective mother, encounters with anti-Semitism, and sexual problems leading him to a career- and a life-threatening stomach ulcer. Psychoanalysis turned out to be his savior as his neuroses dissolved once their causes became clear to him.[6] Lucy Freeman's *Fight Against Fears* of the following year told not just her own story but those of many Lucys whose parents did not or could not give their child what they needed most. For Freeman, the main reason analysts' appointment books were so filled was that these men and women were, like her, unloved as children, the maladjustments of adult life a direct result of the loneliness and misunderstanding they felt growing up. "This is a letter from your daughter, the daughter you didn't want," began one such story in the book, the writer telling her parents how her current unhappiness stemmed from her self-loathing as a child. A big part of Freeman's mission was to debunk many of the myths surrounding psychoanalysis so that others could have the courage to detangle the facts and fictions of their own lives. "In easy-to-read prose, the book removes most of the mystery from the kind of treatment that many people need, others dread accepting, and still others have undergone," wrote Marguerite Clark for *Saturday Review*.[7] Most important, rather than being an escape or indulgence—a common (mis)perception—Freeman made it clear that psychoanalysis was, as Karl Menninger wrote in his review of the book, "an ordeal in which the patient must struggle unceasingly against self-deception and rationalization in the long and painful search to know himself." She considered this the first thing readers should know, whether or not they personally chose to go into treatment.[8]

Philip Wylie was another author to reveal, as his 1956 article in the *Washington Post* was called, "What It's Like to Be Psychoanalyzed." Like Freeman, Wylie wanted to separate truth from fantasy so that others might get their lives back. "This is the day you've dreaded most in your life," he recalled fearfully thinking as he made his way to his analyst's office, angry that a man who had the American Dream—beautiful wife, good kid, great job, big house with two-car garage—found himself in this sorry position. With a variety of unexplainable physical ailments and an onset of intense acrophobia, however, Wylie knew it was time to visit a psychoanalyst after his family doctor suggested it. "By merely lying down on a psychiatrist's couch you've admitted you've reached the end of the line," he felt at the time, the reasonable conclusion being that, "You're a nut." Asked by the analyst to free associate, Wylie casually mentioned that he hated baseball but his father loved it. This was the point where it began to get interesting. The reluctant patient soon found himself recalling painful memories when he was eight, these involving, of course, baseball. In his second session, Wylie recalled another painful memory from when he was five or six, this one (about swimming) also concerning his dad (who threw him into Lake Erie). After a month went by with three sessions per week, however, Wylie was convinced he had made little or no real progress. He intentionally missed an appointment and showed up drunk to another to show his displeasure at how things were going. Eventually they got around to dream analysis, sexual fantasies, and, finally, a memory that hit him "like the blast-wave of an A-bomb."[9]

What was the thermonuclear event? Wylie claimed to vaguely remember being circumcised at eighteen months (something many cognitive experts in the field of memory would today say was impossible), his dad holding him down as he screamed and struggled. Wylie concluded that his lifelong hate, fear, and mistrust for his father stemmed from this experience. The analyst concurred but cautioned his patient that it would be another year or so before he could live a normal life. There was still lots of emotional territory from Wylie to cover, his mother and family life, for example, as his analyst reminded him that, "psychoanalysis is not pill-taking." After a year and change, Wylie felt free from the demons that plagued him and was told by his friends and family that he was back to his old self, a model case of psychoanalysis if there ever was one.[10]

No doubt stirred by such stories, many Americans with much simpler troubles in their lives took to the couch, much to the dismay of orthodox psychoanalysts who believed that their method should be used only for severe disorders. Popular culture too was helping fuel the notion that psychoanalysis could and perhaps should be part of one's mental health routine, not unlike seeing one's medical doctor or dentist to maintain good physical health or clean teeth. In New York City in the early 1950s, for example, one could tune in *Psychoanalysis in Daily Living*, a radio show sponsored by a local psychoanalytic society that discussed ways in which principles of the field could be useful in "normal" situations.[11] Women's magazines also hopped on the psychoanalysis bandwagon, not too surprisingly, publishing articles on the subject that were sure to catch both housewives' and career gals' attention. "Should You Be Psychoanalyzed?" asked *Mademoiselle* in 1953, many women probably asking themselves the very same question. More sensational stories like *Good Housekeeping*'s 1957 "How I Got Caught in My Husband's Analysis" and *Cosmopolitan*'s "Psychoanalysis Broke Up My Marriage" of the following year were also sure to sell magazines. Some women had undoubtedly heard of similar situations among their friends or friends of friends. Having an actual analyst at a dinner party was the ultimate way to dish the psychoanalytic dirt, a way to find out if one's problems (cloaked as someone else's, of course) could be solved on the couch. (Shrinks jokingly called this quizzing "socialized medicine," and explained why they preferred to spend time with their own kind.)[12]

Local newspapers, meanwhile, focused on the scientific aspects of the field, further spreading the psychoanalytic word by reporting new research findings. "Celibacy Can Be Healthy, Doctor Says," went the headline of one such story published by the *Los Angeles Times* on January 1, 1956. The news that single people could be emotionally healthy was generally contrary to mid-1950s popular thought in America. (Lost somewhere in translation was the idea that single people could be sexually active—even more so than married couples.) Even perennial bachelors or unmarried career women could be well-adjusted, sometimes more so than long-wed couples, Abe Pinsky claimed. This was quite the revelation for the many amateur psychiatrists practicing their trade over Manhattans and Rob Roys at cocktail parties and nightclubs. Pinsky, who worked for the American Institute for Psychoanalysis, had recently led a discussion group in New York on "Success in Marriage or Single Life," learning that those who had put career over marriage and those who just preferred being single were not necessarily neurotic. With no instinctual drive to get married—the institution being a socially determined construct—this made sense to Pinsky, although his findings went against the grain of postwar American norms and values.[13]

With more and more ordinary people going into analysis, inspired by personal success stories and influenced by the media, the once rather radical prospect of seeing a shrink had become nothing short of an all-American activity. "Psychoanalysis, which has been installed as a pretty standard fixture in American life, no longer needs its Bohemian prophets," wrote William Barrett for the *New York Times*. Clearly, much of the early edge of the field had now been rounded off. Psychoanalysis, in part viewed as an exciting opportunity to escape one's inhibitions in the 1920s, had a few decades later become a more sober affair, especially among younger Americans. "Young people now look upon it as a very serious and even painful task and not as the gay adventure of release it may have seemed to some people in the most light-hearted decade," Barrett thought. Ironically, Freud's pessimism had been one of the more appealing aspects of the method.[14] Only recently labeled a "voodoo religion," psychoanalysis had, rather suddenly, become popular, but it was hardly a complete victory.

The Case against Psychoanalysis

Indeed, quite a few psychoanalysts were not pleased to see how their field had evolved into a therapy for the masses. "At present this nation has more psychoanalysts—and incidentally more murderers and more comic books—than any other two or three nations combined," observed Frederic Wertham, now director of the mental hygiene clinic of Queens General Hospital. Wertham was of the persuasion that, despite the widely acknowledged shortage of shrinks, there were enough analysts but not enough analysis.[15] Eight out of ten psychoanalyses were not necessary, Wertham believed, and six out of ten actually did more harm than good. Wertham was also dismayed, to say the least, to see psychoanalysis and electric shock treatment being used for the same patient, the two methods considered by strict Freudians to be diametrically contradictory. And although Freud had refused to treat many patients who came to see him, thinking his talking cure was not necessary or the right approach, analysts of the early fifties were telling nearly everyone who knocked on their door to lie down and tell all. Because American society and the world as a whole were sick and neurotic, the general argument went, all of us were by default sick and neurotic and thus eligible candidates for psychoanalysis.[16] While as enthusiastic a supporter of traditional psychoanalysis as anybody, Gregory Zilboorg also agreed that things had got a bit out of hand. "In our age of propaganda and pragmatic go-getting, psychiatry and psychoanalysis have been oversold, as everything we have and do is oversold," he wrote in 1950, unhappy to see a science turned into a fad.[17]

On cue, a bevy of books attacking psychoanalysis was soon forthcoming. Robert Lindner's *Prescription for Rebellion*, Sebastian de Grazia's *Errors of Psychotherapy*, and Calvin S. Hall's *The Meaning of Dreams* were all of the what's-wrong-with-psychoanalysis school, each book explaining in its own way how Freud had got it wrong.[18] In his book, for example, Lindner argued that despite what leaders of the field said, psychoanalysis merely patched up mental patients rather than cured them, and the method fell far short of what psychiatry could possibly achieve. Rather than free their creativity and "natural rebelliousness," he maintained, analysts encouraged patients to feel content and satisfied with their lives. "I have been shocked to learn that they (analysts and patients) have felt themselves to have achieved their analytic goals when they (the patients) became placid, accepting, undisturbed by the condition of man and the world, uncaring for the fate of their fellows and able without guilt or strain to pursue wholly selfish goals," the author of *Rebel Without a Cause* wrote, believing this was a misuse of what was in fact a very powerful methodology. Rather than instill the values of "conformity, surrender, passivity, social apathy, and compliance," psychoanalysts should push their patients to be as individualistic as possible—a "prescription for rebellion" that would be better both for the patient and for society as a whole.[19]

It was another book of 1952, Andrew Salter's *The Case Against Psychoanalysis*, which made the loudest, if not the strongest, complaint. Even more so than in his previous book, *Conditioned Reflex Therapy*, Salter, a well-known New York psychologist, argued that the current vogue of psychoanalysis was more a result of some people having too much time and money on their hands than any real need. For yesterday's "Aunt Hettie," some fine chocolates and steamy novels were a sufficient cure for a bout of "the vapors," Salter wrote, but today's Hetties were being diagnosed by analysts as having psychosomatic illnesses that required years of treatment. Likewise, the country doctor of the past could give top shrinks of the day a run for their money, he felt, the former's "bedside manner" as therapeutic as any psychoanalytic technique.[20] Salter should have stopped there while the getting was good but he could not resist going into areas he had no business going, opening himself to a torrent of criticism. Upon making the case that Freud often contradicted his own ideas and that he was thus his own worst enemy, for example, writers like the *Nation*'s Helen L. Lynd were quick to come to Freud's rescue. Lynd argued in her review of Salter's book that, "It is no criticism of Freud's theories that he himself changed and criticized them and that later workers have continued to do so."[21] Others who knew a thing or two about psychoanalysis panned the book ("Freud would not have bothered to point out all of Salter's inaccuracies," wrote Rollo May in his review in the *New York Times*), but the title alone reinforced the idea that a decent case could indeed be made against the method.[22]

More so than any psychologist or psychiatrist with an ax to grind, it was psychoanalysts themselves who compellingly pointed out real problems in the field. The fact that American psychoanalysts could hardly agree on anything was perhaps the best evidence that the field was in turmoil. In his landmark book of 1953, *A History of Psychoanalysis in America*, for example, C. P. Oberndorf reported that after four years of discussion, the American Psychoanalytic Society determined that it was "impossible to find a definition of psychoanalysis that is acceptable to even a large group of its members." Oberndorf also believed that psychoanalysis "cannot be applied identically by any two persons and each case is a case unto itself." No wonder, then, that analysts could not even agree on a definition of the field.[23] Others suggested that despite its new appeal to the mainstream, psychoanalysis was still an elitist institution, ignoring the needs of average Americans. "Psychoanalysis must come from its clinical ivory tower and acquire a firsthand acquaintance with every-day problems of every-day people," said Alexander Martin of the American Psychiatric Association in 1951. This was a sentiment widely shared by those working in the trenches of the field rather than in "understated chic" offices furnished with leather chairs and plush carpeting.[24]

Although analysts were as unique as their fingerprints, psychoanalysis in America had by the mid-1950s cleaved into two basic groups, the Freudians and the neo-Freudians. The Freudians were aligned with the largest organization in the field, the American Psychoanalytic Association (which in turn had close ties to the American Psychiatric Association and American Medical Association), while the neo-Freudians, whose theory drew heavily from Harry Stack Sullivan, Erich Fromm, and Karen

Horney, were connected to the William Alanson White Institute, the American Institute for Psychoanalysis, and the Association for the Advancement of Psychoanalysis. The divide between the Freudians and neo-Freudians had become wider than ever, the traditionalists hanging onto the sexual instinct as their operative lens while the rebels looked to aggression as human's primary drive. As well, neo-Freudians tended to be warmer, less formal, and more sympathetic with patients than Freudians, their approach more midcentury America in manner than fin de siècle Austria. While both groups agreed on the fundamental aim of psychoanalysis—to free the patient from neuroses and change his or her personality through deep internal insight—and were each now focusing more on current behavior than "forgotten" episodes of the distant past, there was no love lost between them. "These two armed camps generate almost as much mutual bitterness and hostility as did Catholics and Protestants in the days of the Reformation," thought Nancy Lynch in 1957. The Freudians accused their cousins of being superficial, and the neo-Freudians viewed their kin as rigid, authoritarian, and pessimistic to a fault.[25]

If internal infighting were not problematic enough, other psychological methods were encroaching on psychoanalysis, offering troubled Americans legitimate alternatives to the emotional demands of the couch. Carl Rogers and some associates at the University of Chicago, for example, were promoting in the early 1950s what they called client-centered or nondirective therapy, in which a psychologist or counselor (versus psychiatrist or psychoanalyst) identified with his client (versus patient) by seeing the world as he or she saw it. Clients, not therapists, should take the lead in a session, he and his colleagues believed, the former better equipped to direct the conversation. And by taking the client's side rather than staying neutral, Rogers felt, the fear of criticism was removed, making treatment both more effective and shorter. To illustrate, Rogers told the story of a man who was having trouble with his wife, thinking her to be unreasonable, inconsiderate, and unappreciative. If in psychoanalysis, the analyst would have remained objective, simply guiding the conversation to allow the patient to reach his own decision about what to do, if anything. But in client-centered therapy, the counselor would agree with the man's viewpoint, encouraging a deeper understanding of his role in the relationship gone sour and what potential action to take. For Rogers, it was not repression of socially unacceptable behavior that led to psychological problems, as Freud theorized, but rather situations that fell outside of or contradicted an individual's identity. These constituted the issues that should be addressed in treatment.[26]

Other, less scientifically grounded therapies were also making inroads on psychoanalysis. L. Ron Hubbard's 1950 *Dianetics: The Modern Science of Mental Health* was an immediate bestseller, as thousands of Americans rushed to learn how the new therapy could relatively quickly and cheaply eliminate psychological difficulties and psychosomatic illnesses. Just as psychoanalysis had its "neuroses," Hubbard's treatment focused on what he called "blocked engrams," the engram being "a moment of uncon-sciousness containing physical pain or painful emotions ... not available to the analytic mind as experience." Other parallels to psychoanalysis were obvious (therapists were called "auditors," and the patient's goal was to become "clear"), but some of Hubbard's theories made those of Freud seem almost pedestrian. Each cell in the human body had mem-ories that affected physical and mental health, he argued. The key to recovery was to unblock or release the engrams residing within them. Hubbard believed that medical operations had to be performed in silence, as did sexual intercourse, or engrams were created. Needless to say, the psychiatric and medical communities were highly suspicious of these claims. (The fact that early articles about dianetics appeared in the magazine *Astounding Science Fiction* did not help its cause.) Morris Fish-bein, former editor of the *Journal of the American Medical Association*, for example, labeled dianetics the "poor man's psychoanalysis" but, because it was more comical than anything else, something that even a poor man should avoid at all costs. However, the public remained intrigued by dianetics, so much so that clinics had been set up in New York, Los Angeles, Washington, Chicago, and Honolulu, with the New Jersey–based Hubbard Dianetics Research Foundation determined to grab a chunk of the nation's expanding therapeutic marketplace.[27]

Norman Reider, chief of psychiatry at a San Francisco hospital, further warned that "self-starting, free-wheeling mind-peddlers" were continu-ing to plague the field. These twenty-five thousand or more charlatans (some of them having day jobs as plumbers and electricians) were still taking advantage of the fact that no state in the nation required a license to practice mental therapy. Reider had actually once seen a sign in Los Angeles offering "Colonic Irrigations and Psychoanalysis," a good example of the widespread quackery in the field. Much worse than people wasting money on such services was when they received bad advice, as in the case where a self-appointed "marriage counselor" told a woman whose husband was ignoring her to "dress up and stay out all night." The husband subsequently beat her severely.[28] Using a variety of highly suspect techniques—Reichian vegetotherapy and sexual healing, to name a couple—untrained "psychoanalysts" were indeed a menace to society.[29]

After decades of mind-peddling, Senator Samuel L. Greenberg introduced a bill into the New York State Legislature in 1954 to include nervous and mental disorders in the Medical Practices Act, the passage of which would mean that only licensed physicians would be able to practice psychoanalysis in that state. Whether psychoanalysts also had to be doctors had been a source of controversy since the beginnings of the field in both Europe and the United States, so it was inevitable that someone in an official capacity attempted to clarify the matter for legal reasons. French courts had the year before ruled that the practice of psychoanalysis constituted the practice of medicine, and the field seemed to be taking this direction in the United States as well. For years, the American Psychoanalytic Association's authorized institutions had restricted training to physicians, so state laws requiring psychoanalysts to be doctors would formalize the official policy of the field. This would go a long way, many believed, toward protecting citizens from the healing powers of techniques like vegetotherapy.[30]

Guerrilla Warfare

Like quackery in the field, another persistent threat to psychoanalysis—traditional Catholicism—also refused to go away. Much higher officials in the church than Monsignor Sheen, in fact, now began to attack psychoanalysis, perhaps seeing a direct connection between the growing practice of the field, particularly in America, and a decline in its own set of beliefs. In 1952, the clergy of Rome banned faithful Catholics from "indulging" in psychoanalysis; the vicariate (under orders from the Holy See) asserted that the treatment "can easily become a school of corruption." "It is difficult to excuse from mortal sin those who, knowing this, voluntarily submit to this method of cure," read the clergy's bulletin, employing much harsher words than Sheen had ever used.[31] A few months later, Pope Pius II himself entered the fray, condemning "the pansexual method of a certain school of psychoanalysis," that school of course being Freudianism.[32]

Six months later, the pope broadened his attack, now cautioning Roman Catholic psychoanalysts and patients that they were treading on thin spiritual ice, especially when it came to the church's sacred tradition of confession. The pope made it clear that psychoanalysts must not assume priestly duties, while those who went to them "frequently have no rights whatever" to reveal their secrets, even if doing so would be of considerable relief. The sexual orientation of psychoanalysis was again a particular sore spot, the holy man advising that "one should be slow to lower man ... to the level of the brute."[33] The church had faced plenty of threats in the almost two millennia it had been around but, as a modern form of healing, psychoanalysis was being treated as an especially serious one. More missives continued to come forth from Rome, all of them attempts to keep this increasingly popular form of therapy in check. Two years later, for example, the pontiff warned his flock around the world that psychoanalysis could not remove one's guilt "by insinuating that it never existed"; only repentance and submission to God's will was capable of doing that.[34] Orthodox psychoanalysis and orthodox Catholicism appeared to be, in a word, incompatible.

Local shepherds in America tended to temper Rome's orders, especially those belonging to different strands of Christianity. It was possible for psychoanalysis and Christianity to live together peacefully because they had different and, in some cases, complementary goals, many clergy believed. Just a month after the pope's latest warning, for example, the Very Reverend James A. Pike of the American Episcopal Church, and dean of New York's Cathedral Church of Saint John the Divine, declared that while psychoanalysis was indeed very good at "taking people apart," only religious faith could "put a man together again." "Self-understanding brings only distress if there is no way out through grace," Dean Pike explained. Psychoanalysts did not have the priest or pastor's ability to rebuild patients by offering forgiveness and a grand philosophy of life. By working together, however, healers of the mind and of the spirit could help the troubled. The dean thought that programs that gave seminarians three to six months of clinical training in mental hospitals was a good example of how the lion could lie down with the lamb, as were conferences like the one recently held at the Menninger Foundation in which ten psychiatrists and ten clergymen combined their approaches on specific case studies.[35]

Popular personalities straddling the line between the sacred and the secular also helped bridge the divide between Catholics and psychoanalysis. Norman Vincent Peale, the famous Protestant preacher and progenitor of "positive thinking," for example, believed in the curative powers of talking to someone else about one's troubles, taking issue with Fulton Sheen's claim that confession to a priest was the only way to achieve that. Peale went right to the source to show that God wanted all of us to air our troubles "whatever your religion may be," promising "a wondrous sense of peace and joy" to those who did so. Peale pointed to James 5:16—"Confess your faults one to another, and pray for one another that ye may be healed"—as proof that people should unburden their souls "whether it takes place in a church or synagogue or in a psychiatrist's office or that of a trusted physician."[36]

Another formative organization in the 1950s—the Communist Party—was as determined as the Holy See to rid the world of psychoanalysis. Like the Nazis who had in the 1930s banned its practice, communists were hostile to the field, its bias toward an individual's internal forces not aligned with the interests of an all-powerful economic or political system.[37] In Russia, psychiatrists and neurologists were saying *nyet* to psychoanalysis, that country's academy of medical sciences firmly opposed to contemporary Freudianism.[38]

Americans like William L. Alland, a Hollywood producer, also found psychoanalysis to be inconsistent with communism. Alland, one of four witnesses questioned at closed-door hearings in Los Angeles, told a subcommittee of the House Un-American Activities Committee in 1953 that he broke with the Communist Party after being psychoanalyzed. Alland, who coproduced such all-American films as *Citizen Kane* and

Native Son, revealed that he was first exposed to communism in 1940 when he married his first wife, who had been a long-term, active member of the party. After returning from the Pacific as a combat pilot in World War II, Alland decided to join the Reds when he "fell in with what I thought were do-gooders," maintaining his membership for three years. In 1949, Alland underwent psychoanalysis and began to have a change of heart about his politics. "I had a deep feeling of guilt all the time—that I was a criminal every moment," he testified, rebuffing party leaders' attempts to have him rejoin. "The Communists found out I was taking psychoanalysis and told me not to come to any more meetings," Alland explained. He added that he believed 95 percent of the party members were "emotionally and mentally disturbed the way I was."[39]

Communists might have also resented psychoanalysis because some practitioners used it to "cure" them from their wayward political ways. Norbert Bromberg, an analyst based in Tarrytown, New York, found that a child's hostility toward his parents could drive him to communism in his later years. He claimed to have case histories of patients who had gravitated toward totalitarian politics as an act of rebellion. In a twist on the Oedipus complex, sons identified the capitalist system with their fathers, the actual target of their hatred, driving them to seek out an alternative kind of politics. At a 1958 meeting of the American Psychoanalytic Association, Bromberg described one such patient: "Capitalism, like his father, he considered wholly cruel, avaricious, tyrannical, unjust, hypocritical and dishonest," while "the Communist movement, and its leaders like himself, were full of brotherly love, beneficent, freedom-loving, just, forthright, wise and honest." Through therapy, the young man's pinkish leanings waned as the hatred for his father disappeared, an interesting case in which psychoanalysis and politics met face-to-face.[40] Equally interesting, some psychoanalysts believed that racism too was linked to inner, unresolved conflict experienced as a child. Active, racist movement leaders in the South were usually emotionally disturbed, argued Terry Rodgers of New York City at the following year's meeting of the American Psychoanalytic Association; typically, hatred of the father was projected onto a vulnerable group in order to regain some sense of control.[41]

One did not have to be a member of the Roman clergy or Communist Party to find psychoanalysis objectionable. An entire American city, in fact, appeared to be against the technique, or at least one of its classic works, Freud's *A General Introduction to Psychoanalysis*. Pocket-sized editions of the book were pulled off the shelves of Cleveland's bookshops and newsstands in 1953, part of that city's effort to outlaw indecent literature and anything else deemed sinful. Councilman Joseph Flannery was on a mission to clean up his town, banning not just the Freud book but *The Golden Ass* (written by the Roman philosopher Lucius Apuleius about two thousand years ago), as well as a number of other works including Somerset Maugham's *Cakes and Ale*, John Steinbeck's *Wayward Bus*, and even Mickey Spillane's *I, the Jury*. The problem with *A General Introduction to Psychoanalysis* was that it "contained a chapter on sex," as a book distributor who was forced to obey the order explained it, afraid that the police would shut his business down if he did not comply.[42]

Cleveland's ban on Freud's book did not sit lightly with Mel Evans, the publisher of the fifty-cent reprint edition, who was understandably upset about the situation. Evans called the ban "guerrilla warfare" and compared it to another one that had recently been led by the Our Lady Help of Christians Roman Catholic Church in Brooklyn. (That church was following the orders of the Chicago Archdiocesan Council of Catholic Women for the National Organization for Decent Literature, which had compiled a list of books it considered obscene, Freud's work being among them.) Despite the fact that *A General Introduction to Psychoanalysis* was consistently ordered as a school textbook, was accepted in libraries across the country, and was included in the Great Books of the Western World set recently published by Encyclopedia Britannica (which was edited by the former chancellor of the University of Chicago), anyone wishing to find a cheap copy in the biggest city in Ohio would be mostly out of luck.[43] Those with a better understanding of the First Amendment soon took on Flannery and his effort to make Freud persona non grata in Cleveland. Morton B. Icove, chairman of the American Civil Liberties Union's censorship committee, declared that his organization was ready to take on the case, and Bernard Fields, operator of the Fields Book Store, continued to stock books on the list, threatening legal action if anyone tried to stop him from selling any work, whether it was written by Sigmund Freud or Mickey Spillane.[44]

Those with stronger academic credentials than Brooklyn nuns or Cleveland councilmembers were also waging guerrilla warfare against Freud. With his "What Is Wrong with Psychoanalysis?," a chapter in the 1953 book *Uses and Abuses of Psychology*, and his 1956 *Sense and Nonsense in Psychology*, for example, British psychologist H. J. Eysenck vigorously criticized Freudian theory. His own ideas about personality and intelligence offered a much different view on why one was the person one was. Eysenck was not the only intellectual delivering a sharp attack against psychoanalysis as the fifties wound down. *Psychoanalysis, Scientific Method, and Philosophy*, a collection of twenty-eight papers read at a meeting of scholars in March 1958, and edited by Sidney Hook, "is the most devastating criticism of psychoanalysis I've ever seen," declared Rudolf Flesch of the *Los Angeles Times*. Given that half of the book's essays were pro-Freudian (and half anti-), the book had clearly made a strong impression on Flesch. "The Freudians lose and the antis win—by a landslide," thought Flesch, the central issue being whether the field was a proven science or not. A parade of academics including Ernest Nagel of Columbia, Sidney Hook of New York University, Arthur Pap of Yale, and Max Black of Cornell blasted the Freudians, with Swarthmore's Michael Scriven laying down the gauntlet. With psychoanalysis "the most sophisticated form of metaphysics ever to enjoy support as a scientific theory," he asked, how could shrinks justify taking good money from sick people? The nation's eight hundred or so analysts were each making at least $12,500 a year, Scriven figured, collectively robbing Americans of some $10 million.[45]

Perhaps an even greater blow to the field at the end of the decade came from a much more powerful group, the United States Tax Court. Two Washington DC–area psychiatrists had deducted the cost of their own psychoanalysis from their income taxes, arguing that they underwent treatment to improve their skills. The court rebutted that their treatment was not a business or medical expense and thus its cost was not deductible, establishing a precedent for other psychiatrists intending to write off their own therapy. Key to the court's decision was its ruling that psychoanalysis was "a special technique, different from psychiatry," the former not a subfield of the latter as the two men had contended. Despite (or because of) its greater-than-ever popularity among Americans, was anyone not out to destroy psychoanalysis?[46]

Repressed Hostility Blues

Certainly not comedians, given that psychoanalysis was turning out to be the biggest source of material since the knock-knock joke. Contrary to what one might think given the actual experience, psychoanalysis had become by midcentury undeniably funny, used by pretty much everyone trying to get a laugh. Freud "created a whole new field for playful wits," thought Evan Esar of the *New York Times* in 1950—"every other joke today seems to be based on psychiatry." It was true that an inordinate percentage of newspaper and magazine cartoon panels, particularly in the *New Yorker* and *Punch*, featured a psychoanalyst and a patient, sometimes with couch, sometimes without. The subject was also prominently featured in humor stories. There was, briefly, even a comic book called *Psychoanalysis*, the pulpish magazine published by EC Comics in 1955 lasting just four issues. (Its editor, Al Feldstein, moved on to *Mad* magazine the following year, something funny in itself.) As well, the protagonist in jokes, formerly physicians or teachers or some other occupation, were now often psychoanalysts, a symbol of their new cultural power. Mock definitions rooted in psychoanalysis were also popular (a neurotic was a person "who thinks you mean it when you ask him how he feels," went one), as were Freudian slip-of-the-tongue ha-ha's ("It was so nice of us to come," went the punch line of one about a woman who reluctantly attended a party thrown by a person she loathed). In a perfect explanation of the phenomenon, Esar described psychoanalytic humor as "the best evidence that the profession has finally become an important fixture of our society and that its members play a conspicuous part in everyday life."[47]

Psychoanalysis first started to get funny during World War II, Esar argued, "the great number of mental cases created by it" offering lots of material to turn into comedic fodder. Analysts quickly became caricatures, their relationship with patients the standard conceit (with the GI almost always coming out on top, naturally). A typical wartime joke involving a psychiatric board testing a soldier's mentality went this way:

PSYCHIATRIST: Do you ever hear voices without being able to tell
                 who is speaking or where the voices come from?
SOLDIER: Yes, sir.
PSYCHIATRIST: And when does this occur?
SOLDIER: When I answer the telephone.[48]

When the war ended, Esar continued, there followed a postwar boom
in psychohumor as civilians were substituted for soldiers. Once again,
the analyst typically played the role of foil, either not particularly bright
or crazier than the patients he was seeing. Two psychoanalysts meet on
the street, went a classic, one saying to the other, "You're fine. How am
I?" "The mad analyst is more than another passing symbol to indicate
the historic continuity of humor," concluded Esar, he is "an ironic commentary on our modern world, a contemporary Hamlet peering into
the uncertain future of an atomic world."[49]

Humorists of the fifties could not resist offering their own take on
the mounds of decidedly unfunny psychoanalytic literature being published. For the New Yorker in 1955, for instance, Wolcott Gibbs parodied
Joseph Wortis's recently published Fragments of an Analysis with Freud,
with the former's fictional experience quite different from the latter's
real one in the early thirties with the great man. "Go away, I find you
repulsive," were the first words spoken by Freud, Gibbs "recalled," not a
very good start. Herr Doktor eventually took the patient on but had the
habit of slipping behind the couch to go to sleep and, on other occasions,
explaining his own dreams to Gibbs. Freud had a dog (who had once
been a transvestite), Gibbs continued, the mutt (named Jung) often lying
beside or on top of the patient on the couch, something the father of
psychoanalysis found very amusing. After about six months of this, Gibbs
decided to end his treatment with Freud, his story ("A Couch of My
Own") went, leaving readers with a refreshing alternative to all the earnest, profound books and articles on the subject.[50]

Jules Feiffer, already a well-known cartoonist in the late 1950s, definitely found Freud funny, so much so that he created "Sick, Sick, Sick,"
a strip running in the Village Voice. Feiffer was especially fascinated by
nonprofessional analysts—parents, schoolteachers, relatives, random
adults, and contemporaries—who saw Freudian meanings in the actions

of those around them. Immediately from birth, Feiffer mused, a child became a source of study for the amateur analyst. If a son cried frequently, for example, his mother was told by her friends that he was orally fixated. If he rarely cried, these same friends advised her that he was repressed, this serious enough to try to figure out why. Paperbacks were then read on the subject, these saying that nothing was really wrong as long as the mother doled out heaping quantities of love to the little one. Father's coming home and kissing mother was cause for alarm, of course, but nothing that millions of other boys hadn't endured without too much damage. Finger-painting at school was another potential danger zone, the wrong subject or color (black, specifically) warranting a trip to the principal's office for some amateur free association.[51]

For Feiffer, the end of childhood hardly meant the end of amateur analysis. A young man telling his dreams to his girlfriend would inevitably result in her explaining to him what they really meant (to much embarrassment). Friends interpreted his ordering of a hamburger with onion as an antisocial act, they too having read some Freud. "There is no action too insignificant to be traced and brought back to childhood and brought to heel," Feiffer wrote in a 1958 essay for the *New York Times Magazine* titled "Couch-as-Couch-Can School of Analysis," an army of volunteers prepared to plumb the psyches of anyone and everyone.[52] The ultimate form of amateur analysis was self-analysis, with Feiffer offering a not-too-farfetched spoof of what might be heard in an actual shrink's office. "You see," the amateur analyst says of himself,

> I have a need to be guilty. Because when I was a child all the other kids were guilty but I wasn't, so they beat me up for trying to be different. Hungry for their acceptance, I adjusted to their behavior patterns and acted guilty. But I didn't really feel guilty. I was a fraud. I began to feel guilty about not feeling guilty.[53]

Another funnyman of the day, Bud Freeman, used music to get people laughing about psychoanalysis. Freeman's best-selling album of 1958, *Songs of Couch and Consultation*, included twelve tunes sung by Katie Lee such as "Hush, Little Sibling," "Repressed Hostility Blues," and "I Can't Get Adjusted to the You Who Got Adjusted to Me," each one obviously a satirical reference to psychoanalysis. "Whether you're for or against psychoanalysis, it should delight you," wrote Philip K. Scheuer of the *Los Angeles Times* in his review of the album. Sales were especially hot in Los Angeles where, Freeman explained, "psychiatry may be more of a ranking religion."[54]

As in the last few decades, Broadway looked to psychoanalysis for inspiration, but now plays tended to have more of a funny bone. In *Faithfully Yours*, a show playing on Broadway in 1951, for example, Ann Sothern and Robert Cummings play a wealthy New York couple whose greatest fear is that they are normal, something to be avoided at all costs within their strata. The wife's solution to this appalling situation is to see a psychoanalyst to figure out how to make her husband cheat on her, as he was not ordinarily inclined to do so. The remainder of the play consisted of the wife—conspiring with the less-than-ethical shrink—using her new knowledge to persuade her husband to be unfaithful, turning the sexual liberalness associated with psychoanalysis on its head. "This is a good idea for a brisk satire on modern witchcraft," thought Brooks Atkinson of the *New York Times*, the rather loony show playing off the "ironic premise that psychoanalysis is the very disease it professes to cure" (borrowing from a famous saying by Austrian Karl Kraus).[55]

Another show about psychoanalysis popped up on the Great White Way a couple of years later, this one also poking fun at the foibles of shrinks and those of their patients. Atkinson noted that "everybody in the audience seemed to be having a good time" at *Oh, Men! Oh, Women!*, perhaps because psychoanalysis had become "America's leading hobby," she opined. In the comedy, a psychoanalyst about to get married hears some shocking things about his fiancée from a new patient (again, involving sexual affability), creating the spark for what ultimately leads to a group of his patients screaming at and punching each other in a most nonrational manner.[56] A far more sober exercise in dramatized psychoanalysis, *A Clearing in the Woods*, debuted on Broadway four years later in a play about a neurotic woman haunted by memories of her past. Just as in a typical psychoanalytic experience, the woman sorts out her troubled childhood, adolescence, and early adulthood, going through anguish and confusion in the process. In the final scene, she reaches a state of mind in which she accepts that she and the world are less than perfect.

By making peace with her past, she has become a whole human being, a clearing in the woods that many Americans were searching for in their own lives.[57]

All the psychoanalytic goings-on both on and off Broadway had some wondering if the trend was good for the theater and for theatergoers. "Does the dramatist have to be a psychoanalyst as well as a creator?" asked Philip Weissman, himself a shrink and self-described "long-standing and dedicated member of the audience." Weissman, who was on the consulting staff at the New York Psychoanalytic Institute Treatment Center, was frustrated that "the subject of the mentally ill seems to be the predominant preoccupation of the writer and the public," not just on Broadway but on television and radio as well. Fond of going to the theater to escape the trials and tribulations of his day job, Weissman was disappointed to see case histories much like those he worked on embedded into plays like *A Clearing in the Woods*, *The Bad Seed*, and *The Shrike*. (A trip across the pond offered little refuge, with psychiatric plays like *Black Chiffon*, *The Cocktail Party*, and *The Potting Stage* playing on London stages during the fall 1957 season.) Psychopathological characters created by masters like Eugene O'Neill and Tennessee Williams were fine, Weissman griped, but did seemingly every playwright feel compelled to "provide a diagnosis and a pill" on the Great White Way?[58]

Analysts like Weissman found no relief from diagnoses and pills on television of the late 1950s. After attending an advance screening of new shows for the 1958 season, for example, Lawrence Laurent, the television writer for the *Washington Post*, began to wonder about the psychological dynamics of the Old West, specifically, "just how those folks managed to survive without the tender care of Sigmund Freud and the scripts served up by today's psychoanalyzed writers." Laurent posed his own psychoanalytic theories about the villains in the "adult westerns" that were so much a part of the contemporary televisual landscape, seeing in them a rather familiar story. As a whole, the bad guys were not really bad but rather just misunderstood, "their aggressive tendencies ... caused by a lack of parental affection." The heroes of these same shows deserved to be analyzed as well, Laurent thought, their personalities also shaped by neuroses or psychoses. Paladin, for example, the protagonist in *Have Gun, Will Travel*, is unable to choose between a luxurious life in San

Francisco or a rough-and-tumble one on the frontier and so "suffers from schizophrenia, or split personality," he suggested. The hero of *Wanted—Dead or Alive*, meanwhile, suffers from "pangs of guilt," his occupation as a bounty hunter often leading to conflicting feelings about turning a man in (or killing him) for a reward. The hero of a new show called *Lawman* had "already built up a series of neuroses and tension" that was apparent to Laurent in the very first episode. The lead character of another new show, *Bat Masterson*, meanwhile, was an "exhibitionist," his habit of wearing a derby and carrying a gold-tipped walking stick making this clear as day.[59]

Who the Hell Do You Think You Are?

If the shrink had become the premier butt of jokes in the psychoanalysis-happy fifties, his or her sidekick—the couch—was now linguistic shorthand for the field. A mere piece of furniture had become symbolic of the widespread effort to cope with life's problems and emerged as a major source of inspiration for art, drama, and fiction, not the likeliest of scenarios.[60] "The couch is all around us," commented Gerald Walker of the *New York Times* in 1958, a ubiquitous sight in cartoons, television, and the movies as well. Linguistically, the "couch" had displaced the previous generation's pet phrase of "getting psyched." The word had become virtually synonymous with psychoanalysis. "No self-respecting neurotic would enter analysis today without informing his friends with appropriate urbanity that he's either 'hitting the couch' or 'couching it,'" wrote Walker, the smart set knowing that "to sofa was to suffer." The Couch was even the name of a coffeehouse in Greenwich Village, the little enclave in New York that happened to have the highest density of psychoanalysts in the world. Waiters at the Couch wore doctors' smocks and served drinks with psychoanalysis-inspired names like "Psychic Masochist," the "Complex," and the "Dr. Freud" (the latter a concoction of v-8 juice, rum, and lemon peel). Robert W. Mark's recently published novel *The Horizontal Hour* too was a reference to the psychoanalytic lie-down, its protagonist an A-list analyst who marries a beautiful patient, starts to think she means him harm, and ironically winds up in an asylum.[61]

The rampant "couch consciousness" of the late 1950s was a sixty-year-old remnant of Freud's experiments with hypnosis. Freud eventually discarded the technique but kept the trappings of his office. (He used the same couch for most of his long career.) The couch not only put patients at ease, Freud thought, their upward, vacant focus encouraging them to speak freely, but also diverted their gaze from himself (something he could not stand). Freud's chair was always at the head of the couch, placed at an angle so that he did not see the patient and vice versa. Because of the couch, the unseen therapist could more easily take on the role of "the other" (mother, father, whomever), which was thought to help achieve the transference that was such an important part of psychoanalysis. While the couch was indeed a staple of psychoanalytic culture for strict Freudians, the classic image of the (bearded and bespectacled) shrink taking notes was by now largely a myth, considered too much of a giveaway of the analyst's relative level of interest in whatever the patient was saying at any given time. Neo-Freudians such as those belonging to the Karen Horney, Harry Stack Sullivan, and Columbia University schools were not wedded to the couch; the propping up of the patient in a regular (but comfortable) chair was a symbolic rejection of Freud's mustier theories. As well, these groups' view of the analyst as "participant observer" versus anonymous father figure lent itself more to face-to-face conversation, another reason to ditch the couch.[62]

Whatever position they preferred their patients to be in, there were about eight hundred medically trained analysts in practice in 1958, with another five hundred or so lay analysts who had received some psychoanalytic training at one of the nation's seventeen authorized institutes. One thousand more were now currently in training, leading Marion Kenworthy, the new president of the American Psychoanalytic Association, to expect the number of practicing analysts to double over the next three years.[63] With an average age of thirty-nine, newly minted physician analysts were hardly spring chickens, having spent the last eight years in training. This was all after completing a medical degree and, often, an armed services requirement, some very tough hoops to jump through to become a full-fledged psychoanalyst.[64]

Given the challenges these analysts-to-be faced, it was even more remarkable that so many Americans wanted to be one. "For eight or nine hours every day the analyst must sit alone in a room with mother's boys, masochists, frigid women, homosexuals, suicidal depressives and the like, listening to an outpouring of bizarre fantasies, sickly fears, and nightmarish dreams," wrote Morton M. Hunt in 1957. Further, the human punching bag was frequently "assaulted by strangled, explosive talk, angry shouting, painful confessions, or, most baffling of all, hostile silences." Analysts were also often put in a no-win situation by their patients, deemed bored if they listened too quietly, and bossy if they talked too much. "It has been likened to being indoors on a long rainy day with your own kids plus a swarm of the neighbors' kids," said one understandably anonymous psychoanalyst of his occupation.[65] On a bad day, the job could be plainly abusive, as this actual, abridged rant from a female patient of a San Francisco practitioner makes clear:

> I'm fed up. A whole year I've been at this—mixed-up, miserable, wasted year. And for what? Nothing. Not a goddam thing. You say I seem hostile today? God almighty, I don't need *you* to tell me that. I'm not hostile—I'm a mad bitch tiger, that's all. One of these days I'm going to find the guts to walk out on you and not come back. Why should I come back? You do nothing for me, nothing. Year after year, you just listen. How many years do you want? Who the hell do you think you are?[66]

One big question those not in the business often considered was whether emotional illness was somehow contagious, that is, whether analysts could possibly catch their patients' problems. Could a normal person endure a nearly constant barrage of anxiety, guilt, depression, and perversity without being affected by it? one had to ask. Psychoanalysts themselves believed they were immune from such a thing, that the range of emotions they were routinely exposed to was not only expected but useful and interesting, essential steps toward their patients' recovery. Feelings directed their way were, after all, not really about them but about other people in their patients' lives, the analyst vicariously taking the blows through the process of transference. The three hundred or more hours psychoanalysts themselves spent on the couch as part of their training was a big help in their ability to not take things too personally, of course, having walked in their patients' therapeutic shoes.

Outside the office, however, it was a completely different matter. Analysts were probably just as vulnerable to emotional issues in their personal lives as the average man or woman on the street.[67]

Still, being a psychoanalyst was hardly a piece of cake. Understanding patients, especially their provocative behavior, required an extraordinary amount of effort and delicacy. The analyst had to remain open to patients' problems and be sympathetic to them in order to fully comprehend the situation, but also maintain a certain detachment and objectivity, a fine line to walk. Despite their years of training, retaining what was called in the trade "free-floating attention" was particularly challenging. It was not an easy task to remain receptive to anything and everything the patient said or did. Simply keeping one's concentration for fifty minutes a number of times a day without using the selectivity aspect of normal listening was draining, to say the least. As well, dealing with patients' accusations, bouts of silence, and occasional attempts at seduction were also no fun, as were the times when they were late or did not pay their bills. Many believed psychoanalysis to be more difficult than medicine, in fact, the former not having the step-by-step, almost formulaic approach to diagnosis and treatment that physicians employed. Feelings, memories, and emotions were a lot more ephemeral and mercurial than organs, tissue, and bone, after all, and one patient's set of issues was often completely different from another's. As a vital tonic for their own mental health, a good number of analysts took not just August off as vacation but July as well, but even this apparently wasn't enough R&R for some. Although there were no firm statistics to cite, anecdotal evidence suggested that an unusually high percentage of male analysts suffered heart attacks at an early age, a result of the tension that came with the job.[68]

In 1957, *Mademoiselle* did yeoman's duty by interviewing sixteen female psychoanalysts, finding a variety of reasons why they went into the field. (Women comprised a surprisingly high 19 percent of the 702 members of the American Psychoanalytic Association, and were often presidents of local societies and institutes.) Many of the women, as for their male counterparts, turned out to have had less-than-happy childhoods, their careers consciously or unconsciously serving as a way to understand and cure themselves. Loneliness and uneasiness with other people when they were young was not uncommon, as was stress, anxiety, and an inability to express their feelings. (Freud himself suffered from a variety of neuroses as a young man including depression, moodiness, indigestion, migraine headaches, and fear of open spaces.) Only in the field of psychoanalysis could the presence of some kind of inner discomfort and desire to get rid of one's own problems be considered better credentials for prospective analysts than believing it was a good career to go into. Demand for analysts far exceeded supply, meaning one could not only make decent money—$20,000 to $25,000 yearly on average (roughly $160,000 to $200,000 in today's dollars), the magazine estimated—but choose how many hours a week to work. As well, because analysts often had a father or grandfather who was a physician, this may have sparked their interest in medicine and in healing people, whether their ailments were physical or mental. A strong streak of curiosity, of course, was a staple characteristic for psychoanalysts; the possibility of hearing in detail what people really thought was almost irresistible to those thinking about entering the field.[69]

The Psychiatric Revolution

The growing number of psychoanalysts eager, willing, and able to listen to people's problems was indicative that something even bigger was going on in American culture. By the early 1950s, there was little doubt that the West was going through "a psychiatric revolution," as Ernst Kris, a faculty member at the New York Psychoanalytic Institute, referred to it in 1952. Kris believed that key institutions like medicine, education, and welfare were being reinvented as a result of this "mental uprising."[70] Psychoanalysis in particular was having a major effect on Western society as it became much more than a last resort for the toughest psychiatric cases. One did not have to look far to find evidence that psychoanalysis was becoming more central to everyday life in America and familiar to a cross-section of the nation's population. One psychoanalysis clinic in Beverly Hills, for example, had a sign outside that advertised, "Four couches, no waiting," while a Gypsy fortune-teller in Asbury Park had one that said, "Palms read: fifty cents; psychoanalysis, twenty-five cents extra." Sales of patent medicine were reportedly down because faithful users were now seeing analysts to heal their emotional wounds rather than drowning them in alcohol. Not that long ago reserved for severe neurotic disorders, psychoanalysis had become an almost standard part of the American experience.[71]

Another development in the field—free analysis—offered the possibility of making the method even more central to everyday life in America. As a five-year experiment through the early 1950s, free treatment was offered at a clinic in New York, with patients making equal progress with those who paid for it, discounting the accepted belief that results came only with financial sacrifice. Payment was the analyst's problem, not the patient's, it appeared, posing big questions about the future of the field. Was the long-held idea that patients should always pay for their treatment because it was an incentive to get well wrong, as this study suggested? Interestingly, Freud had envisioned a day in which analytic treatment would be gratis for those who could not afford it, a way to lessen the "vast amount of neurotic misery" in the world. "One may reasonably expect that at some time or other the conscience of the community will awake and admonish it that the poor man has just as much right to help for his mind as he now has to the surgeon's means of saving life," Freud said in a 1918 speech in Budapest. He predicted that free psychoanalytic clinics would someday, somewhere emerge as "an urgent duty" of the state.[72]

Freud's prediction had by the mid-1950s come true. With the opening of the Karen Horney Clinic in New York in May 1955, free and low-cost psychoanalytic treatment was available, assuming one could get an appointment. Five hundred people applied for treatment even before the place opened, with more than ten thousand applying over the first twenty-one months that the clinic was in business. Sixty analysts from the American Institute for Psychoanalysis volunteered a total of 150 hours a week to the clinic that operated exclusively on the principles of Horney (who had died rather suddenly at age sixty-seven in 1952), with $6.50 the maximum charge for a session. Only a hundred patients could be treated at any given time, however, meaning there was a very long waiting list to get in the door.[73]

The huge demand to receive psychoanalysis, whether free, low-cost, or otherwise, had much to do with the fear, or actual belief, that one was insane or in the general vicinity. The idea that we could possibly be losing our individual and collective minds was pervasive in the 1950s, although it was difficult to say exactly why. One explanation was the amount of attention mental health had received during World War II, creating the psychology-friendly climate of the postwar years. About nine hundred thousand men had been rejected for military service because of mental illness and other "personality disturbances" during the war years, giving the appearance that insanity was more prevalent in the United States than previously believed. (Nine hundred thousand represented just 5 percent of the eighteen million men examined, a percentage of mental illness not significantly higher than for the general population.) Others took a more philosophical view of our emotional jitters. The poet W. H. Auden famously believed that the postwar years were an "age of anxiety," for example, a crisis in personal identity leading us to think we were dangerously close to a collective nervous break-down.[74] The prospect of a nuclear holocaust, reinforced by civil defense sirens, the building of bomb shelters, and duck-and-cover drills, no doubt caused a significant level of mental strain, and the prevailing consensus of conformity must have served as a pressure cooker for those not particularly well suited for the demands of traditional family life. Whatever the cause, many Americans took the experts' warnings that civilization had gotten so complex that the human mind could very well shatter quite seriously, afraid that rampant mental illness could strike them at any time.[75]

Although mental illness had not in fact risen, experts in such things reported, and one was no more likely to go off one's rocker in Chicago than Peoria, the myth that Americans, particularly urbanites, were perilously close to going insane was persistent. "Nearly everybody is skirting along the edge of sanity much of the time," wrote Howard Whitman, a columnist for the *Washington Post*. The pressures of modern life in America were producing a "vast annual crop of ulcers, neuroses, and the national refrain, 'My God, I think I'll go mad.'" Whitman believed the source of the problem was that Americans were living in the jet age but were equipped with "horse-and-buggy emotions," the pace of life and myriad of distractions simply beyond our mental capacity. Tension and anxiety was the natural result of this mismatch, with what Whitman called a "new kind of calmness" needed to bring ourselves back into psychological alignment. Psychiatric remedies such as psychoanalysis (which Whitman described as "the unpacking of a messed-up suitcase") were fine, but something bigger—a more spiritual philosophy of life, specifically—was needed to help Americans keep sane in a mad society, he proposed. Whitman was essentially recommending that readers not sweat the small stuff, a few decades before such thinking was all the rage.[76]

The psychiatric revolution of the fifties seemed to have no boundaries, with psychoanalysis in particular being used in unexpected ways. In 1953, for example, the city council of Johannesburg, South Africa, decided to send its elephant, Nona, to psychoanalysis, the trouble being that "the peevish pachyderm cannot stand children," as the *New York Times* reported the story. Six months earlier, Nona had suffered a traumatic experience when a sheet of newspaper blew across her path while she was carrying some children, the event turning the elephant into an emotional wreck whenever a kid was within view. With Nona worth $5,600, a few sessions with a shrink seemed like a good investment to city officials, although it was uncertain exactly how the elephant would engage in "talk therapy."[77]

It thus was not too surprising when, a few years after Nona was sent to lie down on what was hopefully a very strong couch, Paxital, a tranquilizer developed specifically for canines, was introduced, its purpose to "make vicious dogs friendly and frightened ones calm." The drug, created by Warner-Chilcott Laboratories in New Jersey, was similar to chlorpromazine, along with reserpine the top sedatives for humans, and fast becoming almost as popular. Initial sales of Paxital were three times what Warner-Chilcott had expected. The company was naturally excited given that there were twenty-five million dogs in the country and only a couple of thousand veterinarians who treated them. Moreover, vets, like psychoanalysts, were concentrated in the Northeast and California, meaning that it was not possible for many "inland" dogs to get professional help and heal their psychic wounds, making a wonder drug that much more wonderful for them (and for the local mailman and milkman suffering the consequences). A variety of "neuroses" did indeed seem to be plaguing the Great American Dog in the 1950s, with many a Fido reportedly suffering from extreme shyness, lack of appetite, hysterical barking, compulsive running, or general nastiness. Whether the cause was biological (from overbreeding, for example) or environmental (such as from trauma resulting from cruelty, overtraining, or overprotectiveness) was uncertain, but it did appear that the nation's canines were as emotionally impaired as their two-legged companions.[78]

In fact, there were signs that dogs could soon be part of the nation's "horizontal hour," eligible candidates for a similar kind of treatment that many Americans were getting. Animal psychology was, according to Joanne Bourne of the *New York Times*, a "lively science" in the 1950s, with research showing that aggressive and unusual behavior among dogs was a result of some inner conflict and would lead, eventually, to an "emotional breakdown." William James of the University of Georgia's psychology department was one such researcher exploring the mental state of canines; his dream was to set up a dedicated Center for the Study of Neurosis in Dogs. C. E. Harbison, meanwhile, was acting as Quaker Oats' "dog psychologist," his expertise residing in how owners could deal with "recalcitrant pets." Harbison, who also edited a dog magazine for Condé Nast, did not believe pooches could have neuroses in the human sense but did agree that they required a lot of care and attention, which is where psychology came in. Some of the same psychoquacks treating people were already offering their services for dogs, suggesting that legitimate psychoanalysis for *Canis lupus familiaris* could possibly be on the way. "If man ever finds a way of giving dogs the necessary self-awareness to resolve unconscious conflicts, it seems highly probable that Coco will wind up on that couch after all," concluded Bourne in what would turn out to be an accurate prediction with the likes of the "Dog Whisperer" looming in the future.[79]

With talk of man's best friend heading to the couch, it was plainly obvious that the vocabulary of the field, already familiar to many, had spread further through the strata of American society. "Today thousands of people who, as late as 15 years ago, didn't know the difference between a neurosis and third base and thought psychosis was something you caught from a parrot, are able to converse learnedly about 'transferral' and 'sublimation' and 'libido,'" thought minister and author Alson J. Smith in 1956. Smith argued that psychiatric treatment "[had] replaced the appendectomy as a subject of fashionable conversation."[80] Intellectuals of the day, at least the pro-Freudians, assigned a much grander role to psychoanalysis, thinking it could be far more than just witty banter. "The intellectual climate of our time has accorded a special position to the insights made possible by psychoanalysis," suggested Jacob Arlow in 1959. Indeed, some looked to the field for "a new morality [or] scientific ethic which would equate evil with neurosis and salvation with deliverance from internal conflict."[81]

Part of the intense amount of attention being given to psychoanalysis in the fifties by both ordinary Joes and the best and the brightest was due to the wide knowledge that a good number of celebrities had personal experience on the couch. It was no secret that Marilyn Monroe, for example, was in psychoanalysis, her treatment beginning in 1951 intended to help her feel more secure in social situations. (Monroe occasionally stammered when under stress, and often could not say a word when she was in a group of strangers.) Given Norma Jean's childhood, it was not surprising that she ended up in analysis as an adult. With no father around and her mother committed to an institution for the mentally ill, the girl was sent to live with a woman named Grace McKee, but this too turned out to provide a false sense of security. McKee was unable to adopt her, and Norma Jean became a ward of the state, living in no less than eleven different foster homes between the ages of three and nine.[82] Psychoanalysis may have been helping her social skills but it seemed to be having no effect at all on another one of her problems, chronic lateness. Bennett Cerf ranked Monroe the "unchallenged champion of the tardiness brigade in Hollywood" in 1959, her lateness in showing up to shoot scenes in Billy Wilder's *Some Like It Hot* soon the stuff of Tinsel Town legend. Monroe was even late for her own operation for appendicitis and once kept the navy waiting for her to christen its new destroyer. Worst of all, perhaps, Monroe typically did not arrive at her analyst's office until her hour was almost over, ironically preventing her from getting the help she obviously needed.[83]

One with the Universe

Whether a patient's problem was chronic lateness or major neurosis, psychoanalysts of the fifties, like those of previous decades, were determined to make their field more of a science. Keenly aware that despite its amazing popularity there was still no hard proof that the method actually worked, analysts actively pursued a wide range of research projects to discover new, more effective techniques. More insight into patients' behavior during the therapy session itself might also produce better results, just one way some of the justified criticism of the field could be quashed. After a five-year study of "how the body speaks," for example, Felix Deutsch, a Boston psychoanalyst, reported in 1950 that talking wasn't the only way patients told their stories. Over the course of three years of treatment, Deutsch found that one of his patients used her fingers to depict her family, moving her two sisters, father, mother, and brother around like it was a puppet show. The patient was quite the puppeteer, able to convey a wide range of feelings—aggression, hostility, friendliness—with each finger movement. It was not clear if shrinks would start analyzing their patients' body movements as much as their conversation but studies such as this (reported in *Science Digest*) were a step in the right direction to bring more credibility to the field.[84]

Some psychoanalysts felt that another way to make the field more of a science and less of an art was to improve training. Reuben Segal, a Chicago psychologist, was trying to get more analysts to film their sessions with patients—a major violation of psychoanalytic standards—as a training tool, something he felt was sorely lacking in their education. Medical students, after all, observed surgical operations as part of their training but, because Freud was adamant that no "third person" be admitted in a session because he believed it hindered communication, films of real sessions were unavailable. By getting permission from both parties, Segal had tested such a thing and found that treatment was largely undisturbed, which encouraged him to persuade training institutes to get behind the idea. In fact, if anyone was disturbed by the presence of a camera, he noted, it was the analyst, not the patient. "The uneasiness stems largely from the prospect of having his techniques scrutinized by his peers," Segal explained.[85]

Franz Alexander, still one of the leaders of the field, had a different idea on how to make analysts better analysts (and patients better patients). Since 1955, Alexander had been working at Mount Sinai Hospital in Beverly Hills, the sixty-seven-year-old Hungarian immigrant and author of nine books as committed as ever to modernizing the field while staying true to its Freudian roots. Acknowledging that there was great unpredictability in therapy, Alexander was working on a project to see whether patients could be matched up with analysts according to their personalities in order to ensure a good fit. Mismatches between patients and analysts continued to be a major problem of the field, with the degree of success largely dependent on how well or poorly the two parties connected. With a $250,000 grant from the Ford Foundation, Alexander had set up a couple of small rooms to house three observers and some electronic equipment that recorded physiological reactions between a therapist and a patient in another room. Skin temperature, heartbeat, and body motions of all five individuals were recorded to determine whether there was a relationship between a patient's emotions and the analyst's responses. Alexander hoped to find a general pattern that could then be used in some kind of matchmaking process. "After 35 years [waiting] for a revelation, I have become impatient," Alexander said in 1958, speaking of how long he had been a practicing psychoanalyst, hoping that experiments such as this one would pave the way for new techniques that would advance the field.[86]

While at Mount Sinai, Alexander was also exploring ways to reduce the time required for psychoanalysis, a pursuit of his for many years. For this project, Alexander was partnering with a local scientist, Arthur Brodbeck, who claimed that the psychoanalytic process could be cut in half by showing patients popular Hollywood movies that elicited powerful emotions and depicted their inner conflicts. Films were chosen by their dominant theme—fear, love, aggression, sadism, for example—and then matched up with a patient's particular problem, with the expectation that the experience of the movie's protagonist would have a cathartic effect on the viewer. "Without being aware of it, the fantasy gets into their dreams, their social relations, their moods," said Brodbeck. He was convinced that the films helped to bring the patient's conflict from the unconscious into the conscious—precisely the purpose of psychoanalysis. After repeatedly showing the motion picture *Wages of Fear* to those with an irrational fear of death, *Miracle on 34th Street* to depressed patients, and *On the Waterfront* to emotionally troubled people regretting decisions they had made in the past, Brodbeck found that three years of treatment could be cut to eighteen months, quite the discovery, if it was all true. Was Hollywood the solution to Americans' psychological afflictions?[87]

It was probably inevitable that psychoanalysis and another dimension of popular culture, subliminal perception—Madison Avenue's "invisible sell" that turned out to be a very visible bust—would cross paths, which they indeed did in 1959. By flashing hidden messages too quickly for the conscious mind to register, those words or images were nonetheless captured by the unconscious, according to subliminal perception theory. A nice idea maybe, but one that had absolutely no validity when put into actual practice by those testing it.[88] Tossed into the dustbin by advertisers hoping it would be the ultimate selling technique, a couple of psychologists at the Menninger Foundation, plucked it out, believing it could have applications in psychoanalysis. Howard Shevrin and Lester Luborsky of the foundation exposed psychiatric patients to pictures flashed so fast they could not be seen on a conscious level and then told them to "dream about it," wondering if this would have some kind of effect on the following day's therapy session. Miracle of miracles, the patients reportedly had a richer pool of material to offer in the dream interpretation portion of their analysis, suggesting that the hidden messages had registered in their unconscious. In quite a leap, the researchers used the results as supporting evidence for a general tenet of the field—that people who "forgot" things had actually repressed them—meaning subliminal perception might have a future in helping psychoanalysts unpack their messed-up suitcases.[89]

More so than any of these new techniques, it was drugs that presented the biggest opportunity for and biggest threat to psychoanalysis. Clinical psychiatrists were increasingly treating the mentally ill, particularly schizophrenics, with what were often called "calming" or "peace of mind" drugs like rauwolfia, a pill derived from a snake-root plant found in India. Reserpine, chlorpromazine, and promazine were also being used by physicians in mental hospitals and outpatient medical practices to help them more easily communicate with their patients and for cases in which psychoses were considered beyond the scope of psychoanalysis. Freud himself recognized that his talking cure would not be successful for extremely serious ailments like schizophrenia, and he looked forward to a new, psychosomatic age of medicine.[90] Hardcore Freudians, such as Zilboorg, remained unconvinced that sedatives could be an asset to mental therapy. "If I hit you over the head and make you bleary-eyed, will you understand me better?" he asked at a 1956 symposium, frustrated to see both drugs and electric shock therapy viewed as immediate, if only temporary, cures to mental illness. Zilboorg accepted the idea that drugs could make patients easier to handle but strongly objected to the claim that they were in any way curative, something that more psychiatrists were coming to believe.[91]

Less orthodox psychoanalysts too were accepting the idea that drugs could be useful in treating neuroses and psychoses. Morton Ostrow, a psychoanalyst, was working with Nathan Kline, a physiologist, for example, on a project involving reserpine and chlorpromazine, two of the most powerful tranquilizing drugs of the day. The pair reported that the drugs reduced the "psychic energy" produced by the brain, making the patient more receptive to psychoanalytic treatment. The study, which was presented at a 1956 meeting of the American Psychoanalytic Association, was somewhat of a breakthrough in that it bridged psychic energy—a Freudian concept, encompassing the libido—with pharmacology, suggesting that the two fields could be synergistic rather than mutually exclusive.[92]

Hopes were also high, so to speak, that a new drug—lysergic acid diethylamide, or LSD—could also facilitate the psychoanalytic process. Isolated from ergot, a rye fungus, by Albert Hoffman, a Swiss pharmacologist, in 1938, LSD was two decades later being used on an experimental basis by a number of researchers around the world including Paul Saltman, a biochemist at the University of Southern California, and Sidney Cohen, a psychiatrist with the Veterans Administration's Neuropsychiatric Hospital in Los Angeles. The pair was particularly interested in how the drug could make those in psychoanalysis better patients by breaking down the barriers to the unconscious, something that often took years to achieve in traditional treatment. "The purpose of psychoanalysis is to discover suppressed memories which are painful to the patients," Cohen said in 1958, explaining that LSD "relaxes the patient's defenses and allows these suppressed memories to rise from the unconscious." It was not uncommon for researchers to occasionally take LSD themselves to get a sense of what it felt like to be psychotic, exactly what

Cohen's partner had recently done. Saltman drank a glass of water with one-tenth of a milligram of L S D and was soon experiencing extraordinary hallucinations, describing the sensation as a "technicolor fantasia." It was not like being drunk, however. Instead, the drug produced a "feeling of unworldliness," Salter explained, the twenty-nine-year-old father of two giggling uncontrollably and seeing a potted plant move, all in the name of science.[93]

By the following year, L S D was being hailed as a new weapon against mental illness, with many an analyst excited about its applications for psychoanalysis. One psychiatrist in Britain reported that the drug was of the "utmost value in psychotherapy." He contended that it made those resistant to treatment more cooperative and sped up the process, something that could potentially revolutionize the field. There were in fact more than five thousand case histories of patients who had been given L S D as part of their psychiatric treatment, with almost 70 percent reportedly "improved" after just a few sessions. Five hundred articles on the subject had been published in medical journals internationally. The *Los Angeles Times* reported in 1959 that "an experienced psychiatrist using L S D can often bring a neurotic person back to good mental health in a tenth of the time taken by ordinary psychoanalysis." By lowering the barrier between the conscious and the unconscious, psychoanalysts explained, the patient could look more deeply inside himself, increasing his understanding of both himself and others. Making a direct connection to classic Freudian theory, British novelist Aldous Huxley envisioned great possibilities for L S D (no doubt seeing some parallels with his fictional drug "soma," described in *Brave New World* as "euphoric, narcotic and pleasantly hallucinant"). "One has a sense of transcending the subject-object relationship and becoming one with the nature of things," Huxley thought, after dabbling with L S D, explaining that "this is what Freud called the 'oceanic' feeling of becoming one with the universe."[94]

Although it was unclear whether Americans would soon be dropping acid as part of their psychoanalytic treatment, there was little doubt that drugs would represent an increasingly important part of the psychiatric (and cultural) revolution. Assigned a greater role as mental illness in all its stripes rose to the forefront of the nation's concerns, psychoanalysis became an integral part of American culture in the 1950s. With more analysts and more patients than ever, psychoanalysis was undeniably a hot field, the status attached to it far greater than during the previous era between the wars. Most important, there was clear evidence that psychoanalysis continued to help people, whether there was scientific proof or not. Still, the field was in a precarious position as outside criticism intensified and as practitioners themselves fought over which direction psychoanalysis should take. As well, an increasing number of alternative therapies were beginning to challenge psychoanalysis for dominance in the marketplace, meaning that the future of the field remained highly uncertain. Like the nation as a whole, psychoanalysis would set a new course in the decade to come, another leg of its long, strange trip about to begin.

CHAPTER 4: The Pernicious Influence

> Life itself cures more neuroses than all psychoanalysts combined.
>
> ANONYMOUS PSYCHOANALYST, 1961

In May 1962, Adeoye Lambo, a Nigerian psychiatrist, made headlines around the world with what had to be one of the most unusual application of psychoanalysis ever conceived. Lambo was integrating psychoanalysis with African witchcraft to treat patients in his country, creating something that could be called with no exaggeration a "voodoo religion." Lambo, who got his degree in psychological medicine from Britain's Royal College of Surgeons, mixed and matched Freudian theory with "magical" native techniques such as animal sacrifices, rituals, and dances for Africans who found the couch more terrifying than their anxieties (which included things like infertility among women and being bewitched by tribal enemies among men). The work Lambo was doing at his eight-year-old hospital for nervous disorders in the village of Abeokuta was getting a lot of attention in mental health journals and at medical conventions. The thirty-nine-year-old "headshrinker" was even invited by Stanford University to spend a year at its Center for Advanced Study to share his findings with some very curious Westerners.[1]

While the Nigerian village of Abeokuta may have presented a major growth opportunity for psychoanalysis, it was in the United States where the influence of the field could be most felt. The 1950s had been the best decade yet for psychoanalysis, its popularity peaking as both a therapy and a theme in American culture. John R. Seeley, a professor of sociology and psychiatry at the University of Toronto, fully recognized the impact psychoanalysis had had on American culture and was continuing to have in the early 1960s. In a 1961 article titled "The Americanization of the Unconscious" published in the *Atlantic*, Seeley described how the biggest of Freud's ideas had added an entirely new dimension to society, a "radical act" equivalent to the one that sparked the founding of the new nation.[2] "This development in America, and it has still to run the major part of its course," Seeley wrote,

> makes for a change in the very nature of the society, comparable in the magnitude of its effect to the original American revolution. But that was a revolution of mere externa; this is of interna, ultima, privatissima. We are confronted by the possibility—perhaps, now, the inescapable necessity—of a highly self-conscious society of highly self-conscious individuals. . . . We are in the process of producing, if we have not already produced, a distinctly American unconscious.[3]

At the zenith of its influence, it can easily be seen how Seeley and others believed that even greater things lay ahead for psychoanalysis, "the major part of its course" yet to be run. Seeley's "highly self-conscious society of highly self-conscious individuals" would indeed come to pass over the next couple of decades, but psychoanalysis would no longer be a primary contributor to this major transformation of American society. In fact, psychoanalysis was about to embark on its roughest ride since the 1930s—like then, its present a constant source of controversy, and its future very much uncertain.

The Great American Game

With the presence of psychoanalysis a formidable one in the early sixties, few could have predicted its rather rapid decline. "The Great American Game is no longer baseball," Ralph Schoenstein wrote for the *Saturday Evening Post* in 1962, thinking that psychoanalysis was now the nation's most popular sport. Ironically, in some circles, people who were not in therapy were considered odd and suspect, as if there was something wrong with them. People who thought they were happy, upon going into analysis because it was the thing to do, were finding out they were "sick," capable of committing the most heinous of crimes in the right (or wrong) circumstances. As well, anyone claiming to be happy without having been analyzed was subject to mockery and derision, his or her friends knowing much better. "Psychoanalysis has become a fashionable pastime for mild neurotics who are trying to keep upset with the Joneses," Schoenstein quipped, calling the phenomenon "Freudian fever." More seriously, Schoenstein thought Americans' obsession with psychoanalysis had made us a "nation of psychic Peeping Toms," with more sophisticated folks routinely examining the psychological works of everyone they met. Besides being rude, he felt, widespread familiarity with Freud's theories had made it seem as if no one was really crazy anymore because we were all in our own way a little crazy. Those who did bad things were also now getting off the hook by being seen not as evil but as suffering from a disease, not really responsible for their actions. Was this raging "Freudian fever" a good thing? Schoenstein had to wonder.[4]

Given the degree to which psychoanalysis shaped patients' lives and society at large, that was a very good question. Those in treatment often felt they had to get their analyst's permission before making any major or not-so-major decision—for example, whether to have a baby or go on a trip. Analysts would, on occasion, even consult with each other if their respective patients wanted to get married, a double whammy of responsibility shirking. Friends and family of someone in analysis often could not help playing shrink, seeing things not as they were but as symbolic of something else. Adventurers, such as those risking their lives to swim the English Channel or to climb Mount Everest, were not heroes but simply people who were seeking approval because they had been rejected by their parents or had a death wish, those with Freudian fever might say. A long-held complaint about psychoanalysis—that it sucked the romance out of life like a Hoover vacuum—also continued to rear its ugly head. "Love" was now defined by those fluent in Freud as a "mutually compulsive and complementary interrelationship of egos" or, alternatively, a "wish-fulfillment fantasy between two people with dependent ids." Most perversely, feeling good was particular cause to see an analyst, some felt, since this was obviously just an emotional cover-up for some deeper, truer underlying issue or issues.[5]

America's continuing love affair with psychoanalysis was all the more amazing given that in Europe the method remained cultlike. Its relatively small group of followers was the target of considerable hostility by traditional psychiatrists and psychologists. (The field had been essentially wiped out there during the war, with most analysts either fleeing from or killed by the Nazis.) The European public generally shared this negative view toward the field, showing contempt for not just those who practiced it but for those who had elected to be in analysis. (Lingering anti-Semitism was no doubt part of this hostility.) With the exception of rural New England and certain parts of the South, where one would probably not want to tell one's neighbor one was in psychoanalysis, however, being in treatment in the United States was something to brag about, as if one belonged to a special kind of club. Geoffrey Gorer, the well-known British anthropologist and author of *The American People*, argued that any sort of sickness or weakness, physical or mental, was considered "un-American" in this country, perhaps accounting for our attraction to something that promised to make people better and stronger. "Psychoanalysis has been accepted in the United States, mainly as a system for explaining the failure of individuals to achieve their potential goodness, health, and happiness," Gorer wrote in 1961. He considered the discovery of what made a person maladjusted or antisocial to be a positive step in turning him or her into a good citizen. As well, psychoanalysis offered scientific explanations for individuals' aberrant behavior, this too an appealing concept for Americans. Although Freud had no way to imagine that his theories would be interpreted (and distorted) this way, the "un-Americanness" of neuroses and repressions did indeed seem to have propelled psychoanalysis to an unparalleled position in the world.[6]

Male psychoanalysts had of course become an immediately recognizable cultural archetype by the early 1960s but little or no information was known about their wives, something that was about to change. "Gradually, the spotlight of the public's interest in psychoanalysis has been enlarged to include not only the practitioners themselves but also those shadowy and generally forgotten women—their wives," observed Joan Ormont in 1961, considering them to be "a very special breed." Psychoanalysts' wives played prominent roles in the Broadway show *A Far Country*, Joyce MacIver's novel of 1961, *The Frog Pond*, and in *I Married a Psychiatrist*, a nonfictional work in which Louise Pfister told her personal story, raising awareness of the "peculiar conditions" that came with this particular territory. The wife and kids of an analyst were, for example, presumed to be unemotional and have no real problems, the simple fact of having a shrink for a husband or father making them immune to such ordinary concerns. Ormont, herself an analyst's wife, also found that her marriage to an analyst not only heavily defined her role within the community and her social life but her own identity as well, a result of being married to a man working in such a sensitive field. Although she rarely knew the names of patients and usually could not recognize them by sight, they would often figure out who she was after being introduced at some kind of gathering, which is when the games would begin. Social encounters with one of their husbands' patients were especially delicate situations that called for great tact given that the patient had most likely developed elaborate fantasies about not just the analyst but also his wife. Being constantly stared at by the patient at a party was just the beginning; the analyst's wife knew that she would likely be a topic of discussion at his or her next session as well. Because of this, analysts' wives would be very careful about what they said at get-togethers, and they expected to pay the price of being seen as social bores unusually interested in the weather.[7]

Even in a big city like New York, it was a relatively small world when it came to psychoanalysis. This made it necessary for the wives of "Thinkmen from Psycheville," as the latest nickname for analysts went, to keep a low profile. Running into not just patients but friends of patients or even patients of friends was a daily concern, since any information at all about the psychoanalyst's personal life was considered desirable. Analysts knew the most intimate details of their patients' lives, after all, making it perhaps human nature for patients to try to even the score given the opportunity. Evasion and ignorance thus became the wife's stock in trade; she would be very careful not to reveal anything about her husband's outside-the-office personality (but tempted to innocently mention that he had another wife, just for kicks). Transference, though a natural and desired part of the therapeutic process, was a particularly tricky issue, the wife knowing that some women patients (and no doubt a few men) were likely to be in love with her husband. If the husband was treating a beautiful or famous woman, this discovery represented yet another potential landmine. Telling herself that the beautiful woman was "just another patient" was simply not of much comfort. Finally, it was not always jealousy of a specific person but of an analyst's cumulative commitment to his patients and job with which wives had the biggest problem; their husbands were often emotionally drained when they came home. Not being able to talk about his work in any significant way left a gap in the typical marriage between an analyst and his wife, just another fact of life for the Thinkmen from Psycheville and their better halves.[8]

Fortunately, parties consisting mostly or entirely of their own kind offered analysts and their wives an opportunity to let down their hair and get a little crazy, so to speak. "A cocktail or evening party of analysts is a cross between a Mexican square on market day and a teenager's birthday party," thought Ormont, a rare chance for shrinks to express themselves, show off, and poke fun at themselves and their work. "They tell the latest sick-analyst jokes, quote or make up witty sayings of real or fictional patients, extol the virtues of one analyst as compared with another, or even burst into spontaneous songs and dances," she told readers, who were no doubt glad to hear that shrinks were human after all. Psychoanalysts not only preferred to hang out in their spare time with each other but with those of the same school as well, that is, Freudians with Freudians, Sullivanians with Sullivanians, and Jungians with Jungians. At gatherings in which members of different psychoanalytic schools were present, sparks were likely to fly, the underlying cause of human behavior as touchy a matter as politics or religion. Unaware that the party he was going to would be a shrink-fest, the stray writer or artist invited as a guest could often be found in a corner of the room with a group of the analysts' wives, talking safely about some topic that had nothing to do with repression or neuroses.[9]

At your average get-together in the early sixties, it was Freudian fever rather than the Freudians themselves that shaped the tone and tenor of the evening. Rilyn Babcock of the *Atlantic* thought psychoanalysis was putting a distinct damper on conversation at cocktail parties, with guests afraid that anything they said would be interpreted as something else (usually hostility) or read as a Freudian slip. In the good old days, she recalled, the two big taboos of politics and religion would regularly be brought up after a couple of drinks, after which a verbal brawl would inevitably break out. But this was a good thing, Babcock felt, with every-body leaving mad but happy to come to the next one to do it all over again. Now, with what was sometimes referred to as "fractured Freud" or "addled Adler," people spoke in a kind of code at get-togethers, using psychospeak to have a normal conversation. "It's good to ventilate your emotions" meant "Let's gossip," for example, while "He's definitely schiz-oid" translated to something like "My husband no longer loves me." Perfect strangers were, after twenty minutes, discussing their compulsive-ness, tendency to "block," and need to escape reality, all this leading her to conclude that "the fifty-minute-hour has replaced the vodka martini crowd" as "the voice of the neurotic is heard in our land."[10]

Dating too was affected by psychoanalysis. Not surprisingly, the dynamics of relationships were heavily influenced by one or both of the party's experiences on the couch. As it occasionally did (and still does), *Mademoiselle* invited male perspectives on the mating dance; its Novem-ber 1964 "Man Talk" column was devoted to the role of psychoanalysis in relationships. David Newman and Robert Benton saw "the $25 hour" as something that directly impacted not only their girlfriends but those of their own gender, and not in a particularly positive way. "Many girls (and you may be one of them) are rushing headlong into analysis with-out any thought for the true victim of the process," they began, insisting that it was not she, Mom, or Dad who suffered most from the experience but "the poor guy" with whom she happened to be going out. If a woman started analysis while in a relationship, she would eventually discover that she was seeing him to fulfill "neurotic needs," and it would soon be splitsville, they firmly believed. "So it's good-bye, Charlie," Newman and Benton warned, with really nothing the poor sap could do to prevent this from playing out.[11]

If in a relationship with a woman who was near the end of analysis, it was a much different story, Newman and Benton thought. "The girl by this time relates *everything* to the inner ordeal she suffers on the couch," as the two saw it, meaning their boyfriends were martyrs for staying with them when they were less enlightened. Although appreci-ated and trusted, men were hardly out of the woods. "Suddenly he finds that his most innocent moves are suspect," Newman and Benton wrote, everything he did subject to "deep analysis." "Girls in analysis, nearing the end, like to make like analysts, too," they warned, the pseudo-shrinks having learned the tricks of the trade. Why does he like this? Why does he dislike that? The endless series of questions were really things she was asking herself, of course, but knowing that offered little comfort or compensation for the unlucky lug. "In short, this man doesn't ever know what's coming next," the pair concluded. The complete lack of control was foreign territory for most men a half-century ago.[12]

The Primal Horde

The popularity that psychoanalysis was enjoying in the early 1960s as the Great American Game led top representatives of the field to think it was about to reach even higher plateaus. Although he was unquestionably jumping the gun, David Beres, the new president of the American Psychoanalytic Association, confidently told his colleagues at their 1963 annual meeting that their field was now "secure enough to assert itself as a member of the scientific community." Analysts were indeed more determined than ever to bury the ghosts of psychoanalysis past, specifically the snickers that almost inevitably could be heard whenever the sexually charged subject came up. The first order of business was for the field to prove that the treatment actually worked via a new "scientific" study, the last such one having admittedly been a dismal failure (despite the use of one of those newfangled, vending machine–sized IBM computers to sort through the mounds of data). Beres had two other ideas on how the field could be recognized as more legitimate. Addressing social problems and their impact on patients' lives would help a lot, he thought, as would teaching psychoanalytic principles to social workers, nurses, pediatricians, and others in the more broadly defined mental health community.[13]

Beres and his colleagues saw other opportunities to make psychoanalysis both bigger and better. Expanding the field's boundaries beyond the stereotypical patient—the well-off, middle-aged adult having some sort of midlife crisis—would go a long way to making psychoanalysis more relevant; there was no reason to ignore the mental health problems of children, adolescents, and seniors, they argued. It was also readily apparent that psychoanalytic theory had applications across everyday life in America, an asset that could be more fully leveraged. A couple of papers presented at the 1963 conference that addressed the intersection of psychoanalysis and sports, for example, made this vividly clear. One, "On Play and the Psychopathology of Golf," made the case that people who chose to spend hours chasing little white balls around may have some issues, while another, "Baseball and the Primal Horde" (in which that sport was defined as "a highly organized and regulated game in which the rebellion of man against authority and the competition among rivals are reduced to a safe game"), suggested that even the most wholesome of activities had a psychological backbone.[14]

If golf and baseball could be explained by psychoanalysis, some thought, so could things like traffic accidents or even adolescents. Trying to learn why cars smashed into each other or people on the street with unusual regularity, the New York City Traffic Department asked a group of local psychoanalysts to analyze accident victims, thinking the findings could help reduce future mishaps. Taxi and truck drivers also were asked to lie down on the couch, all this part of the department's safety education program "designed to make the public aware of the psychological factors involved in traffic accidents."[15] A few years later, the versatility of psychoanalysis again became clear when shrinks were asked to help New York City's finest deal with the rising tide of youthful offenders. "One problem in identifying with the client is that you can overidentify," said a real-life Officer Krupke from Staten Island to an on-staff psychoanalyst from the Postgraduate Center for Mental Health. The burley veteran patrolman was one of 131 cops learning how to better deal with "juvies" through psychoanalytic principles.[16]

Psychoanalysis in action went well beyond the confines of New York City, entering the orbit of America's space program as a potential way to make sure astronauts had "the right stuff." Not surprisingly, the United States Air Force psychiatrists thought long and hard about the kind of man that should be launched into space, especially as the country got closer to landing on the moon and began to think about interplanetary travel. Longer flights would require a different sort of person than the ones who took the big ride in the Mercury, Gemini, and Apollo programs, the air force believed, the intense "man of action" with a military background probably not right for the job. "Close interpersonal relationships present more difficulties for them than for many other men," suggested Lt. Col. Terence McGuire, head of psychiatry at the USAF School of Aerospace Medicine. He cautioned that the typical type-A pilot might go berserk sitting in a tin can for anywhere from one-and-a-half to three years. As well, a flight to Mars would consist mostly of monitoring instruments rather than rocketeering, McGuire told the Southern California Psychiatric Society in 1967, a situation likely to make control freaks start to snap at each other like chickens in a henhouse.[17]

How, then, could the air force find and, ideally, prepare this new kind of spaceman, McGuire and his fellow flyboys wondered? Having candidates go through psychoanalysis would not only reveal a tremendous amount about their personalities, he thought, but also allow each individual to have a better understanding of himself and what he was capable of. However, because of the time requirements, both on a weekly basis and over the long term, psychoanalysis was impractical, McGuire believed; the method was also likely to lower candidates' productivity as they became introspective. Astronauts in training, like other high-achieving, independent spirits, tended to view any and all psychiatrists as a threat, he added, not at all comfortable being the subject of intense scrutiny by headshrinkers trying to find potential defects. This too would make psychoanalysis probably not the best choice to select and train spacemen of the future, McGuire concluded, with other methods a better fit. Educational programs to teach astronauts about psychology and its role in human behavior would be a good choice, for example, a lot quicker and less confrontational than having speed demons lie on a couch talking about themselves for years.[18]

However, the myriad ways in which psychoanalysis was applied and could potentially be useful was impressive, especially given the fact that the method was now a relatively small piece of America's psychiatric pie. About fifteen hundred of the nation's twelve thousand psychiatrists were estimated to be bona fide psychoanalysts in the early 1960s, with maybe fifteen thousand Americans currently in treatment. Although these numbers were undeniably small, American psychiatry was still heavily psychoanalytic in practice, with about three-fourths of psychiatrists teaching at medical schools focusing on Freudian theory. The rise of psychosomatic medicine too was largely credited to psychoanalysis, with Freud and his followers early to recognize the link between mind and body. Much more significant was the imprint psychoanalysis had made on American culture, its impact on literature, humor, education, philosophy, and even the way children were raised impossible to dismiss or ignore.[19]

Despite its weighty presence in the psychiatric community and on the national scene, dark clouds were appearing on the horizon. "Psychoanalysis, the vogue that caught the fancy of an estimated 20 million American neurotics, may soon be relegated to the county fair side shows along with its ancestor, phrenology," wrote Norma Lee Browning in 1961, not a very happy birthday present to the field, which was officially celebrating its fiftieth year in America. Its popularity beginning to wane and a good number of its disciples deserting, psychoanalysis was facing the real danger of losing its status as a recognized specialty within psychiatric medicine, something that would spell virtual doom for the field. "The reaction has set in against psychoanalysis and the pendulum is swinging the other way," said Francis Gerty, still one of the top psychiatrists in the country. Gerty credited Freud with arousing interest in the psychological factors that influence human relationships and behavior but saw his theories as now having limited value for treating the mentally ill.[20]

The therapeutic value of the method, or lack thereof, was naturally the focus of critics' attention. Psychoanalysis was a relatively easy target given the lack of scientific proof that it worked even a fraction of the time. One study showed that two out of every three severe neurotics made at least some improvement over the course of a couple of years with little or no treatment at all, the same general success rate most psychoanalysts claimed. Some analysts readily admitted this. "There is no reason to assume that [the results of analytic treatment] are better than the results attained by any other method of psychotherapy or, perhaps, than the results of spontaneous recovery," said Melitta Schmideberg, a well-known psychoanalyst (and daughter of Melanie Klein). The official stance of the American Psychoanalytic Association was to make no promises at all when it came to results. Freud himself famously discounted the therapeutic value of his theories and techniques, becoming more and more skeptical about the benefits of his talking cure as he got older. It appeared that any number of methods ranging from hypnosis and electroshock to cold baths, tooth extraction, placebos, prayer, and the laying on of hands offered pretty much the same results as expensive, time consuming, and emotionally painful psychoanalysis, making many reasonably wonder why anyone at all would voluntarily choose to go through it.[21]

Still, the Catholic Church remained very much concerned that psychoanalysis could cast a powerful spell over anyone who encountered it. In 1961, the Vatican banned Roman Catholic priests, nuns, and religious brothers from both practicing psychoanalysis and undergoing it (except in "grave" situations and with permission from their bishop, regarding the latter), stepping up its decades-long opposition to the field. It was specifically the sixth of the ten commandments that led Pope John XXIII to his decision, concerned that clerics exposed to the method would change their views about the sin of adultery (and about their own vows of chastity).[22] Cracks in the church's official position began to appear in the 1960s, as members of the faith around the world found value in the method. "It is impossible in this day and age to consider man without using many of the ideas and concepts formulated by Freud," wrote one of them, Sister Michael Marie, in *Catholic World* in 1967. "Psychoanalysis properly understood and used is one of the most penetrating instruments for studying the concrete meaning of human behavior," Marie argued, "and so it is only proper that the Church take advantage of it." Besides being a nun, Marie also happened to be a medical doctor, her experience as a resident psychiatrist at St. Vincent's Hospital in New York no doubt shaping her views. Marie believed that the Vatican's objection to the method was that a number of Freud's views—his blatantly antireligious stance, theories of sexuality, and denial of free will, in particular—directly contrasted with those of the church, leading it to confuse the messenger with the message. "Truth sets one free and is never opposed to the highest good of man," Marie reminded her fellow Catholics. Marie saw in Freud's work some basic truths that could indeed lead to a greater understanding and appreciation of the human experience.[23]

No one agreed with Sister Michael more than a group of monks in Mexico who were ignoring the ban by going through analysis (something the Vatican was not at all happy about when it finally learned of it, especially because the analyst was a woman). The twenty-two Benedictine monks at the Monastery of Santa Maria de la Resurrección in Cuernavaca saw psychoanalysis simply as a modern interpretation of a very old Christian ideal—"Know thyself"—but the Holy See saw things very differently, "suppressing" (suspending) the monastery's operations. "I think the technique of psychoanalysis at present is the only means available to the average man to acquire a level of knowledge he cannot attain in any other way, because it takes into account their subconscious," said Father Gregoire Lemercier. Lemercier, who had been prior at the monastery, still believed that the method was "the first step toward the underground of any person." Concerned that many men had entered the cloister because they feared the outside world or felt sexually inadequate, Lemercier encouraged the monks to join the group therapy sessions, a way to determine if they had a true calling or should be doing something else.[24] The Belgian monk believed the Vatican viewed psychoanalysts as rivals of priests, and that this was the real reason why the church labeled the method a mortal sin. Despite no longer being recognized by Rome, the monks continued to live at the monastery through the 1960s and enjoy their favorite pastimes—producing religious and secular art and undergoing analysis.[25]

A Hit-or-Miss Affair

The beliefs of a nun and a couple of dozen Mexican monks notwithstanding, psychoanalysis came under full attack in the 1960s as its opponents recognized an opportunity to turn it into a bad chapter in the history of psychology. With shades of the 1930s, more physicians and social scientists were lambasting psychoanalysis not just as a psychiatric method but, according to Browning, because of "its influence on all phases of American life, from the schoolroom to movie and TV screens." Simmering for a half-century, the controversy surrounding the Freudian movement was coming close to boiling over, its enemies determined to rid the nation of this thing that had ballooned to enormous proportions. Two southern psychiatrists, Corbett H. Thigpen and Hervey M. Cleckley, were now leading the charge; their mission was to save psychiatry as a medical science by killing off its bastard child.[26]

Thigpen, author of *The Three Faces of Eve*, had a clever strategy to stop or slow the growth of psychoanalysis, lecturing at medical colleges across the country to convince physicians-to-be that the field was pure bunk. "Where is the proof?" he asked future doctors, blessed by the American Student Medical Association to pose such questions to its members. By appealing to Western medical students' number one concern—science— Thigpen, who taught at the Medical College of Georgia and at the state's University Hospital, knew he had a captive audience. Other psychiatrists on staff at major American hospitals made their voices heard. Benjamin Boshes, a Northwestern University professor and chief psychiatrist at Wesley Memorial in Chicago, considered Freudian analysis to be "a lot of long-haired mumbo jumbo," delighted to see his field gravitate toward true medicine. A colleague of Boshes's at Northwestern, Jordan M. Scher, had recently introduced a new, distinctly anti-Freudian kind of therapy. His "existential psychiatry" provided yet more evidence that psycho-analysis was being pushed to the sidelines.[27]

Even worse for the field, some leading psychoanalysts were defecting. Thomas S. Szasz, who had once been on staff at the Chicago Institute for Psychoanalysis, had just written a book called *The Myth of Mental Illness* in which he argued that a neurosis was not a medical problem but a moral conflict—an outlook that was anathema for orthodox Freudians. Yet another psychiatrist at Northwestern, Jules H. Masserman, who was a graduate of the Institute for Psychoanalysis, used satire to make Freud-ians look silly. In his article "Psychosomatic Profile of an Ingrown Toenail," which somehow got published in the *American Journal of Psychiatry*, Masserman described the toenail in phallic terms, concluding that an ingrown one was a symbol of "masculine aspirations and intrauterine fantasies." Proving his point that virtually anything could be interpreted by Freudians as somehow libidinal, some psychoanalysts took Masser-man's article seriously, congratulating him on his psychosomatic reading of onychocryptosis (medicalese for the podiatric condition).[28]

The anti-Freudian revolt was spreading like wildfire through the social sciences as the fifty-year war against psychoanalysis led by American psychologists reached its greatest intensity. As always, science, or more precisely the lack of it, was the main issue, the field's theoretical strengths a weak substitute for empiricism. In his new book, *The Crisis in Psychia-try and Religion*, for example, O. Hobart Mowrer, former president of the American Psychological Association, saw nothing to suggest that "psychoanalyzed individuals permanently benefit from the experience." The field was "in a state of virtual collapse and imminent demise," he opined. And in his own hot-off-the-press book, *The Freudian Ethic: An Analysis of the Subversion of American Character*, Richard La Piere, a Stanford University sociologist, labeled psychoanalysis a "pernicious influence" that was "bringing our very civilization and way of life into jeopardy." The American Medical Association had yet to criticize psychoanalysis (or endorse it, for that matter) but members of local medical societies were making their views known. "From a pure medical science point of view there have been no controlled tests to prove its therapeutic value," said Theodore Van Dellen, president of the Chicago Medical Society. (Chicago was a stronghold of the field, with psychoanalysts accounting for about one-third of the city's psychiatrists.) But since 1947, in fact, the American Psychoanalytical Association had been trying to prove quantitatively that the method worked, an effort that to date had failed. "The classifications were so vague and unusable that the entire result, statistically, did not amount to very much," bemoaned Gerhart Piers, director of Chicago's Institute for Psychoanalysis. As well, the spread of psychoanalysis into arenas like marriage counseling and religion was only drawing more criticism to the field, making even its most ardent supporters question whether the method's next half-century in America would be as good as its first one.[29]

Of course, some of the problems of psychoanalysis were inherent to the field, its greatest strengths also its greatest weaknesses. Because of its intensity, analysts could not have more than eight or nine patients at any given time, while medical doctors could see that many people in a day or possibly even an hour. Admittance to one of the country's eighteen authorized training institutes now required not just a medical degree but a year of general internship and two years of full-time psychiatric residence, sharply limiting the number of practitioners in the field. Add four more years of education at a cost of about twenty thousand dollars, and it was not surprising that only about a hundred new analysts were hanging out their shingle each year. The field's refusal to budge much from Freud's theories and techniques was also a major constraining factor, its failure to progress in any significant way something for which practitioners could only blame themselves. "Analysts have been too busy with endless ruminations and rhapsodizings, with variations on original analytic themes and theories," thought Lawrence Galton of the *New York Times* in 1961. As much as anything else, this complacence was making the method "a hit-or-miss affair." Still, a half-century was not much time in which to create an entirely new science, especially one dealing with the human mind, making one wonder if critics were being too hard on the field.[30]

The differences in opinion about psychoanalysis were not limited to those with advanced degrees. "Which side are you on in the cocktail party battle?" Morton Hunt and Rena Corman of the *New York Times* asked in 1962. The subject of psychoanalysis was usually the kindling for "a raging argument in which dear friends find themselves on opposite sides of a line as sharp and impassable as those that separated Blue from Gray." Few people seemed to be neutral on the subject, believing that it either worked wonders or did not work at all. The portrayal of psychoanalysis in movies, television, and plays was not really helping matters; many considered that the classic trope of a paralyzed woman suddenly able to walk upon learning in analysis what caused her condition was not remotely like real life. Which side one took had a lot to do with how one defined "cure," or even "improvement," the "deliverables" of psychoanalysis ranging from mild emotional relief to a complete personality overhaul. Analysts were admittedly thrown whenever the issue of evaluating the results of treatment came up—a legacy of Freud's reliance on individual case studies as scientific data—but it was getting more and more difficult to push the issue aside as psychoanalysis became increasingly scrutinized. Something more than the one-third cured, one-third improved, and one-third unchanged rule had to be produced for the field to retain any credibility at all.[31]

Much of the controversy swirling around psychoanalysis in the 1960s was a direct result of the arrival of new, or the revival of not-so-new, therapies that promised better and faster results. Behavior therapy was coming on strong in the sixties, its practitioners buoyed by new research showing that rats and cats "learned" neuroses and thus could "unlearn" them much like how Pavlov's dogs were taught to salivate at the sound of a bell. If true, people's fears and anxieties could be reduced or elimi-

nated more effectively by "correcting" neuroses through behavior therapy than by psychoanalysis, another serious blow to Freud's followers.[32]
Joseph Wolpe of the University of Virginia School of Medicine was a
leading proponent of behavioral therapy in the early sixties, claiming
that 90 percent of his 210 patients had been cured or improved through
his "reciprocal inhibition" technique. One woman afraid of heights went
up to the ninth floor of a building after being treated and was about to
take a flight on an airplane, Wolpe reported, something years of psychoanalysis had not come close to achieving. Wolpe and his colleagues
argued that behaviorism represented a truly scientific approach to psychology, while Freudian theory was merely metaphysics.[33]

While Wolpe's research was impressive, Eric Berne's 1964 *Games People Play: The Psychology of Human Relationships* would become the biggest
thing in behaviorism since John Watson put it on the map in the 1920s.
By 1967, the book had finally dropped off the bestseller list, after 111
weeks and sales of 650,000, but the paperback edition—with a print run
of two million copies—was ready to hit the shelves. What was the big
draw? Berne offered a user-friendly (and jargon-filled) guide to the
dynamics of relationships. His approach was steeped in Watsonesque
behaviorism, and advocated the distinctly non-Freudian idea that people
were products of their environments and were thus "conditioned" to do
the things they did. Although many critics found the book an insult to
the psychiatric profession ("The cynicism, the cult of self, the lack of any
philosophical, historical or religious perspective . . . is thoroughly American, and awful," bewailed Robert Coles in his review for the *New York
Times*), *Games People Play* made psychology, for better or worse, arguably
more popular than ever.[34]

Other less popular but certainly more erudite thinking came forth
to try to knock psychoanalysis off its roost. Martin R. Haskell, a sociologist who headed up the American Society of Group Psychotherapy
and Psychodrama, proposed that Freudian principles be replaced with
something he called "socioanalysis," the time long overdue to send psychoanalysis to the old folk's home. Haskell (and others of the socioanalytic school, like Jacob Moreno) felt that Freud's theories just did not
play well in contemporary American society. The fundamental concept
of early childhood experiences as the root cause of adult personality

disorders was the product of a very different time and place. Socioanalytic theory "corrects this mistaken reversal of cause and effect," Haskell argued; its focus on interpersonal relationships and one's peer group was much more relevant than Freud's omnipotent father figure.[35]

Reality therapy too was making headway in the 1960s, its supporters also challenging the basic tenets of psychoanalysis. Reality therapy rejected the very concept of mental illness by holding the patient responsible for his or her behavior, and further distanced itself from psychoanalysis by focusing on the present instead of the past. As well, no kind of transference was sought in reality therapy, nor was any attempt made to identify unconscious conflicts. Again, the patient was held fully accountable for his or her actions. And unlike in psychoanalysis, where issues of morality were essentially ignored, reality therapy subscribed to the idea of right and wrong; this too was an attempt to get patients to do the right thing for themselves and others. To that point, reality therapy practitioners offered solid advice regarding how their patients could and should behave, rejecting the "don't get involved" philosophy adopted by psychoanalysts in order to remain as impersonal and objective as possible. Rather than just offer insight, in other words, the goal of reality therapy was to teach patients how to solve their problems, or to practice what William Glasser of the Los Angeles Orthopaedic Hospital called "a special kind of education . . . to live more effectively." How could psychoanalysis compete with something as compelling as that?[36]

Challenge to the Couch

Maybe it could and maybe it couldn't, but with the publication of an article by William Sargent in the July 1964 issue of the *Atlantic Monthly*, the row between those for psychoanalysis and those against it got only that much more intense. In the article, which was part of a special supplement on "Disturbed Americans," Sargent, a British psychiatrist, claimed that the number of American mental patients was steadily rising despite (or because of) the psychiatric community's Freudian orientation. In Britain, meanwhile, the number of patients was declining, a result of that country's nonpsychoanalytic, more pragmatic approach. It was true that the Brits preferred biological and chemical treatments like electroshock, surgery, drugs, vitamins, and even penicillin to talk therapy, believing that the former delivered better, faster results. Just this would have been more than enough to get people's attention, but Sargent was not done. The United States was "almost completely isolated ideologically from all the rest of the psychiatric world," he suggested. Sargent claimed that the Freudian loyalists even barred those with opposing views from university teaching jobs.[37]

Sargent's article struck a nerve at a time when more and more American psychiatrists were themselves losing faith in Freud and gaining faith in pharmacological alternatives as they gradually improved. An editorial (titled "Challenge to the Couch") soon appeared in the *Boston Globe* (the *Atlantic* was also based in Boston, hence the local interest), not so much endorsing Sargent's view as simply saying that, with his "foreign eye," he could be on to something. However, after reading the editorial, leading members of Boston's psychiatric community bombarded the paper with a series of letters discounting Sargent's claims. American psychologists had not been "duped" or "imprisoned" by the Freudians, experts from the Boston University School of Medicine, Harvard Medical School, Tufts University School of Medicine, and the Boston Psychoanalytic Society were quick to point out (with no particular school dominating any other). Non-Freudian psychology was, in short, not banned in Boston or anywhere else in the country.[38]

For the psychology consumer, the American psychiatric landscape of the mid-1960s was undoubtedly a diverse one, with psychoanalysis on one end and "supportive" therapy—involving a half-hour-a-week pat on the back and maybe a handful of tranquilizers—on the other. In between were some forty other schools, with some very important issues—where illnesses originated, how much the therapist should talk, whether the patient should sit or lie down, if the focus should be on the past or the present—up for grabs. Many therapists in fact customized their approach according to their personal style and the needs of the individual patient, with eclecticism prioritized over orthodoxy. Although it was this ambiguity that perhaps most defined psychotherapy (one critic called it "an unidentified technique applied to unspecified problems with unpredictable outcomes"), all practitioners would likely have agreed that two conditions were necessary for success: one, that the patient wanted to get "better," and two, that there had to be some level of rapport between patient and therapist. This was all the more true for psychoanalysis because the rebuilding of at least part of a patient's personality over the course of several years was heavily reliant on the two parties working together toward a common goal.[39]

While a team approach toward therapy certainly made a lot of sense, those who had split off from Freud to follow or form their own psychoanalytic schools remained convinced that American psychiatry needed to be reinvented. Erich Fromm firmly believed so, making the case in 1966 that the heart of Freud's theories—the individual's "instinctual urges"—were now not very relevant or important, replaced by the modern pressures of boredom, alienation, anxiety, and hopelessness. Basic drives or family pathologies were not the source of emotional problems but rather issues of conformity, Fromm argued, shifting the focus from the individual to society. One did not have to be a cultural anthropologist to realize that sexuality was a much different thing in the 1960s than in the 1910s, making Freud's ideas of unconscious repression appear, at the very least, outdated. "Sex is something to 'get,' something cheap and relatively accessible," Fromm said. Repression was now more likely to come from underlying feelings about the meaninglessness of life than unsatisfied physical desires.[40]

Rollo May, the leader of the existential school of psychoanalysis, also saw the challenges of the modern age as responsible for the emotional woes of Americans. Like Fromm, May had split off from classic Freudianism, looking to philosophers like Kierkegaard and Sartre to inform his own heady psychoanalytic theories. May believed that a society's mythologies enabled the individual to handle feelings like anxiety and guilt, things that were on the rise because our mythologies were disintegrating. "You might say that ours has been the myth of a mythless society," he said in 1968, our pronounced faith in rationalism and reason leading us down a wayward path. History has shown that individuals always suffer in mythless societies, May argued, comparing the countercultural interest in altered states to the medieval search for meaning in witchcraft and sorcery. Even the growth of psychiatry, including psychoanalysis, was a result of the breakdown of myths, our collective mental health in need of aid because of the lack of a guiding sense of purpose. Eventually, our dying myths based in competition and nationalism would disappear and be replaced by ones emphasizing cooperation and collectivism, May predicted. An emotionally healthier "new age" was waiting in the wings.[41]

Even Anna Freud, who made a rare visit to New York in 1968, admitted that her father's version of psychoanalysis was becoming increasingly passé, especially among young people. The seventy-two-year-old told a packed house at Hunter College exactly what many critics had been saying for some time: "Young people now are not interested in man's struggle against himself, but in man's struggle against society." Despite acknowledging this and a number of other problems in the field—the encroachment of medical-based therapies, the lack of solid research, questionable training, and that analysts had first to be physicians (something she was not, nor for that matter was fellow analyst Erik Erikson)—Freud somehow remained hopeful. "Psychoanalysis will grow and it will take us deeper and deeper into life," she promised. Freud believed that the movement her father had founded three-quarters of a century ago would not only survive but thrive.[42]

Others were less optimistic, especially when it came to the touchy matter of psychoanalysis as an alleged science. "It has become increasingly obvious that psychoanalysis is a system of creed, code, and cult—in short, a religion," observed Alan Watts of the New Republic in 1965, not denying its therapeutic value but dismissing its proponents' claim that it was a science. The pursuit to quantify the motivations of human behavior was ultimately a doomed one, he felt; there were too many variables in the real world to allow any kind of controlled experimentation. "There may come a time when this field can be mapped with scientific precision," Watts mused, "but as things are now even the 'inner environment' of the nervous system is far from being understood."[43]

Thomas S. Szasz, who a few years back had made his thoughts on psychoanalysis quite clear in The Myth of Mental Illness, could not have agreed more. In reviewing Psychoanalysis Observed, a 1967 collection of essays edited by prominent British psychoanalyst Charles Rycroft, Szasz reminded readers that Freud himself was not sure whether what he created was a natural science or a moral one. What Szasz called "this fateful inconsistency" now was at the forefront of the field, with Rycroft and his contributors definitely leaning toward the moral side. Neither a heavily objective science like physics nor a purely subjective one like poetry, psychoanalysis was simply a study of human experience, Szasz believed; the notion that neurosis was a disease was an entirely fictional one. Szasz and his colleagues argued that psychoanalysis needed to be relocated from the world of medicine and biology to sociology and philosophy, and they were convinced that a shift of this nature would help to restore the reputation of the field.[44]

The following year, Szasz, then a psychoanalyst and professor of psychiatry at the Upstate Medical Center in Syracuse, was even less bullish on the field's future. "Psychoanalysis is vanishing," he said in 1968. He declared the method to be "as moribund and irrelevant as the Liberal party in England." Another leader of the field, Judd Marmor (who had actually been president of the American Academy of Psychoanalysis), was almost as pessimistic. Marmor was of the opinion that the field was close to "receding into an unimportant sidestream" of psychiatry. Bruno Bettelheim, who was, with Fromm and Anna Freud, one of the most prominent figures in psychoanalysis in the late sixties, considered Sigmund Freud's theories "time-bound, very shaky, very dubious," something you might expect to hear from someone of a different school but not from one of their own. Virtually everyone in the field agreed that a crisis was at hand, the salad days of the fifties gone for good. External criticism, internal strife, and new kids on the block were destroying what had made psychiatry not just prestigious but glamorous.[45]

The facts bore out all of these concerns. Of the roughly forty recognized forms of therapy in the United States, classical psychoanalysis was now the least practiced, according to the National Institute of Mental Health, used with just 2 percent of psychiatric patients. (It should be noted, however, that many patients were in "psychoanalytic-based" therapy.) Worse, that number was decreasing, as "community psychiatry," with its quicker, cheaper (and typically federally funded) therapies, threatened the method with extinction. Just one out of twenty psychiatric residents was now choosing to become a psychoanalyst versus one out of seven in 1945, another sign that the field was about as hot as big band music. Enrollment in the twenty approved training institutes was actually up 1 percent since 1960 but the adult population of the United States had risen 10 percent, indicating that the field was definitely losing ground. "There's a feeling it's no longer the frontier," explained Robert Jay Lifton, a psychiatrist at Yale's School of Medicine. Instead, the new frontier of "hard" studies—neuropharmacology, genetics, and brain research—was understandably pulling in the best and brightest. Most depressing, so to speak, was that some believed that standards to get accepted at a psychoanalytic institute were dropping just to fill the slots, suggesting the troubling possibility that shrinks of the future were not going to be as good as those of the past.[46]

So what does any organization do when its business is heading south and its public image is suffering? Hire a public relations consultant and hold a press conference, of course, which is exactly what the American Psychoanalytic Association did in 1968. The organization invited a group of reporters to see for themselves that psychoanalysts were not sex-crazed Freud look-alikes and talk-alikes but rather nice, normal people with good intentions. This was in fact the first time in the organization's fifty-six-year history that it formally met with the press, a belated coming-out party for a discipline often shrouded in mystery and secrecy. One attendee, Willard Clopton Jr. of the *Washington Post*, was definitely impressed and a little surprised by the ordinariness of the seven representatives who spoke at the all-day affair at the Waldorf-Astoria. Only one speaker had a detectable accent, and he was from Brooklyn, not Vienna, reported Clopton. Only two men there had beards, and they were fellow journalists. Another stereotype—that psychoanalysts were rolling in dough—was shattered when they learned that many if not most other doctors (especially surgeons), and even dentists, earned more money. It was not until he chatted with the analysts at the cocktail party at the end of the day that Clopton fully realized how pedestrian they were. "They are not a superior breed of humankind, immune to the stresses and sorrows that afflict the rest of us," he surmised; most of them were "family men with mortgages, balky cars, and kids who misbehave." It appeared to Clopton that the men also worried, argued with their wives, and even occasionally lost their tempers, this too dispelling the popular image of the holier-than-thou, never-can-be-rattled psychoanalyst.[47]

More than just an open house at the Waldorf would be needed to get psychoanalysis back on track, however, as new community mental health centers with an array of nonanalytic tools threatened to push the field to the margins of psychology and psychiatry. Analysts freely admitted that Freud's theories could be completely lost in the mental health shuffle and considered too obtuse and clunky in a time demanding faster therapy for more people. The psychoanalytic community had long been wary of the press, the natural result of decades of misinterpretation, resistance, and hostility, but public recognition for being involved with social issues was one way for the field to demonstrate that it was not just about treating rich people. Three out of the five major task forces on the Joint Commission for Mental Health of Children were headed by psychoanalysts, the American Psychoanalytic Association told the media in 1968; it also pointed out that sessions on social issues (hippies, sex education, and youth unrest, to be specific) were held at the organization's last annual meeting. Psychoanalysts also now wanted to be identified as such when referred to in newspaper and magazine articles, no longer content with being called psychiatrists. Desperate times called for desperate measures.[48]

A Far Country

Now fighting back, leaders of psychoanalysis made it clear that nails were not yet in the field's coffin. "There are always fashions, fads, and pendulum swings," announced Leo Rangell, past president of the American Psychoanalytic Association. Rangell asserted that analysts were still very much in demand at elite psychiatric institutions and that no other single theory had yet pushed psychoanalysis off its pedestal. The quick fixes that were now all the rage would eventually be exposed as superficial and even dangerous, Rangell warned, with no drug, direct suggestion, or conditioning technique able to replace the unearthing of the deep roots of conflict. "Other therapies attack the discrete manifestations of mental illness; psychoanalysis addresses itself to the underlying vulnerability," agreed Mortimer Ostow, president of the Psychoanalytic Research and Development Fund.[49] The real problem with psychoanalysis, Rangell felt, was that it had been "oversold" to the public by the media after World War II, and that Americans truly bought into the idea of a future society free of crime, divorce, and learning problems. "Now there's a big letdown, particularly among the intelligentsia," he concluded, even though psychoanalysts themselves had never made such utopian promises.[50]

Psychoanalysis certainly was not dead within popular culture, the subject still a powerful plot device or rich source for social commentary. Jules Feiffer continued to scribble cartoons featuring the subject although now they appeared in the opinion section of the Sunday *New York Times*, quite a promotion from the *Village Voice*. Fellini followed up his 1963 masterpiece *8½*, in which a film director much like the Italian auteur psychoanalyzes himself, with *Juliet of the Spirits*, this too a psychic wonderland of the workings of a troubled mind.[51] It would not be until the end of the decade that psychoanalysis would reach full bloom as creative inspiration. The couch served as the perfect vehicle for the guilt-ridden hero of Philip Roth's *Portnoy's Complaint* to vent to his shrink about his parents and about other assorted middle-class neuroses. "Let's put the id back in yid!" Alexander Portnoy exclaims at one point, trying to come to terms with his sexual peccadilloes against the backdrop of a traditional Jewish upbringing. Fittingly, the novel ends with Doctor Spielvogel saying his one and only line: "So. Now vee may perhaps to begin. Yes?"[52]

Much less hilarious was *A Far Country*, a play about Freud and the origins of psychoanalysis, which opened on Broadway in 1961. In the hit show, the young Freud is faced with the challenge of determining why a woman with perfectly good legs cannot walk, the story based on a real case when "Elizabeth von R." met with the unknown doctor in 1892. The playwright, Henry Denker, had almost as tough a challenge in making psychoanalysis seem fresh "some 30 years after those discoveries have been accepted as basic ground rules for half the serious plays produced on Broadway," as Walter Kerr wittily put it. The "far country," need it be said, was that of the mind. ("The soul of man is a far country which cannot be approached or explored," said Heraclitus, the pre-Socratic Greek philosopher.) In the play, Freud urges his patient to "remember ... things from the past," things which turn out to be buried deeply in her unconscious. Denker came up with the idea for the play when he himself was in analysis, reading everything he could find on the subject when his treatment ended. (Analysts typically asked their patients to avoid reading anything about psychoanalysis while in treatment because conflicting theories could muck up the works.)[53]

Even more ambitious was John Huston's much-anticipated *Freud: A Secret Passion*, which was released in the United States by Universal Pictures the following year. By far the boldest effort yet to try to capture the essence of psychoanalysis on film, the movie covered just five years of Freud's life (1885–90), intertwining the case of Cecily Koertner with the man's own struggle to get his ideas accepted. Huston had Jean-Paul Sartre, who wrote the script, borrow heavily from Freud's works to lend a strong sense of authenticity to the film, the exterior location shots also bringing viewers back to turn-of-the-century Vienna (the interior scenes were shot in Munich). With Montgomery Clift (who looked quite a bit like the young Freud) playing the leading man, Huston had high hopes that viewers would agree that his film would be, as he said while shooting it, "one of the most exciting mysteries of our time."[54] Not coincidentally, perhaps, Huston (along with Clift, Clark Gable, and Marilyn Monroe) had just finished *The Misfits*, this film also an intense exercise in soul searching. (Philip K. Scheuer of the *Los Angeles Times* described the Arthur Miller script as "elliptical psychoanalysis," considering the film "one of the strangest pictures ever made.")[55]

Although he did not catch the irony, Huston admitted that his obsession with Freud for the past eighteen years was what had driven him to tackle such a difficult subject (and one which clearly violated Hollywood's golden rule of "action, action, and action"). "Very few of man's great adventures, not even his travels beyond the earth's horizon, can dwarf Freud's journey into the uncharted depths of the human soul," the director said when the film opened, with "no spectacle to rival the fantastic revelations spun out in the nightmare world of men's dreams."[56] The film received mixed reviews, and at least two audience members clearly did not like what they saw. When the film opened in London a year later, Freud's children, Anna and Ernst, protested it, reasonably arguing that no movie could accurately capture the life and work of their father.[57]

Complementing the portrayal of psychoanalysis in American popular culture was the profound, personal interest taken by celebrities in experiencing the ways of the couch. Marlon Brando was one such celebrity, seeing in psychoanalysis a way to gain a deeper understanding of himself and the human condition. Psychoanalysis in fact changed the way Brando felt about acting, and was the reason he was choosing to spend more of his time off-screen in the early sixties. (Brando acted in just two films in the late 1950s, spending more of his time producing and directing.) "Acting by and large is the expression of a neurotic impulse," he said in 1960, believing that actors chose their profession because "it gives them sustenance for their narcissism." Based on his fluency in psychospeak, it was clear that Brando had spent considerable time on the couch, quite well versed in Freudian theory. "The actor is released from the confinement of neurotic inhibitions by being—so to speak—the part he plays," he continued. Brando concluded that being a movie star was not much more than a "false form of love and attention." Brando was even thinking about retiring from acting completely, although he did have one reservation. "The principal benefit acting has afforded me is the money to pay for my psychoanalysis," he admitted. It seemed likely that more movie roles were in store so that he could continue his soul searching.[58]

Brando was just one of many notables to credit psychoanalysis as a life-altering experience. Cary Grant said that psychoanalysis had "made him a new man," something that had also happened to retail magnate Marshall Field III.[59] Field was living the life of a millionaire playboy, nice work if you can get it but not very satisfying for the grandson of the founder of the Chicago department store. After going through psychoanalysis with Gregory Zilboorg, Field found purpose in his life, devoting himself to humanitarian causes.[60] Dustin Hoffman also found psychoanalysis to be a profound experience, relishing his twice-a-week visits to his shrink in New York. "It's probably the most important thing in my life," Hoffman said in 1968, not yet comfortable with his newfound fame after making *The Graduate* and *Midnight Cowboy*. "Psychoanalysis is my way of escaping this stuff and I know it has helped me," he explained. Hoffman may have thought it was not right for someone who was crazy, but it was evidently quite beneficial to someone like himself, "just an average neurotic." Hoffman also credited his time on the couch for helping him in his work "because in acting, the more you know about people the better you'll be," something that could perhaps be said about any profession.[61]

Other celebrities had much less success with the method. "I think that analysis had a lot to do with her change of personality," said Virginia

Thompson, Judy Garland's sister, in 1969, blaming her time on the couch (rather than Hollywood executives) for leading her to alcohol and pills. Garland was about nineteen when she started psychoanalysis, Thompson recalled, remembering her as "an unusually healthy girl" before that.[62] Psychoanalysis also turned out to be a bad choice for another popular singer, Kitty Kallen. Kallen, who had been named Singer of the Year and Most-Played Female Vocalist in 1954 by *Billboard* and *Variety* after having a big hit with "Little Things Mean a Lot," found herself with a mysterious case of laryngitis whenever she performed in front of a live audience. Her voice was fine when she sang in a recording studio, making her realize the problem was psychological rather than physical. Kallen began treatment with a well-known Freudian analyst, a decision she later regretted as she recounted in 1960. "For five 'lost' years, I've been in the clutches of psychoanalysis," she told the *Washington Post*, her twenty-four-hours-per-week sessions not only costing a small fortune but almost ruining her marriage.[63]

Unhappy with her analyst's recommendation to give up both her husband and religious faith, Kallen went next to a disciple of Wilhelm Reich, author of the infamous orgone theory. This experience, which involved being completely nude and some odd contraptions in their sessions, turned out to be worse than that with the Freudian, leading her to an "adviser" who practiced "antipsychoanalysis" based on "conditioned reflexes." After this did not work out either (he too recommended she leave her husband, with whom she stayed married for forty-five years until he died), Kallen's next move was to an endocrinologist whose specialty was hypnosis and posthypnotic suggestion. Coming to the conclusion that hypnosis was ultimately a crutch she did not want to lean on, Kallen serendipitously found peace of mind through faith in God, a story similar to that of Clare Booth Luce. "The greatest psychiatrists were the wise men in the Good Book," she concluded, the so-called wise men she had earlier put her faith in just false prophets.[64]

Libido Lane

Celebrities back east may have gravitated to psychoanalysis as a way to deal with their demons but Hollywood folks considered it a virtual necessity. Psychoanalysis and Tinsel Town were a perfect match, the method helping actors deal with the intense pressures that came with being a performer and public figure. In 1960, for example, Elaine Stritch left Manhattan for Hollywood to make a television pilot for *My Sister Eileen*, a big move but something for which she felt she prepared. "I'm no nut, but I'm glad I went thru [sic] four years of analysis," she explained, believing that time on the couch "helps you get ready for TV in Hollywood."[65] Earl Holliman, a Hollywood television and movie workhorse, was hitting the couch five days a week despite being a tall, handsome, rich, and otherwise healthy bachelor in his early thirties. "I'm unhappy and honestly trying to find peace," Holliman said in 1962, everything he already had apparently not providing it.[66] Like psychoanalysis in general, Hollywood's dependency on the method seemed to be a distinctly American phenomenon. "We don't have the wholesale rush to head shrinkers that you do," Peter Sellers told Hedda Hopper on his first visit to Hollywood that same year. "The analyst's couch isn't the answer for us." Sellers thought it was Britain's experience in two world wars that made psychoanalysis unnecessary for its actors (and citizens in general), the beating the country took putting career worries and personal issues in perspective.[67]

Natalie Wood was going through quite a personality makeover in the mid-sixties, with psychoanalysis the reason for what an industry insider called "the whole Pygmalion bit." "Have you heard about Natalie Wood?" the reliable but unnamed source whispered to Peter Bart of the *New York Times* at a Hollywood cocktail party. Rumors had already been flying through the town that the film star was now collecting art and taking courses in English literature at UCLA. Upon investigation, Bart found the rumors to be true, with Wood the new proud owner of a Bonnard and a Courbet as well as a reading list of works by Burns, Blake, Shaw, and Eliot. Her recent plunge into the literary world and rather sudden interest in art grew out of her time on the couch, during which she realized she "lacked the ability to enjoy [herself], to enjoy being alone." As a child actor, Wood was constantly surrounded by people, depriving her of the chance to develop her true identity. (Wood started making movies at age five, and by the time she was twenty-seven, in 1966, had appeared in forty films.) Now pulling in a million dollars a year, Wood was making up for lost time, going on a cultural binge which, as she put it, "brought out my latent interests." Now that Wood had apparently found herself, would she continue with psychoanalysis, Bart had to ask? "Oh, I don't know," she replied, adding the very true words, "It's very hard to start and it's very hard to stop."[68]

Given that Hollywood was what Joe Hyams called "the most psychiatrically oriented community in the nation," it was not surprising that industry people wanted to make movies that they knew something about. While John Huston was making *Freud* in Vienna in 1961, Warner Brothers was shooting *The Chapman Report*, a film exploring the sexual psyches of four women, with another psychiatrist-as-hero flick, *The Couch*, also in the works. It could be said that art was simply imitating life. A three-block stretch of Beverly Hills was so populated with psychiatrists it was known as "Libido Lane," the West Coast equivalent of the shrinkvilles of Central Park West and Greenwich Village. There was one psychiatrist for every 169 residents of Beverly Hills—more than eighty times the national average—most of them specializing in what were referred to in the trade as "film star problems." Although just some of the 182 psychiatrists in Beverly Hills (with over a third of them on Libido Lane) were full-fledged psychoanalysts, Freud's presence could not be missed, his ideas as popular in Tinsel Town as the Brown Derby.[69]

In fact, psychiatry was so popular in Beverly Hills in the early 1960s that analysts there were not taking on any new patients except in cases of real emergencies (like an actor not getting a role he or she coveted). Indeed, many of the celebrities making a trip to Libido Lane (a very long list including the likes of Jerry Lewis, Ava Gardner, and Jonathan Winters) had personality and identity issues, their public personas not aligned with their personal ones. "They are almost always people who never found themselves in adolescence," said Herbert J. Kupper, a top analyst on Roxbury Drive in the heart of Libido Lane, speaking of his rich and famous clientele. Kupper felt that many actors went into the profession to find themselves through different roles but hit the wall when part after part did not lead to an epiphany. "The great actors are ones who learn to put up with the realization that between roles they are very ordinary, often dull people," Kupper thought. Kupper considered that the scads of less-than-great actors were in for a rude surprise when they discovered they were not really the dashing figures they were on the big screen. Sudden fame and wealth was a perfect recipe to knock one for a loop, with nothing really to prepare one for becoming an overnight success.[70]

While all suffered from "film star problems," the particular reasons actors flocked to psychoanalysts of course varied. At the suggestion of director Blake Edwards, Tony Curtis went to see Marcel Frym of the Hacker Psychiatric Clinic, a course of treatment that lasted three years. Curtis was depressed, not sleeping at night, and fighting with his wife, Janet Leigh, all classic symptoms, Frym decided, of "sudden success syndrome." (The Bronx-born Bernard Schwartz had recently starred in *Sweet Smell of Success, Some Like It Hot,* and *The Defiant Ones,* the latter earning him an Academy Award nomination.) Leigh, a successful actress in her own right (she had just finished *Psycho*), seemed to be bearing the brunt of Curtis's issues, believing that "marriage is particularly difficult for the wives of stars." Rhoda Borgnine, wife of Ernest (who had won an Academy Award in 1955 for his role in *Marty*), had a similar story to tell ("Living with a star is like walking on eggs," she confessed), making it understandable how analysts' waiting rooms were filled with damsels in distress. "The film star receives inordinate adulation at the studio all day and is subjected to flattery from beautiful and available younger women," putting wives in a very tough spot, explained an anonymous analyst. Male stars and, no doubt, some leading ladies would also frequently have romantic dalliances to prove to themselves they were the sexpots they portrayed on screen, this too not a very good way to keep a marriage together.[71]

Like Curtis, Ben Gazzara had a three-year stint on the couch, his problem an inability to cope with the self-absorption that acting required. "It disgusted me and still does sometimes," he said, "but thanks to analysis I've adjusted now and have perspective about myself and my craft." Nanette Fabray had a full-on breakdown in the 1950s but, through psychoanalysis, recovered, something for which she was deeply appreciative. "Thanks to psychoanalysis and my own efforts I have made the storm-tossed trip back to mental health," she publicly announced, hoping others would do the same if in similar straits. Gene Tierney also admitted to having hit rock bottom in the fifties, first entering a sanitarium in

Hartford, Connecticut, and then going twice to the Menninger Clinic before returning to acting (and marrying a Texas oilman). Sid Caesar was equally open about his time on the couch, wisely seeing psychoanalysis as something that could not make one's problems disappear but could enable one to maneuver around them. Rod Steiger had a similar experience, explaining that psychoanalysis had "enable[d] me to substitute one set of problems for another but the second set was easier to cope with," a sentiment many ordinary people shared after their own extensive sessions of talk therapy.[72]

With all this analysis going on in Beverly Hills, a number of local couch manufacturing companies were doing quite the business, as were interior decorators who specialized in psychiatrists' offices. Waiting rooms were almost inevitably painted pastel green, wall-to-wall carpeted, and lit softly for a soothing effect. Prints of Impressionist paintings and classical music completed the scene, the room as art-directed as a Hollywood production. Shrinks' offices often included a tan vinyl couch for the patient and a Danish contoured rocking chair for the analyst, each of these decidedly more modern than the furniture typically found in the inner sanctum of a New York psychoanalyst. And while the psychoanalysis scene was beginning to lose some of its luster in the Big Apple, being in therapy still commanded a considerable amount of status among the Hollywood crowd. "On the first visit of a star I have to find out why he or she is visiting me," noted Kupper, uncertain if it was because "psychiatry is fashionable or because he really needs help." Even more fashionable than Libido Lane (where sessions went for twenty-five to thirty-five dollars an hour) was going to a private class led by Laura Huxley. Huxley, wife of psychoanalysis devotee Aldous, offered physical and mental therapy for friends and friends of friends, the self-described "lay analyst" helping actors more effectively use their creative talent. Other industry people, looking for a way to better understand not just themselves but the human condition, took a more academic route by attending extension classes in psychology and psychiatry at UCLA. Whatever the setting, psychoanalysis was boffo business in Los Angeles in the sixties, an opportunity to reconcile reality with illusion.[73]

How Can I Help You?

The popularity of "the cure" among celebrities was vivid proof that, despite all the criticism being directed at it, psychoanalysis was still a powerful force in the 1960s. Aaron Karush, assistant director of the Psychoanalytic Clinic for Training and Research at Columbia University, knew exactly why ordinary people, and not just the famous, remained faithful to the method. "What we try to do, really, is to give people a second chance in life," he told *Today's Health* in 1968. Karush and his colleagues believed that they provided their patients with something undeniably valuable—a fresh start. Difficulty coping with problems in ordinary aspects of life—work, marriage, and parenthood—was now the most frequent reason for patients to go into psychoanalysis; their "disease" was instead some kind of personality distortion that could be treated and, hopefully, eliminated.[74]

Hendrik M. Ruitenbeek, editor of the 1964 book *Psychoanalysis and Contemporary American Culture*, agreed that the days of "hysterical" patients marching into psychoanalysts' offices en masse were over, and that the day-to-day business of the field was now a much different thing than in Freud's time or even up to the Second World War. Today it was "individuals distracted by the problem of who they are—that is to say, anybody" that were coming in for help, as Harold Rosenberg of *Commentary* described it in his review of the book. Now it could be said that the analyst's main objective was to get his patient to "recognize himself." With crisis of identity "the spiritual hallmark of our time," Rosenberg thought, neo-Freudians like Karush were sensibly adopting the philosophical and religious angst of postwar American society as their reason for being.[75]

Still, there was much opportunity for psychoanalysis to move forward as a field, with emerging technologies offering exciting possibilities. As many critics had pointed out, psychoanalysts could see only a handful of patients (about five) a day, and the method's time intensiveness was clearly a real liability when demand for therapy exceeded its supply. Kenneth Mark Colby of Stanford University was working hard to change that in the late sixties, seeing the computer as a way for literally hundreds of patients to get treated simultaneously.[76] Via "high-speed time sharing,"

Colby thought, an IBM 7090 could have a "dialogue" with a patient much like this one conducted in his lab:

COMPUTER:	How can I help you?
PATIENT:	I am sick and tired today.
COMPUTER:	Do you have any idea why?
PATIENT:	Yes, I am old.
COMPUTER:	Please go on.
PATIENT:	I seem to have lost interest in everything.
COMPUTER:	Tell me more about such feelings.
PATIENT:	I have some idea why I feel this way, too.
COMPUTER:	You have?
PATIENT:	It seems that I miss having a family.[77]

Importantly, Colby would have a real analyst monitoring these "conversations," ready to add the human touch that was missing from what he called the "auto-couch." Colby envisioned creating a number of programs—one about family relationships, one to address sexual issues, and so on. The technology was based on key words fed into the computer, which then prodded the patient to say what he or she was thinking. Colby even had a "neurosis program," able to translate patients' language into psychological terms like deflection, projection, and reaction formation. While Colby admitted his gizmo could not pick up nonverbal cues, recognize lies or jokes, or know anything about the patient's history, it could help them express themselves and articulate their problems, which could be an exercise of considerable value in itself.[78]

Colby was not the first to wonder whether computers could play some kind of role in psychoanalysis. Joseph Jaffe, head of research at the William Alanson White Institute, was pursuing a somewhat different path in the 1960s, focusing on the language used by patients when they were in analysis. Computers would "notice" repetitive themes that suggested certain patterns of behavior better than an analyst could, Jaffe thought, and could even recognize unspoken material that was potentially significant. If a woman talked at length about her family and did not mention her mother and father in the same sentence, for example, the computer would immediately identify that as unusual. "Human beings notice what is there, but computers can pick up what is missing," Jaffe said in 1965, believing that the emerging area of psycholinguistics could have interesting applications for the field. Jaffe foresaw that if all analytic sessions could be taped, transcribed, and card-punched into a computer, which then tabulated and classified a patient's language into specific emotions and kinds of conflicts, the output might provide a valuable tool for the analyst to use in his or her treatment. Having what Jaffe called a "semantic road-map of the patient's sentence structure" could tell analysts which subjects or events were the most problematic, potentially reducing the time needed in therapy. "Although no sophisticated person today should be impressed by a row of blinking lights, there will come a time when the use of the computer will revolutionize psychoanalysis," Jaffe predicted. Four decades or so later, Jaffe would be proven right.[79]

New ways to apply psychoanalytic principles in the business world, too, could be a way for the field to reinvent itself, some thought. Scientific Methods, an Austin, Texas–based consulting company, for example, had come up with something the two psychologist founders called the Managerial Grid, a performance assessment tool. Forty-five of the top industrial corporations in the United States had, by 1969, hired Scientific Methods to assess their employees. "This is routinely a disturbing, difficult but highly rewarding experience," said Robert R. Blake, one of the founders, his grid typically showing that executives were not the great leaders they thought they were. Many of the ideas central to psychoanalysis—suppressed conflicts between individuals, resistance to change, self-delusion—surfaced in the exercise. One's score on the rating system (which measured concern for people and concern for production, the higher the better for each) was often a rude awakening for late-1960s businesspeople. In fact, the only problem with the Managerial Grid seemed to be that an inordinate number of managers were fired or resigned after being put on the griddle because the process had revealed that they were entirely unfit for their jobs or, perhaps worse, unnecessary to the companies' operations.[80]

If computers and managerial grids did not suggest that change was in the air for psychoanalysis in the late sixties, some new thinking about shrinks' August vacations—a sacred rite of the profession—surely did.

For decades, it had been well accepted that patients went on a collective emotional bender when their therapists left town, left to deal with their demons on their own. But now a couple of top analysts were saying that their colleagues' annual pilgrimage might be healthy for patients, an opportunity for them to make further progress in their treatment. "A certain amount of integration takes place during the period of a layoff," thought Joseph L. Schimel, medical director of the William Alanson White Institute. Lawrence Kolb, director of the Psychiatric Institute of Columbia-Presbyterian Medical Center, agreed, believing that "patients discover their personal strengths" while their analysts were sunning, swimming, and sightseeing. Given that Schimel's employer completely shut down in August, as did the New York Psychoanalytic Institute and the Karen Horney Clinic, it would be a mighty good thing if the thousands of patients in treatment could go happily analysis-free for the month. Just in case, the Postgraduate Center for Mental Health was leaving a skeleton crew around to handle "emergency cases," knowing that at least a few New Yorkers would be unable to cope without talking to someone about something.[81]

Regardless of the fresh air blowing into psychoanalysis as the counterculture raged, most observers had serious doubts about the future of the field. "A vastly different and more anxious time has bred problems—and demanded solutions—that Freud never envisioned and that analysis was not designed to treat," wrote *Time* in its 1969 swan song to psychoanalysis, sensing the buzzards circling overhead. Faced with new competition and growing skepticism among a younger generation of psychiatrists, psychoanalysis was "in search of its soul," the magazine told readers. Its phenomenal run during the postwar years was clearly over. "It has nothing to say to us, and there is nothing we can do for it except ensure a decent burial," chipped in H. J. Eysenck, happy to see the mainstream media announce that psychoanalysis was on the ropes if not down for the count. Out of touch and out-of-date, psychoanalysis seemed to be gasping for air in the late sixties, struggling just to keep alive. The next couple of decades would prove to be an even more challenging time for psychoanalysis as the field's search for its soul led it down some very unusual paths.[82]

CHAPTER 5: The Impossible Profession

> It's different from any other human relationship that
> I know of, in its combination of deprivation and
> intimacy.
>
> Leo Stone, the eighty-three-year-old unofficial
> "dean" of psychoanalysis, speaking of the dynamic
> between an analyst and a patient, in 1988

In February 1970, a book called *The Psychiatrists* was published, very likely the most thorough and detailed peek into the lives of psychiatrists and psychoanalysts ever attempted. In his book, Arnold A. Rogow served up a mother lode of information about shrinks, including everything from what they read to how they voted to how often they committed suicide. The author, a professor of political science at the City University of New York, learned, for example, that psychiatrists and psychoanalysts leaned left politically, ranked just seventh in earnings in the ten largest medical fields, and got divorced much less frequently than the average American. Other interesting tidbits were that there were no psychoanalysts at all in sixteen states, just one in six other states, and 314 in New York, making one wonder what it was about the Empire State that made it such a fertile place for shrinks to set up shop.[1]

In the process of digging up these and other juicy nuggets (80 percent of psychiatrists and psychoanalysts regularly read *Life* magazine, in case anyone was wondering), the author learned something much more important. After speaking with hundreds of therapists, Rogow came to the conclusion that the profession was having its own identity crisis, unsure of what it was or what it should be. "Never before has there been so much collective soul-searching and self-examination, so much questioning of theory and technique, so much discussing of principles, problems and policies," he wrote in the first chapter. Rogow believed that it would not be an exaggeration to say that both psychiatry and psychoanalysis were going through "a crisis of doubt and uncertainty about the present status and future direction of the profession." Some of those interviewed for the book believed it was time for the sibling fields to make some kind of quantum leap equal to that made from alchemy to modern chemistry, with talk therapy seen as perhaps the psychiatric equivalent to leeching. Could a "space-age aspirin" be developed to cure mental disorders, some wondered, or the computer used to provide a more efficient and scientific form of therapy?[2]

The early 1970s identity crisis within psychoanalysis was just the beginning of a two-decade stretch that would test the field as no period before in American history. An abundance of new, hipper therapies were nipping at its heels, for one thing, making psychoanalysis seem dowdier and more over-the-hill than ever. Other challenges from feminists and by critics accusing Freud of being a world-class fraud made the next twenty years a time in which the field's very survival would be seriously questioned. Against all odds, psychoanalysis would not only withstand the turbulence of the 1970s and 1980s but develop into a more stable field, a prime example that what does not kill something may very well make it stronger.

The In Thing

In the bell-bottomed, tie-dyed days of the 1970s, however, psychoanalysis was definitely squaresville compared to other therapies bursting on the scene. "Now the encounter group is the in thing," wrote May V. Seagoe, in the *Los Angeles Times* in 1970, believing that psychoanalysis had begat neo-Freudian psychotherapy, which begat group therapy for individuals, which begat the group encounter. Three new books on the subject had just been published, in fact: *Encounter: A Weekend With Intimate Strangers* by John Mann (founder of the Esalen Institute), Martin Shepard and Marjorie Lee's *Marathon 16: New Concept in Therapy*, and Jane Howard's *Please Touch: A Guided Tour of the Human Potential Movement*. The basic concept of the Human Potential Movement (HPM), as the group-encounter faithful referred to their larger cause, was that people could learn a lot about themselves and others through an intensive experience, for example, "emotional reeducation." The key difference from traditional therapies was that encounters involved moving and touching rather than talking. Freeing the total self by bringing to the surface one's fears and "hang-ups" was the ultimate goal. Ideally, each member gained greater sensory awareness, creativity, and social skills in the process.[3]

The ironic thing about "the in thing" was that it was not really new (although members frequently did find themselves in a full-day session and, occasionally, naked). Jacob Moreno, a contemporary of Freud, had developed his "psychodramas" decades earlier; the new group encounter was merely a more sophisticated and decidedly groovier version of the older interactive therapy. (The Moreno Institute in New York and the Institute of Psychodrama in Los Angeles were two organizations offering training in the technique in the seventies.) And like old-school psychoanalysis, group encounter called for open. communication, demanded complete honesty, and was typically disturbing as insights about oneself began to emerge, making it less innovative (and bizarre) than it perhaps appeared.[4]

The most important thing about group encounters as far as psychoanalysis was concerned was that it illustrated what was perhaps the talking cure's biggest drawback during the counterculture years: the inability of those in treatment to *feel* as a result of what Alvin Toffler called "culture shock." (His bestselling book of that name was published in 1970.) Even dyed-in-the-wool psychoanalysts were in the early 1970s coming to believe that it was not their patients' aberrations that prevented them from discovering and expressing their feelings but rather society and, specifically, its pathologies. The Human Potential Movement challenged the solitary probing of the distant past that was psychoanalysis, making the case that since we lived in groups it could only be in groups that we could get in touch with our true feelings. A growing number of its leaders believed that greater sensitivity, awareness, and understanding within families, the business world, and even between religions and races could result from the emotional revelation of HPM. An even larger number of followers were coming to believe the same thing.[5]

Although it was itself a cultural phenomenon, HPM was actually part of a much bigger philosophical shift that had been kicking around for

thirty or so years. Like other countercultural goings-on, such as meditation and "rap sessions," encounter groups fell within the domain of
humanistic psychology, this branch of the tree opposed to the principles
of both psychoanalysis and behavioral therapy. Self-concept theory, per-
ceptual psychology, and transactional psychology were previous articu-
lations of humanistic psychology, with proponents of HPM the latest in
a long line of people like Carl Rogers and Abraham Maslow to take on
what they saw as the manipulative aspects of psychoanalysis and the
mechanistic nature of behaviorism. Rather than view people as products
of an imperfect childhood (psychoanalysis) or passive organisms in need
of "reconditioning" (behaviorism), humanists focused on the uniqueness
and autonomy of individuals. Many found this perspective quite refreshing and liberating. The decline of psychoanalysis was thus part of the
counterculture's rejection of external discipline, the time's mantra to
"do your own thing" bad news for any and all authoritarian, rigid schools
of thought.[6]

Not bound by time, done in public, and relying on touch, the Human
Potential Movement was indeed quite a different animal than the fifty-
minute, private talking cure that had dominated psychotherapy for
three-quarters of a century. Toe-touching, "trust marches" (in which
people with their eyes closed were led by strangers), or just jumping up
and down in ecstasy were a few activities commonly encountered in
encounter therapy, techniques traditional psychoanalysts considered a
lot of sizzle but precious little steak. Writing for the *New York Times* in
1971, David Dempsey considered the movement to be "to orthodox psychoanalysis what the Reformation was to Catholicism," an easier-to-
understand language of therapy designed to appeal to more people. By
breaking down the invisible barriers that separated individuals from
each other, those in the movement believed, personal alienation would
dissipate, a goal few could argue was not well-intentioned if not noble.
Dempsey had recently returned from Miami where he attended a convention of the Association for Humanistic Psychology, the "mother
church" of the HPM. The movement's unofficial leader, Rollo May, was
there, plugging the eight hundred attendees into the positive energy of
his brand of humanistic (or "third-force") psychology. Using concepts
like creativity, self-actualization, love, naturalness, and warmth, May and

his fellow humanists were like day to traditional Freudians' night, their sunny view of human nature an attractive alternative to the darkness of the human unconscious and biological urges.[7]

Most analysts shrugged off May's approach as, at best, a watered-down version of psychoanalysis: "He seems to be unaware of the richness, complexities and subtleties of the Freudian position, and offers instead a popularized and simplistic view of man which has great appeal precisely because it is so simplistic," sniffed Michael Beldoch, a New York old-liner. But many Americans found the approach useful and meaningful during the major bummer that was the early 1970s. (Stagflation, an energy crisis, and the Vietnam War, not to mention Richard Nixon, were just a few things bringing us down.) May's recently published book *Love and Will* was not only selling well but a number of universities across the country had designed courses around it, the post-Freudian's focus on "higher values" a breath of fresh air in the cultural smog of the times. And unlike "scientific" psychiatry, humanistic psychology was unapologetically spiritual, its ethical foundation making it an inclusive, one-stop shop for whatever problems one may have. "Our society is sick because it has lost the language by which it communicates with the meaningful crises of life," went a typical May observation, wise words for those wondering why success had not brought happiness in the bargain. Rather than one's libido, society was the problem, he preached; the only real solution for our collective anxiety was to declare our own personal humanity.[8]

Lousy Therapy

Other great minds who had lost faith in classic Freudianism weighed in on why psychoanalysis was ultimately a losing proposition. Jean Piaget, the eminent child psychologist, agreed that the method was in decline but thought it would be science that would spell doom for psychoanalysis rather than humanism. Freud's theories were "provisional" because of emerging medical research, the seventy-six-year-old told a packed house at City University of New York in 1972; it was just a matter of time before psychoanalysis was exposed as not much more than an interesting fairy tale. "When the endocrinologists find certain answers, much psychoanalytical theory will be found entirely mythical," he thought, but many of the students there to see the legend were not at all happy about what they just heard. "Sure, they're upset," said Harry Beilin, the clinical psychology professor who had hosted Piaget, fully aware that the man's opinion "[implied] that their house is resting on quicksand."[9]

More bad news for psychoanalysis was feminists' growing objection to it as both theory and therapy. Feminists had been making their opinion about psychoanalysis quite clear for a few years but in 1971 their sentiment reached critical mass, labeling the method as another example of male bias and discrimination. At the Women's Liberation Center in Los Angeles that summer, for example, a group of women shared their experiences about analysis, concluding that it was "lousy therapy." Freudian thinking had "done more harm than good [and] made [women] feel worse about themselves," said Miriam Berger, a psychiatric counselor from New York who led the discussion. Its view of women strictly as wives, mothers, and sex objects was its most disturbing feature, she pronounced. One woman at the "rap session," as the *Los Angeles Times* called it, explained that she was told by her analyst to forget about her art career and "find a husband and have children." Others believed that male therapists simply did not and perhaps could not understand women. "We need female therapists with the philosophy of the Women's Liberation Movement rather than with the old sexist attitudes," said another, the group considering psychoanalysis a classic case of the gender inequality of the times.[10]

Two prominent feminists, Kate Millett and Germaine Greer, were particularly vocal about Freud and women psychoanalysts who supported his theories (such as Helene Deutsch, author of *The Psychology of Women*). In her *Sexual Politics*, for example, Millett wrote, "All the forces of psychoanalysis came to be gathered to force woman to 'adjust' to her position"—that position being of course marriage and family. Greer, author of *The Female Eunuch*, too looked to male-oriented psychoanalysis as something which had held women back, with fulfillment to be realized only by rejecting the social norms of Freud's era. "Every vigorous social movement needs a scapegoat, and Women's Liberation has accused Freud and psychoanalysis of chauvinist dogma that has reduced women to crawling about on their hands and knees in kitchens and nurseries," observed Anne Roiphe in the *New York Times* in 1972, confirming that stories of evil psychiatrists were a staple of women's consciousness-raising groups.[11]

Over the next decade and change, Freud would be public enemy number one among feminists. His male-centric theories of gender development, penis envy, castration anxiety, and Oedipal love provided rich fodder for skewering. Freud's famous question of 1933—"What do women want?"—seemed to say it all, proving that, when it came to half the population, the man was very confused if not a dolt. In 1984, a truce of sorts was called when a few hundred mental health professionals gathered at UCLA for a two-day conference, "The Many Faces of Eve: Beyond Psychoanalytic and Feminist Stereotypes." Harriet Kimble Wrye, the organizer of the conference, believed the two fields no longer had to be bitter enemies. "Both within psychoanalysis and within feminism, there has been a trend of convergence," Wrye asserted. New research was showing that men and women's brains were fundamentally different, for one thing, and recent anthropological studies suggested that personality development between the sexes varied significantly as well. "We are looking beyond the old stereotypes and can now begin to see the uniqueness and intercomplementarity of the feminine and the masculine," she added, with attendees at upcoming conferences in Boston and San Diego also planning to call off the fatwa on Freud.[12]

For hardcore (and mostly male) behaviorists, the bigger problem with psychoanalysis was not its gender issues but that it was pure and utter nonsense. "We are at last facing departure from speculative conjecture and mythology," said Zev Wanderer, director of the Center for Behavioral Therapy in Los Angeles in 1973, very pleased to see that his brand of treatment was thriving. Freudianism was fine as a diagnostic tool, Wanderer thought, but an abundance of sympathetic and expensive listening only served to reinforce patients' problems rather than alleviate them. All psychological problems ultimately led to anxiety or "unidentified fear," Wanderer was convinced, with reality therapy or behavioral modification the best tool in the toolbox to get people to change course. Human beings were animals, after all, meaning that most if not all of our bad habits could be "modified by a process of retraining," not much different than pigeons taught to play ping-pong with their beaks through performance and reward.[13]

For those who had gone through psychoanalysis in their formative years, like Anatole Broyard of the *New York Times*, behaviorism was sapping all the joie de vivre out of the therapeutic experience. Broyard and his kind looked to the method as a sort of graduate school, their neuroses taking on literary and even mythological dimensions as they described them to their European, classically educated analysts. Although it was known as "the talking cure," the idea of actually being cured was simply unheard of—another thing making therapy in the seventies "just no fun anymore." "These brash new therapists in turtle-necked sweaters think nothing of tampering with the lives of their patients," Broyard wrote, disturbed at how they had their "clients" sit up in chairs, looked them directly in the eye, pried into and criticized their behavior, and, worst of all, offered actual advice. To his dismay, all this "curing" was making many of Broyard's friends "normal," something which definitely would not have happened in the good old days when psychoanalysis ruled. "The sweet exchange of symptoms, the talk about the weather of the self, used to be good for an evening," he wistfully remembered, the verbal swapping of humiliations and cruelties (either sustained or inflicted) like "food and drink." The decline of the neurotic was a major blow to American society, Broyard had come to believe, "the grandeur of his delusion the last gasp of the epic or heroic mode in the twentieth century." Broyard dreamed of starting up an "Institute of Regression," where the cured could go to find their old, neurotic, and much more interesting selves.[14]

Like behavioral therapy, Gestalt too was gaining followers in the 1970s at the (high) expense of psychoanalysis. Founded by Frederick (Fritz) and Laura Perls in the 1940s, the goal of Gestalt therapy was and is for clients to "become aware of what they are doing, how they are doing it, and how they can change themselves, and at the same time, to learn to accept and value themselves," as Gary M. Yontef described it in his book *Awareness, Dialogue, and Process*. Gestalt therapy prioritized process over content. Focusing on the "here and now" rather than the past, and incorporating the body instead of just the mind, Gestalt was fast becoming a darling among both psychiatrists and those who had never seen the inside of a college classroom. Psychoanalysts like Richard Cook of Chicago had recently traded in their couches for a chair (nicknamed the "hot seat") and disposed of the rest of Freud's trappings, seeing role-playing as more effective and quicker than talking (and talking and talking). By integrating opposing forces in one's life and recognizing that conflicts with others are actually conflicts within oneself, Cook and other subscribers to Gestalt believed, a patient had a better chance to work out their anger and other negative emotions. Also aligned with the Human Potential Movement, Gestalt was one of various group therapies making headway; the idea that others could provide valuable feedback was trumping the iconic image of the solitary, often silent psychoanalyst.[15]

Even more group-based and expedient (and loud) was primal therapy; its inventor, Arthur Janov, claimed it was nothing less than "the cure for neurosis." Everybody was to some degree neurotic, Janov, a Los Angeles psychologist, thought (a result of early trauma, often the birth process), meaning that patients had to free or unblock themselves from that experience to be healed. Having a "primal," which typically involved the famous scream, was the way to completely access one's feelings, the theory went, with Janov turning the novel idea into a tidy little business. Fourteen to twenty patients a month were signing up for one of Janov's "therapy packages" in 1975, in fact, and the $6,000 price tag was making psychoanalysis seem like a relative bargain. But with allegedly clear evidence supporting his theory (Janov claimed to have observed forceps marks and the impression of an obstetrician's hand on patients in the midst of a primal), the money seemed well worth it to many. Primal therapy could cure everything from ulcers, epileptic seizures, high blood pressure, insomnia, and drug dependency, he told those therapy shop-ping, making Janov either the most brilliant psychologist ever to practice or a conman every bit as good as those who used to hawk medicine tonic for those same ailments. Janov even had the good sense to trade-mark the term "primal therapy" but other psychologists around the country were employing a remarkably similar method called "intensive feeling therapy," this too usually involving a very loud, piercing high-pitched cry as cathartic release.[16]

While such "feeling therapies" were specifically designed to get patients (customers might be the better word) in touch with their emo-tions (often literally so), rational emotive therapy was intended to get them to resolve their trauma by talking themselves out of it. In this twist on psychoanalysis, its creator, Albert Ellis, argued that just discussing one's problems with a therapist did not go far enough. By rationally talking through the issues involved with a particular situation, patients could convince themselves of the right thing to do, a more productive approach. The Chicago Institute for Rational Living was one such clinic doling out rational emotive therapy; its focus on action rather than just understanding was a compelling draw, especially for psychoanalysis dropouts. Transactional analysis (TA) was positioned even more directly as psychoanalysis for the masses, its three ego states (Parent, Adult, and Child) obvious knock-offs of Freud's superego, ego, and id. TA's focus on the present and on interpersonal relationships was different enough from psychoanalysis to make it another popular choice for those in the market for a therapy in the 1970s, a number which was growing as what would soon be known as the Me Decade rolled on.[17]

One did not have to be an expert to recognize the flaws in psycho-analysis that the entrepreneurial creators of these different types of therapies were exploiting. A 1977 letter to Ann Landers, of all things, pretty much said it all. "I'm a college sophomore entering my eighth month of psychoanalysis," wrote "Anonymous, Of Course":

> Talking to someone about yourself for an hour or two a week may give a person a lot of insight, but by the time you solve the problem ...a new one crops up and you have to start all over again. . . . A steady stream of problems, even though they may be of minor significance, can keep you in therapy forever. If you don't establish some goals early, you can get hooked on a very expensive habit. Ninety percent of the decisions that come out of therapy are arrived at by the person who is in treatment. Please get this idea across to the thousands who lean so heavily (and for so many years) on their shrinks.[18]

The diva of advice agreed with Anonymous, by the way, thinking as a general rule that "after three years of shrinking, the patient should be given his 'diploma.'"[19]

Junior-Grade Jungs

Psychoanalysis may have been in decline as a therapy in the seventies, but its role in everyday life seemed to be as big as ever. Amateur shrinks, or what a writer for the *Los Angeles Times* called in 1971 "junior-grade Jungs," for instance, continued to make their presence known at parties by analyzing anyone and everyone in sight. "Just make a statement— about anything—and you're in for it," the reluctant partygoer sighed; one would inevitably learn that one was sublimating, compensating, repressing, fantasizing, or free-associating. Bumping into someone "getting help" was an opportunity to not only discover what you really meant when you said something and why you said it but to have your problems solved, free of charge. The gum chewer or nail biter was just asking for it, the diagnosis oral-compulsiveness, mental strain, or some combination thereof. Worst of all was when your new friend opened up to reveal his or her own issues, the result of many hours, dollars, and tears. "Listening to people discuss their own analysis is enough to drive you crazy," she concluded. The hostess's couch apparently acted as a kind of stimulus for the analyzed to launch into an extra fifty-minute session.[20]

Thankfully, leaders of the field looked to other, more formal ways to promote psychoanalysis as its popularity waned. In 1972, the American Academy of Psychoanalysis (AAP) stepped up its efforts to get its members more involved with community issues, which was in part a long overdue response to critics' continual complaints that psychoanalysis was primarily a rich person's plaything. Eight hundred of them were told at their biannual convention at the Plaza Hotel that analysts should play a "wider, vital" role in helping reduce urban problems such as drug addiction, drinking, and gambling, things the organization admitted its members had yet to seriously address. Those with addictive personalities were notoriously difficult to handle, making it not surprising that psychoanalysts preferred to pick the lower-hanging fruit. Compared to the American Psychoanalytic Association, the AAP (which had been formed in 1956) was less steeped in Freudian theory; its members were more likely to see personality disorders as a result of severe environmental stress rather than traumas experienced in childhood and, therefore, more treatable. "It is incumbent upon us as scientists and members of society to work toward reduction of alienation in the community," said Martin

Symonds, one of the chairs of the convention. Symonds's view was perfectly consistent with the organization's mission to better understand why people behaved the way they did.[21]

Some analysts were finding their own unique ways to reenergize psychoanalysis. Although it was not quite as unique as Adeoye Lambo's fusion of African witchcraft and psychoanalysis, Leon Hammer, a physician in East Hampton on Long Island, was creating his own interesting hybrid of therapies. Hammer was trained in both psychoanalysis and acupuncture and was finding that East and West had more in common than one might think, using needles to treat neuroses. "Both are bodies of knowledge based on experience," Hammer said in 1974, seeing Chinese medicine's focus on the senses and intuition as perfectly consistent with Freud's theories. As well, each approach concentrated on causes of illness rather than symptoms. "Add the concept of crisis in cure that exists in both, the use of dreams in diagnosis, and the importance attached to the therapist, and you have an extraordinary similarity," Hammer felt; he was certainly one of few people to make such a link.[22]

Hammer's story was an interesting one. Unsatisfied by "the way psychoanalysis worked and the way psychoanalysts worked with it," as he explained it, Hammer started to explore alternatives and found himself to be an accidental acupuncturist after studying it on his own. Hammer soon started using acupuncture on his psychiatric patients who complained of physical ailments, a decade or so ahead of the mainstream movement in holistic or complementary medicine. His therapeutic one-two punch came in particularly handy with two suicidal patients, with acupuncture proving to be more effective than the talking cure in persuading them not to take their own lives. Absolutely convinced that it worked, Hammer integrated acupuncture into his analytic regime for all of his patients, except one who wanted nothing to do with needles. Sticking people in the right places could "balance a person's energies, break down old ways and provide a release of awareness," he had come to believe, and, like psychoanalysis, get patients "to be themselves." Based on his case histories, Hammer had given a couple of talks to colleagues at the William Alanson White Institute and had written an article for *Contemporary Psychoanalysis*, finding the psychoanalytic community to be more responsive to his ideas than he anticipated. Next on Hammer's plate was charting out in detail the relationship between emotions and acupuncture's five elements (wood, fire, earth, metal, and water); this would be the real litmus test of whether other therapists would start treating their patients as pincushions.[23]

Eastern medicine was not the only discipline psychoanalysis was merging with in the 1970s, as many found it to be quite a handy and flexible theoretical tool (just as Freud had imagined). Psychohistory—history which utilized psychological, and mostly psychoanalytic, insights—had been around for decades, but was now all the rage as more biographers found Freud's theories a powerful way to paint a compelling portrait of a well-known person. Freud himself used psychohistory (or applied psychoanalysis, as it was also called) in his 1910 biography of Leonardo da Vinci ("The excessive tenderness of his mother had the most decisive influence on the formation of his character and his later fortune," he wrote of the genius). Erik Erikson's two works of psychohistory, *Young Man Luther* and *Gandhi's Truth*, were considered the best of the genre. Contemporary authors were taking the approach to a whole new level, seeing in psychoanalysis an ideal set of concepts to analyze complex, controversial figures of the day. Bruce Mazlish, a historian at MIT, for example, had written psychohistories of both Richard Nixon and Henry Kissinger—it would be difficult to imagine better choices circa 1976. David Abrahamsen, a New York psychoanalyst, had also written a psychohistory of Nixon, the ex-president's personality profile apparently too juicy to resist. "His self was splintered, broken, but many pieces of his personality still hung together," wrote Abrahamsen in his *Nixon vs. Nixon: An Emotional Tragedy*, adding that Tricky Dick "was not a whole person." At the time, Mazlish was collaborating with another writer on a psychohistory of then presidential candidate Jimmy Carter, positing that the peanut farmer's becoming "reborn" in the sixties was actually a "third birth," the first his literal one in 1924 and the second occurring in 1953 when his father died.[24]

As America celebrated its bicentennial, more innovative psychoanalysts began to explore an aspect of the field long acknowledged but generally ignored. A not-so-well-kept secret was that patients would sometimes fall asleep on the couch, even this for most analysts symbolic of something deeper than that he or she had simply found a comfortable place to catch forty winks. One of David M. Hurst's patients did just that, prompting the New York psychoanalyst to write a fourteen-page case history on the incident for a 1976 meeting of the American Psychoanalytic Association. "His voice trailed off," said Hurst, recalling what was this patient's twelfth session, noting that the man's speech had become slurred and nonsensical. Hurst asked his patient if he was all right, but "there was no response save his deep, regular breathing," this interesting turn of events integrated into the therapy process. Hurst suggested to his awoken patient that his catnap was an attempt to escape something but the groggy man disagreed, saying he was just "tired and bored." Falling asleep during his session turned out to be a regular feature of the man's treatment. But this behavior was too meaningful for Hurst to ignore. His patient's *zzzzz*s (which were sometimes accompanied by snoring) were an unconscious effort to avoid "unacceptable impulses that are breaking through the barrier of response," Hurst concluded, a psychoanalytic interpretation of the first degree.[25]

Expectedly, some colleagues of Hurst's were not so sure. Ralph B. Little, a Philadelphia analyst, did not initially see much significance in "couch naps," as he called them, though he let his patients snooze as long as they liked on his sofa. In fact, the naps provided Little with fresh dreams to interpret, a very good thing in the process, he felt. Another analyst was on the fence about patients' occasional siestas, of the opinion that they could be significant but usually were not. "Falling asleep can mean anything from not having gotten enough sleep the night before, which is not often enough the meaning attached to it, to some form of resistance, which is too often the meaning attached to it," he sensibly explained. "What happens more often is that the analyst falls asleep," the New York shrink admitted, leading another, Bertrand R. Jacobs, to quip, "The one thing I've never heard of is both of them falling asleep."[26]

A Giant Mental Clinic

Fortunately, most patients (and analysts) were able to stay awake through their fifty-minute sessions. Influenced by the broader therapeutic movement sweeping through the country, psychoanalysts were by the late 1970s treating many patients who needed good advice more than a personality makeover because of a major disorder. "When psychoanal-ysis originally offered its explanation of emotional life, its use was lim-ited to helping people with severe problems," observed Suzanne Gordon, in a 1978 essay for the *New York Times* titled "A Freud in Every Pot." Gordon viewed the talking cure as now just another part of the nation's psychiatric equivalent to home improvement. It was not Freud who was at fault for the democratizing of therapy in America but his fol-lowers, Gordon made clear, but it did not change her opinion that the simultaneous expansion and simplification of psychiatry in general was a bad thing for individuals and society at large. The perception that illness was everywhere implied that we were indeed a sick culture, she argued, which was "threaten[ing] to turn America into a giant mental clinic."[27]

Others were disturbed by the giant mental clinic that was America in the 1970s. Seventeen years after his *The Myth of Mental Illness*, Thomas Szasz published *The Myth of Psychotherapy*, an even more critical portrayal of psychoanalysis and therapy in general. The subtitle of the book— "Mental Healing as Religion, Rhetoric, and Repression"—neatly captured his argument that psychoanalysis and psychiatry were not medicine or science because it was only the body, not the mind, which could be ill. Szasz was especially tough on Freud, accusing him of not just making "false and fraudulent" claims but running the business of psychoanaly-sis "much as a Caribbean dictator, called upon to democratize his regime, might conduct his government"—quite the comparison. (As consolation for psychoanalysts, perhaps, Szasz also panned drug therapy, considering the biggest thing in psychiatry in the last thirty years just "fakery.") Another book published in 1978, Martin L. Gross's *The Psychological Society*, was equally critical of psychoanalysis and psychiatry if less ven-omous. Psychology had turned America into "a conformist society in which we are taught not only what to think of ourselves and others, but how to feel," Gross wrote. Our "natural emotions" had been turned into something not just "undesirable but abnormal."[28]

Movies of the time reinforced the idea that we had become a bona fide therapeutic culture obsessed with our individual selves. One did not have to look further than *Interiors*, Woody Allen's 1978 cinematic exercise in psychoanalysis, to get a full blast of egocentric angst. The film was less than well received by critics, not surprising given that viewing it was not unlike watching people act out someone's therapy session (and, at ninety-three minutes, almost a double one at that). Lines like "I want to do something with my life" and "I don't want to talk about that" seemed to make up the whole film, noted Judith Martin of the *Washington Post*, surprised that the Allen could make such a boring film. (The therapy scenes in his previous film, *Annie Hall*, had deftly and hilariously captured the stark differences between psychoanalysis and behaviorism.) "If this is what Allen dug out of his soul in analysis, it would perhaps have been better not to spread it beyond him and his doctor," she thought. Even the fine performances of an all-star cast were unable to save the script's hollowness. "Let's all hope he gets over his problem and becomes his old self again," Martin wrote, something most filmgoers heartily agreed with.[29]

Psychiatrists of all stripes were soon ubiquitous characters in films, and usually not in a particularly positive way. In early 1981, Linda B. Martin of the *New York Times* viewed more than a dozen recent films in which shrinks played a role. "For the most part, it seems, the psychiatrist these days is seen as a false god fallen from customary grace," she thought, an attitude probably reflecting Americans' "displaced anger" at any kind of authority figure. Although Tyrone C. Berger, the Judd Hirsch character in *Ordinary People*, was certainly a kind (if unkempt) man (the director of the film, Robert Redford, was flooded with letters from psychiatrists praising the portrayal), the (never seen) analyst in *Fame* was described by one character as "some sort of witch doctor" prone to prescribing tranquilizers to patients and nonpatients alike. The failure of Goldie Hawn's character's brief marriage in *Private Benjamin* was due to her therapist's "neurotic need to find a father figure," she said in the film; and the psychiatrist in *Ten* is an eye-rolling, chain-smoking grouch when Dudley Moore's character visits him (after complaining of "male menopause"). Michael Caine's character in Brian de Palma's *Dressed to Kill* is much worse, a psychotic psychiatrist who occasionally dresses in women's clothes and, oh yes, murders any woman who sexually arouses him. Last but not least, Woody Allen's character chases a hairy creature ("rage") taking away his mother in a dream sequence in *Stardust Memories*, his latest jab at the couch. "Stop! I'm a psychoanalyst! This is my pipe!" Allen yells at the creature, like other film directors no doubt expressing his love-hate relationship with the profession.[30]

As filmmakers used psychoanalysis as a dramatic device or comedic foil, the world's leading analysts took time to debate the relative health of their field. The thirty-first congress of the International Psychoanalytical Association held in New York in 1979 was an ideal opportunity to check the field's vital signs, with different doctors having different opinions after careful examination of the patient. "Psychoanalysis is in danger," thought P. J. van der Leeuw, a psychoanalyst from Amsterdam, with Jacob Swartz of the Boston Psychoanalytic Institute countering that "It's not a deathbed scene." Robert Jay Lifton, the Yale psychiatrist (and now psychohistorian), had a far more favorable assessment, arguing that the Freudian revolution was not only still alive but still in its "early phases." If there was a consensus among the 2,500 analysts from thirty-four countries, it was that while psychoanalysis as a therapy or treatment was certainly not as popular as it had been in the 1950s and 1960s, its theory was flourishing not just within psychiatry and psychology but in other fields like social work, history, and the arts. Almost a century after Freud created it, psychoanalysis was turning out to be much as he imagined it would and should be, a powerful set of theories complemented by some limited therapeutic value. The mere fact that so many people had traveled so far to talk about their profession was a very good sign, everyone believed—firm evidence that Freud's ideas were not on life support.[31]

Other signs were good for the field as the Me Decade wound to a close. Surprisingly, the number of full members in the American Psychoanalytic Association had climbed 50 percent through the seventies, and the number of students in the twenty-six psychoanalytic institutes approved by the association had held steady. Thirty of the nation's 120 psychiatry departments in medical schools were headed by psychoanalysts, proof that the field remained firmly embedded within the academic community. As well, almost all of America's most distinguished psychiatrists were psychoanalysts (including Alan A. Stone, president of the American Psychiatric Association), and more than half of the members of that group identified themselves as analytically oriented. Psychologists too tilted heavily toward psychoanalysis, with many of the myriad of psychotherapies in play resting on its core theories: the importance of the unconscious, that inner conflicts lead to neuroses, and that the past was often prologue. One psychologist, Kenneth Keniston, freely admitted that psychoanalysis had its faults but that most critics were wrong to dismiss it entirely. Psychoanalysts could be accused of many things but one could not take issue with their respect for the individual, pursuit of understanding over illusion, refusal to overpromise, and unshakable belief that life was often complex, sometimes tragic, and occasionally wonderful.[32]

Some of those in analysis, understandably jealous at seeing their friends make what appeared to be great progress via less traditional techniques, ultimately came to the same conclusion. "Why had I chosen psychoanalysis as nobody does these days?" wondered Jane Shapiro in *Mademoiselle* in 1979; her circle seemed to be getting emotionally healthier through Rolfing, rebirthing, screaming, and other assorted popular therapies. Aware that the method was not about making people happy per se, Shapiro had the perfect answer to her own question. "Psychoanalysis has helped me to understand my life beyond my expectation," she wrote, while the trendier therapies fell short on that all-important measure. Est (short for Erhard Seminar Training, named after its founder), for example, seemed to have come and gone, its weekend marathon sessions certainly intense but of little long-term value. Shapiro even had high praise for her analyst, able to see beyond the ringer he regularly put her through. "In infrequent but elaborate soliloquies, he has emphasized how life has a continuity I hadn't quite noticed before," she thought, crediting him for getting her to focus on Freud's two essentials—love and work.[33]

Others in analysis proved beyond a doubt that, despite having been in decline for almost a generation now, the method was still offering some people relief from their emotional woes. Personal stories like that of "Elaine Kolberg" (not her real name), a thirty-one-year-old Chicagoan, resonated, her three and a half years of treatment allowing her to control her depression resulting from an early trauma. At the age of twenty-two months, Elaine and her two older siblings had been temporarily sent away to live with relatives while her mother had another baby. This was the event, she believed, that had prevented her from getting true joy out of life as an adult. Psychoanalysis was ideal for this kind of neurosis, thought her analyst at the Chicago Institute for Psychoanalysis, her separation anxiety (like repressed anger, loss of something or someone loved, or early failure to build self-esteem) very responsive to the talking cure. Kolberg, who told her story in the *Chicago Tribune*, figured out that she had been angry at her parents for sending her away but did not vent it, afraid that she would be cast out for good. Any kind of loss later in life would bring back this anger but she would repress it, resulting in depression and an inability to be completely happy.[34]

Kolberg's success with psychoanalysis was not surprising given that her particular problem was where the method excelled. According to classical analytic thought, self-esteem in adulthood is directly linked to the love and caring a child received from his or her mother, the lack of which often leads to depression, stress, and other neuroses later in life. By helping patients understand the source of their feelings of loss, anger, and disappointment, psychoanalysis could disrupt the pattern, making all the difference in the world for those who had suffered all their lives. Advocates of drug therapy had a different opinion, of course, believing that depression had more to do with chemical imbalances in the brain than early childhood experiences. Ronald R. Fieve, author of *Moodswing*, argued that psychotherapy was a good idea only after deeply depressed patients started taking lithium, antidepressants, or both, an example of the chicken-or-egg debate going on in psychiatry. Did psychological factors trigger a chemical change in depressed people or did all roads ultimately lead back to biology? While the answer to that question remained unsure, a shotgun approach to treating depression was emerging as the 1980s beckoned, with everything in the psychiatric sink—drugs, psychotherapy, behavior modification, and lifestyle changes—thrown at the problem to increase the chances of solving it.[35]

A Ho-Hum Attitude

The kitchen sink at psychiatrists' disposal was a very large one. As Ronald and Nancy Reagan moved into the White House, there were no less than two hundred varieties of sixty-seven types of therapies available to the eight million Americans getting some kind of psychological counseling (and spending forty billion dollars a year in the process). "We are obsessed with maturation, repetitive 'identity crises,' and a new, narcissistic devotion to the 'self,'" wrote Lance Lee of the *Los Angeles Times*, in early 1980; our need to "get our heads together" had become a cultural mantra. The strange theories Sigmund Freud had developed almost a century earlier had exploded into a powerful social movement, reshaping the contours of personal identity and interpersonal relationships. "Psychoanalysis and the American belief in the preeminence of the individual conscious are a perfect marriage," Lee wrote. The method fit beautifully with the nation's commitment to the "pursuit of happiness." Ironically, psychoanalysis had remained remarkably unchanged, refusing to budge from its focus on the individual, in-depth approach, and reliance on talking as the means to well-being. Dismissing both the long, steady encroachment of drug therapy and the constant parade of here-today-gone-tomorrow techniques as cheap substitutes (including quasi-psychological "courses" like est and Scientology), psychoanalysis was, for better or worse, staying true to its roots. The experience of a patient free-associating and having his or her dreams analyzed in a session in 1980 was virtually identical to someone who had done the same in 1920, the desired goal of reigning in the forces of the unconscious unchanged.[36]

All this had come at a significant cost. "A ho-hum attitude has sprung up about psychoanalytic thought," Lee observed. Perhaps its assimilation into the discourse of everyday life in America had diluted its intellectual capital. New theories from the likes of Melanie Klein and Heinz Kohut had occasionally spiced things up but, for the most part, psychoanalysis was largely resistant to innovation. This had much to do with the New York–based American Psychoanalytic Association (considered by some to be "the Vatican of American psychoanalysis"), which allowed precious little deviation from its orthodox views. (In practice, some analysts were known to act quite differently than their American Psychoanalytic Association–approved training would suggest, adopting a more flexible, open-ended approach with patients.) Although its intellectual capital had perhaps diminished, another kind of capital associated with psychoanalysis was definitely on the rise. The cost of a session was in 1980 about seventy-five dollars, translating to as much as twelve thousand to fifteen thousand dollars a year for treatment. With such a price tag, it was no wonder that psychoanalysts now had on average just two patients in full analysis.[37]

The good news, financially speaking at least, was the United States Tax Court's overruling of the IRS's decision to make psychoanalysis non–tax deductible for those who considered it a business expense. The (routinely violated) IRS rule was that while psychoanalysts were allowed to deduct the cost of their own treatment (patients could deduct only an amount exceeding 3 percent of their adjusted gross income), others who considered it a form of education could not. This meant that those in quite a few occupations—social workers, teachers, ministers, probation officers, and psychiatric nurses—could now deduct the cost of their analysis as a business expense, saving them hundreds or thousands of dollars a year in taxes. The IRS was considering appealing the tax court's 1980 decision, but until then people like Marilyn and Harry Voigt of Chevy Chase, Maryland, were jumping for joy. "It's a definite benefit for anyone getting into analysis to enhance their job skills," said Mr. Voigt speaking of the six thousand dollars his wife had paid an analyst to improve her credentials as a clinical social worker. Mr. Voigt, a lawyer, had handled his wife's case, the bonus being that he could also deduct the cost of fighting the IRS in court.[38]

Even if psychoanalysis had become a ubiquitous (and, for some, tax deductible) feature of American life, psychoanalysts remained largely a mystery to the public. Janet Malcolm's *Psychoanalysis: The Impossible Profession* changed a lot of that, throwing considerable light on what at least one of them was thinking in and out of the office. For her book's title, Malcolm, a staff writer for the *New Yorker* and daughter of a psychoanalyst, borrowed Freud's observation that psychoanalysis was one of three "impossible professions," with education and government also inevitably delivering "unsatisfactory results." Malcolm used "Aaron Green" as the source of her exposé, the forty-six-year-old classical Freudian analyst from New York eager, willing, and able to tell all about his job. Green, it turned out, had as much anxiety about his career as any of his patients, desirous of becoming a bigger player in the field but not sure how to do it. Larry Kart, in his review in the *Chicago Tribune*, surmised that with much of the material in the book first published in the *New*

Yorker (a staple in analysts' waiting rooms), Green was "sure to become the No. 1 topic of gossip in the tightly knit world of psychoanalysis."[39] Many had assumed some kind of voyeurism was at the heart of psychoanalysts' choice of professions, but Green's admittance of such was shocking nonetheless. Green's perspective was, as he told Malcolm,

> that of an outsider looking into the bedroom: feeling excited and scared, getting aroused . . . but not having to get involved, not having to risk anything. I could have become a Peeping Tom, for one extreme possibility, but I became a scientist instead—a psychoanalyst.[40]

After reading such revelations, Kart concluded that psychoanalysis was neither a science nor an art but rather a "sublime comedy," not any more or less impossible than life itself.[41]

Like the greater interest in "the impossible profession," more attention began to be paid to another key player in the process—the spouses of the analyzed. Since the beginning of psychoanalysis, it had been accepted that a husband's going through treatment was difficult on his wife and vice-versa, but little or nothing was done to prepare the spouse for his or her experience. Steven M. Sonnenberg, head of the Washington DC School of Psychiatry, cautioned, "The poor spouse just doesn't know what's going on." Divorce was not an uncommon occurrence after someone started therapy. (Many of these marriages were likely shaky to begin with, of course.) Even psychoanalysts were not immune to the pressures put on their marriages when their spouses began treatment. When the wife of Howard F. Wallach, a Los Angeles analyst, started to hit the couch, for example, he began to get jealous, and not because he thought she would have an affair with her male shrink. "She would talk about how wise and clever he was," Wallach complained, no doubt echoing the same thought running through the minds of many a husband whose wife was in treatment, analyst or otherwise. A patient becoming withdrawn, depressed, or preoccupied often came with the territory, with the spouse and other family members bearing the brunt of his or her emotional rollercoaster. (Analysis was particularly tough on a patient's parents, making them wonder what terrible things they had done to make their child have to spend years of his or her life and thousands of dollars to recover.) If and when transference—the critical stage in which patients transferred feelings about key people in their lives onto the analyst—was achieved, all bets were off, with family members the recipient of great affection, deep hostility, or anything in between.[42]

The chances of some kind of friction were exponentially multiplied if the patient and analyst were of different genders, with the always-combustible dynamics of love sometimes thrown into the mix. "I think the husband who has a wife in analysis has to learn to share his wife—to learn that she has other loves," said Harvey Rich, a Washington DC analyst. Rich's experience was that women often thought they loved their shrink (although it was more of a fantasy than reality). The presence of a third wheel in a couple's relationship could understandably bring distance between a husband and wife, especially because that wheel was someone whom one of the parties had probably never met. "A third person is present in the bedroom and the house," explained one woman from Pittsburgh whose husband was in analysis, feeling threatened and angry that their privacy had been compromised. Few would argue that running into one's spouse's analyst in public was positively dreadful; the experience was tantamount to encountering his or her lover who was privy to all the intimate details of their personal lives. "I felt . . . that he had been there in bed with me and my wife," said one unlucky fellow who had it happen to him, the imaginary ménage à trois not erotic in the least.[43]

Having an analyst in the family had other vexing if less invasive drawbacks. Because no major decisions could be made in the analyzed person's life, the spouse inherited that condition as well, meaning no additional child, bigger house, or better-paying job. A couple's life was thus essentially put on hold for years, not exactly a good way to build a successful marriage. Furthermore, the time and money invested in one member of the couple's psychoanalysis was typically an issue that put additional pressure on a relationship that was, again, often already strained. Less obvious things—like having to take vacations when the analyst took his or hers in August—also added fuel to the fire. Occasionally, the spouse would urge his or her partner to call it quits or, failing that, even try to sabotage the therapeutic process to bring it to a crashing halt. The perfect revenge was for the spouse to begin treatment himself or herself, an outcome that occurred quite regularly. While tag-team analysis cost a bundle and a half, this was the ideal situation for therapists and patients alike, the blame game instantly dissolved and the couple kept on an even developmental plane.[44]

The Assault on Truth

Impossible or otherwise, psychoanalysis remained a desirable profession for some, with top-of-the-line training available only at the nation's dozen or so American Psychoanalytic Association–approved institutes. One of them, Chicago's Institute for Psychoanalysis, celebrated its fiftieth birthday in 1982—the shrink factory was clear proof that despite the continual stream of alternative therapies (now including biofeedback and sensory deprivation), psychoanalysis was very much in business. With a staff of two hundred, a $1.3 million annual budget, an academy training a dozen or so students a year, and a clinic serving a thousand outpatients, the institute was no mom-and-pop operation. Other such institutes in other cities had split into pieces or dissolved, a result of internal strife, but Chicago remained a bulwark of the field. The key to Chicago's success was that it was able to accommodate a wide range of psychoanalytic thought, even that which strayed from Freudian doctrine. The case of the recently deceased Heinz Kohut was a perfect example. Kohut, a Chicago Institute graduate, president of the American Psychoanalytic Association, and author of the breakthrough *The Analysis of Self*, was unafraid to look elsewhere than the Oedipal conflict to explain human behavior. (It was parents' support, pride, and affection for their children, or lack thereof, which determined the relative mental health of an individual, Kohut thought.) Unlike its stick-in-the-mud cousin in New York, Chicago was unafraid to dabble with ideas not tied to the premise that people were, above all, animals with physical drives. Best of all, the Second City chapter was doing everything critics of psychoanalysis said the field should be doing—reaching out into the community, offering affordable therapy (albeit for a select few), and doing actual research.[45]

A number of scholars were, meanwhile, pursuing research on none other than Sigmund Freud himself, digging deeper into both his theories and personal life. "They are looking for secrets," said eighty-five-year-old Anna Freud in 1981, "but there are no secrets." Already arguably the most analyzed person in history, Freud was still a subject of fascination, some of his unpublished letters perhaps revealing new, critical insights into the thinking behind psychoanalysis. As well, negotiations were going on with the Library of Congress to allow scholars access to more of Freud's materials over the next twenty years rather than await the planned, very far-off date of 2151. "It seems to be a sort of renaissance in a way," gushed Mark Paterson, especially excited about the new interest in Freud given that he managed the rights to the man's works on behalf of his heirs. Four new biographies of his client had been published in just the last couple of years, and Freud had become once again a popular topic in academic papers, more evidence that the father of psychoanalysis was making a major comeback.[46]

Nothing in recent memory brought more attention to the field than a paper given by Jeffrey Moussaieff Masson to the Western New England Psychoanalytic Society in June 1981. Masson, a nonpracticing psychoanalyst who had been selected by none other than Anna Freud to be the projects director of the Sigmund Freud Archives, argued that Freud's decision to abandon his early theory on the origin of neurosis was "a personal failure of courage." It was sexual trauma suffered in childhood that caused hysteria in adults, Freud had written in 1896, his "seduction theory" one of the key ideas of psychoanalysis. But Freud later recanted the theory, judging patients' experiences to be more often fantasy than fact, a decision Masson believed was necessary for him to continue developing other important concepts (including the Oedipal complex). Another possible reason that Freud abandoned his theory was to regain favor with Vienna's medical community. Masson suggested that Freud had been "suffer[ing] emotional and intellectual isolation as long as he held to the reality of seduction."[47]

Very soon and rather expectedly, the forty-year-old Masson (who had been a Sanskrit scholar before becoming a psychoanalyst) was sacked by the thirteen-member board of the Freud Archives. "Would you make director of the archives someone who writes plain nonsense?" asked Kurt Eissler, the archive's secretary. Anna Freud simply commented that she regretted the publicity surrounded the event. (She died the following year.) Essentially accusing Freud of being responsible for "the present-day sterility of psychoanalysis throughout the world" certainly did not help Masson's cause, nor did his later comment that if his (Masson's) theory was accepted by the field "they would have to recall every patient since 1901." The situation was looking a lot "like the [Ford] Pinto."[48] Masson was not done, expanding his argument in a 1984 book, *The Assault on Truth: Freud's Suppression of the Seduction Theory*, keeping the dustup going for yet a while longer. If that was not enough, Janet Malcolm wrote her own book on the matter, *In the Freud Archives*, this too contributing to the feeding frenzy. Most psychoanalysts believed Masson was overstating his case and that the controversy would not have much impact on Freud or the field over the long term, each too deeply entrenched to be significantly swayed by virtually anything.[49] "This won't change the way anyone does anything," thought Bruno Bettelheim. Daniel Goleman of the *New York Times* came to the similar conclusion that "psychoanalysis appears stung but little harmed."[50]

More kindling was put on the fire Masson had started. Peter Swales, a thirty-six-year-old Welshman living in New York in 1984, was a self-described "punk historian of psychoanalysis," his perspective of the field making Masson's seem positively tame. Rather than see Freud as an anachronism, as many critics did, Swales, who had once been a promoter for the Rolling Stones, looked to Freud's early experiments with cocaine as very much in sync with the times. Psychoanalysis was "addictive," many of those in therapy were known to say, this too making Freud quite at home in the just-say-yes eighties. Along with Masson, Swales was a big part of Malcolm's *In the Freud Archives*, he too rocking the staid world of psychoanalysts with his own research showing that Freud was a fraud. Through self-published essays and what came to be recognized as a legendary lecture at NYU in 1981, Swales took one of the arguments in David Bakan's 1958 *Sigmund Freud and the Jewish Mystical Tradition*—that Freud had made a pact with the devil—to an entirely new level. While Swales's ideas were outrageous if not mad (Swales maintained that Freud's theories were less about the unconscious and sexuality than of narcotics and Satanism), they did rather ironically help to revive interest in the field. Swales had a feature article in *Rolling Stone* magazine in 1984, in fact, exposing Freud to an audience more familiar with the likes of Duran Duran, Van Halen, and Cyndi Lauper.[51]

Even if Masson and Swales's accusations were true, as some pointed out at the time, Freud would still have been in some very good company, historically speaking. Galileo, Newton, and Gregor Mendel had all accentuated the positive and eliminated the negative in the process of proposing their respective grand new theories—the bigger cause considered more important than some of the messier details. As well, Masson and Swales's bold moves may have had a bigger sting had they not come at a time when the field was pretty resilient to such attacks. There were 2,800 members of the American Psychoanalytic Association, matched by a similar number of nonmembers who considered themselves psychoanalysts in 1984, quite a jump in the last few years. Considering there were roughly 85,000 psychotherapists in the country, psychoanalysis was still a niche approach, but there was no doubt that the field was continuing to rebound from its two-decade slide.[52]

The revival of psychoanalysis in the 1980s went hand-in-hand with new efforts by researchers to determine whether the method was or was not a true science. Jonathan Winson, a neuroscientist at Rockefeller University and author of *Brain and Psyche*, for example, was finding in 1985 that some of Freud's concepts such as the libido and the death wish just did not "make sense in terms of the reality of the brain." Many other ideas, however—the existence of the unconscious, the importance of early childhood experiences, and the idea of transference—were not incompatible with modern neuroscience. Proponents of behavioral and cognitive psychology naturally scoffed at the mere idea of spending good time and money investigating whether psychoanalysis was a science; they already knew the answer. "Are you better off trying to use the scientific method to extract the small part that is testable, or should you chuck it and test a theory that is more plausible from the outset?" asked Stephen Harnad, a cognitive psychobiologist and the editor of the journal *Brain and Behavioral Sciences*. Harnad was so convinced that psychoanalysis could not stand up to scientific testing that he was devoting an entire issue of the journal to the subject, asking no less than fifty authorities to offer their opinions. Others were equally confident that the field would do just fine in the lab. "Mainstream cognitive psychology is rapidly converging on many of Freud's key insights," said Matthew Erdelyi, author of *Psychoanalysis: Freud's Cognitive Psychology*. Erdelyi, a psychologist, argued that not just the unconscious but things like hidden meanings and repressed memories would be found to be scientifically sound.[53]

As more interested parties weighed in on the issue, it became clear that psychoanalysis was reaching a showdown in the mid-1980s, its scientific validity literally put to the test to either elevate the field or take it down. The unscientific nature of psychoanalysis, more or less canonized by Sir Karl Popper in 1957, when he put it in the same camp as Marxism and astrology, was now being reexamined. A gauntlet of sorts had been thrown by University of Pittsburgh professor Adolf Grunbaum. Grunbaum admitted that the scientific foundation of psychoanalysis was "impoverished," but believed that new efforts might prove that many of Freud's theories were true. While many analysts remained resistant, declaring that their process and the scientific method were fundamentally incompatible, others supported Grunbaum's challenge. "Psychoanalysis has been enormously successfully clinically and vastly important culturally," said Arnold Cooper, past president of the American Psychoanalytic Association, "but the time has come to recast psychoanalytic assumptions so they can be tested scientifically." Why the surge in interest to determine whether psychoanalysis was a science? One big reason was the rise in health maintenance organizations (HMOs) and their mandate to pay only for therapies that were "effective," putting pressure on psychoanalysts to produce something a lot more substantive than its "one-third" rule. "Psychoanalysis makes claims about the mind, and it has to justify them scientifically," agreed Marshall Edelson, a psychoanalyst at Yale's Medical School. Edelson urged his colleagues to face the truth whether they wanted to or not.[54]

Edelson and Grunbaum had both just published books on the subject, in fact, each laying out his respective picture for the future of psychoanalysis. In the former's *Hypothesis and Evidence in Psychoanalysis*, Edelson was cautiously hopeful that psychoanalysts would embrace rigorous research to prove their field was a legitimate science despite the fact that they "still feel free to indulge in their delusion that their heaps of clinical observations, case reports, vignettes, and anecdotes do meet scientific requirements for empirical evidence." In his *The Foundations of Psychoanalysis: A Philosophical Critique*, Grunbaum was less optimistic, arguing that the roots of Freudian theory were planted in weak soil and that it was likely just a matter of time before psychoanalysis died on the vine. "It would scarcely be excessive to conclude . . . that psychoanalysis is little more than a collective contagious delusional system," Frederick Crews wrote in his review of the two books in the *New Republic*, locating Freud alongside other great philosophers and literary figures rather than Copernicus and Darwin. "The outcome of the game is no longer in doubt," he concluded. Crews maintained that the problematic issue plaguing psychoanalysis since its beginnings—its dearth of scientific credentials—ultimately spelled doom for the field.[55]

The Century of Freud

Having heard it all before, psychoanalysts were not going to let a few death sentences for their field ruin their big party. The year 1986 was the one-hundredth anniversary of the founding of psychoanalysis (using Freud's work with Charcot at La Salpêtrière as the official birth), and plans to commemorate the occasion had already been made. "The Century of Freud" conference at UCLA that year was one such celebration, this meeting of academics not dredging up the man's musty theories but providing an opportunity to apply his thinking to current issues. "Freud and Terrorism" was one talk given at the conference, for example; the speaker, Abe Kaplan of the University of Haifa, understood violence to be "a way of dealing with inchoate, confused and conflicted feelings." In her talk "Updating Freud's Views of Women," Doryann M. Lebe of UCLA turned the tables on the man, acknowledging he was a genius and had encouraged women to enter the field but had major blind spots because of his "phallocentric bias." How psychoanalysis could and should deal with issues emerging in the mid-1980s such as genetic engineering, new drug therapies (both legal and illegal), and holistic healing also was batted around. No one at the conference doubted that Freud would have some place in the psychiatric landscape of the future.[56]

Psychoanalysts had good reason to think their days were not numbered, as some critics predicted. There were now about three thousand psychoanalysts (compared to thirty-five thousand psychiatrists) in the United States, the hemorrhaging of the field seemingly over. A lot had certainly happened in the century of Freud (and in the seventy-five years since the founding of the American Psychoanalytic Association, in 1911, and the thirty-year history of the American Academy of Psychoanalysis) but, in the big scheme of things, the method had remained remarkably the same. Unlocking the secrets of a human being was, after all, still the heart and soul of psychoanalysis, the desired goal to alleviate psychic pain resulting from childhood traumas. After an analyst "recreate[d] the psychological moments in a person's life when they suffered hurts," as Stefan Pasternack, clinical professor of psychiatry at Georgetown University Medical Center put it, the patient was usually better able to recognize his or her "infantile distortions." This expected outcome of the method too was little changed. Although Freud's theories had certainly undergone some modifications over the years (primarily a shift in emphasis from the id to the ego) and would inevitably develop further, the consensus among practitioners was that they were still the best way to understand a human being. "The basics will ... probably stay forever," said Ernst Ticho, a Washington DC analyst. Ticho, like his colleagues, was confident the method would be able to survive the two hundred and fifty or so different kinds of talk therapies now believed to exist. Unlike most of these "drive-through approaches," a soup-to-nuts psychoanalytic regime could now cost upward of one hundred thousand dollars, the price of a decent house, making the approach still far too expensive for the average person.[57]

Of course, investing a hundred grand and a handful of years of one's life in psychoanalysis did not guarantee success. A flurry of stories told in the late eighties revealed as much, stark reminders that the century-old therapy was still, at the end of the day, mostly just a theory. Some thirty years after he began treatment, for example, novelist Dan Wakefield was finally able to tell his story, and quite a story it was. In his 1987 *New York Times* article, "My Six Years on the Couch," Wakefield went back to 1956 when he was "approved" for psychoanalysis by a "Dr. Ernest" from the New York Psychoanalytic Institute. (Not everyone was considered intelligent, inquisitive, and perceptive enough to qualify for the method, illustrating how elitist it truly was at the time.) Twenty-four years old and impotent (and with writer's block, to boot), Wakefield was desperate, a (rather feeble) suicide attempt reason enough to try to come up with the six thousand dollars a year cost, somehow, some way. Turned down for a scholarship (the institute sometimes offered a free ride for those with little cash but a particularly interesting problem), Wakefield's parents agreed to foot the bill. (He vowed to pay them back and did so years later.) Wakefield started to see a "Dr. Stanley," disappointed to learn that Freudian analysis was more free association than conversation ("Yes, go on" was about all he heard from the man). Successfully making love to a woman about a year into treatment, Wakefield thought he was cured, but was told by Dr. Stanley that his impotence was merely a symptom of the real problem deeply rooted in his unconscious. "So I settled back on the couch," he recalled, his five-days-a-week sessions continuing for years.[58]

Realizing one day that he did not like Dr. Stanley and that Dr. Stanley probably did not like him, Wakefield began treatment with another analyst also named, oddly enough, "Dr. Stanley." Upon hitting the five-year mark at age thirty, Wakefield began to seriously wonder if all (or any of) the time and money had been worth it. These doubts were not eased by meeting people at parties who had been in analysis for ten or fifteen years, their epiphanies also not yet realized. Wakefield informed Stanley II, as he called him, that he would give it one more year and then, cure or no cure, call it quits. "Then it came," Wakefield told readers, "it" being a terrifying nightmare that he had with just three months to go before his self-imposed deadline. In the dream, Wakefield saw one of his best friends with a disfigured face, finding the image to be even more sickening when he told Stanley II about it. "I tried to shake it, but it only came back, multiplied in greater distortion," he remembered, unable to get it out of his mind. The image soon morphed into a human skull, this even worse than the disfigured face. "I knew it was death, and I knew death was luring me," Wakefield chillingly wrote, convinced he would soon go crazy if his fixation would not go away. "The living-hell of the ever-changing hallucinations," as Wakefield vividly described his condition, lasted almost six weeks, with Stanley II not very helpfully explaining that they had simply entered "the heartland" of the analytic experience. Mad as hell at both Stanleys and the entire process, Wakefield retreated to a small house in New Hampshire by a pond, finding comfort in country life and the Twenty-third Psalm. "Though I walk through the valley of the shadow of death, I will fear no evil; for thou art with me," Wakefield repeated over and over, his soul restored after being led by the still waters of his mind. "I know it was my own dark night of the soul, in the deepest sense of that concept," he concluded, a quarter-century later, his personal psychoanalytic journey a literal nightmare.[59]

Thea George's story was not as horrendous but still not particularly pretty. For her 1988 article for *Mademoiselle*, "I Hate Myself! Am I Crazy?," George published part of her diary that documented her four years of psychoanalysis. At twenty-four, George was miserable although she did not know why she felt "so bad, so ugly, so evil, so filled with dread," having a good job, a nice apartment, and a boyfriend who wanted to marry her. After having a nightmare and feeling it was a bad omen, George was off to see "Dr. M.," hoping he "could stick a suction pump into my brain and suck out all the poisons." (On her insurance forms, George was far less poetic, describing her condition as "generalized anxiety disorder"). Four mornings a week before work, George walked across Central Park to get to Dr. M.'s office on Manhattan's Upper East Side, the months ticking by as she talked about her self-loathing and described her dreams. As is typical, little progress was initially made, much to her disappointment. Expecting "some intense transference/abandonment experience" when Dr. M. went on vacation in August, she scribbled in 1984, George was simply "relieved that I don't have to get up so f——ing early in the morning and talk about sex and then go to work tired with my face all swollen and blotchy." After a little more than a year and still not much improvement, George offered what had to be one of the best descriptions of analysis ever offered: she compared it to looking for a diamond in a ten-mile-high mountain of garbage in the middle of a swamp, the search requiring close examination of every piece of trash (including "rotting meat, dead hamsters, and soiled tampons"). A decision to move out of town would put a rather sudden end to her analysis (referred to as "termination" in the trade) but, after four-plus years of garbage hunting, she felt her "horrible feeling of badness" was largely gone.[60]

As he thoroughly explained in his article for *Esquire* the following year, "Confessions of a Head Case," Peter Freundlich had as much frustration about psychoanalysis as George but less success. Freundlich believed that, for all the thousands of dollars he had paid his shrink, his head would by then have been effectively shrunken, all its excess juices extracted. But that was not the case at all, he was sad to say, his head "the same malarkey-filled melon" he always had. "In every hidey-hole an armed idea crouches, waiting for an enemy notion to show itself," Freundlich complained, the war inside his brain still raging. Going into analysis, he had expected little but hoped for much more, specifically clarity, certainty, and, most of all, peace. In fact, Freundlich was of the opinion that his years on a Naugahyde divan had not shrunk his head at all but instead had expanded it, the human brain like a folded and compressed parachute just waiting to explode open if the right cord was pulled. With his head getting yet bigger rather than smaller, Freundlich was beginning to think that his analyst was an "off-brand," and, as in everything else, you get what you pay for. At this point, Freundlich also had doubts about the entire process, with Sigmund Freud himself perhaps unable to bring his battle to a close, if he had still been around. "Can so much self-introspection be a good thing?" he wondered, something many others on the same Naugahyde divan had certainly also asked themselves.[61]

With such stories floating in the ether, it was not surprising that many Americans opted for one of the many less Draconian therapies readily available. In fact, because there just were not enough patients to go around in the late eighties (Robert Michels, chair of the psychiatry department at New York Hospital–Cornell Medical Center, estimated that just one in ten thousand Americans was in analysis), many analysts were being forced to devote part of their practice to general psychotherapy. As well, many psychoanalysts had dropped the words "cure" and even "insight" from their vocabulary, now talking more about patient "change" and improving their "capacity for self-observation." Freud, Inc., continued to be a big business, however, with Peter Gay's "definitive" biography of the man, *Freud: A Life for Our Time*, the latest book to stir the pot. The relationship between universities and Freud too remained intimate, especially in humanities departments. "It's still very much a one-man science, as if physics had been limited to only what Newton or Einstein had said," thought Theodore Shapiro, editor of *The Psychoanalytic Quarterly*. For Shapiro, though, Freud was still the undisputed heavyweight champion of psychoanalysis. What was clear was that the depth of the field's ideas now exceeded its therapeutic value, its basic concept of the unconscious serving as an extraordinarily powerful paradigm for human behavior.[62]

A blessing in disguise was about to inject new blood into therapeutically anemic psychoanalysis. After being kept out for more than half a century, therapists without medical degrees were finally granted admittance to the major psychoanalytic institutes in the United States, something that could mean huge changes ahead for the field. Although Freud felt that learning or using his method did not require one to be a physician, a sentiment Europeans took to heart, it had been a different story in America where only medical doctors were allowed into American Psychoanalytic Association–approved training institutes. But now, in a settlement reached after a lawsuit, psychologists and social workers, and not just psychiatrists, could be accepted at the nation's premier psychoanalytic institutes to receive full training. The agreement was good for practitioners other than physicians wanting to become psychoanalysts, of course, but consumers too could benefit from this big turn of events. For one thing, the cost of analysis would probably drop dramatically as new players changed the competitive landscape of the field, allowing more people to participate in the talking cure. Equally important was how the method itself could possibly be affected by opening itself up to practitioners who were not also medical doctors. Could those with different backgrounds alter the very nature of psychoanalysis, turning it into something other than it had been for the last century?[63]

Other events suggested that a kinder, gentler psychoanalysis was emerging. By the late eighties, the Macy's and Gimble's of psychotherapy—psychoanalysis and behaviorism—were showing signs of not only calling off their war but of going into business together. An integrated approach combining various schools of therapy was best for the patient, many psychologists were coming to believe—the walls that practitioners had constructed over the decades were not good for anyone. Paul Wachtel, a psychologist at the City University of New York Graduate Center, was a part of this new movement promising synergistic results. "The search is on now for a super-therapy that combines the most effective elements of all the types of psychotherapy," he wrote. Could Freud really get along with his behavioral, cognitive, and drug-friendly cousins? The fact was that many therapists had already mixed-and-matched disparate psychological approaches to create hybrids all their own. Whether called eclectic, integrated, or multimodal, the growing movement was also seeping into university graduate schools, with psychotherapists in training less likely to subscribe to one particular approach. Once bitter enemies now seemed ready to declare a truce. "When you clear away the jargon, you find there is much in common," said Marvin Goldfried, a psychologist at the State University of New York at Stony Brook.[64]

A (literal) meeting of the minds in psychiatry would certainly be nice, but Mike Feder, a contributor to WNYC, the public radio station in New York, had what was perhaps an even better "super-therapy" in mind. "Every day, in every city in the country, people are steaming with anger over something," Feder's monologue from March 1989 began, the usual suspects—bad bosses, useless teachers, malicious friends and lovers, obnoxious kids, and fault-finding parents—making Americans crazy. Other problems of the day—money (or, more precisely, the lack of it), crime, and that everything seemed to cause cancer—only added to the need for some affordable (and legal) way to vent one's frustrations. The answer? "McFreud's," a surefire business idea that even the dozens of fast and cheap talk therapies could not match in speed, efficiency, and price. No appointments would be needed at McFreud's, Feder jested, with "McTherapists" just happy, friendly folks rather than "your usual stuffy degree-laden pedants—stiff self-tortured souls who use big words that leave you more confused than you were when you came in and who charge you outrageous fees." And instead of "a long, difficult process with no guarantees," Feder continued, McFreud's promised "no mysterious silences or incomprehensible theories, just good old-fashioned advice." If that were not enough, an eight-ounce charburger, double fries, and large Coke would be thrown in for each session at McFreud's, a deal that Feder believed most Americans just could not turn down.[65] Funny, perhaps, but as we headed into the final turn of the twentieth century, it would remain Freud himself to whom many Americans would look for therapeutic nourishment.

CHAPTER 6: The Comeback Couch

> The important thing is for your mother to repress what happened, push it deep down inside her so she'll never annoy us again.
>
> HOMER SIMPSON to his daughter, Lisa, in "Fear of Flying," a 1994 episode of *The Simpsons*

In March 1998, three dozen psychoanalysts gathered at Mount Sinai Hospital in Manhattan to talk about the latest thinking in the field. The get-together was, as Sarah Boxer of the *New York Times* described it, "like one big session on the couch," with another observer seeing it as "a Woodstock of epistemology." The gaggle of shrinks had convened to try to reach consensus on some of the key theories of psychoanalysis as the field moved further and further from Freud's century-old ideas. Concepts like seduction, trauma, reality, and fantasy were, more than ever, up for grabs as practitioners struggled to forge a psychoanalysis that was relevant for the twenty-first century. "Psychoanalysts seem to be obsessed with what they know and don't know, how they know and don't know it, and what their patients think they know and don't know," Boxer summarized the situation; the existential crisis perhaps reflected a meta-version of some of therapy patients' own nagging self-doubts. Should psychoanalysts try to have their patients remember the truth of their past? Or was it their job to help patients construct a useful narrative or mythology that could best serve them in the future? More to the point, which was more important as a therapeutic device—reality or fantasy?[1]

The Sartresque questions raised at the 1998 summit captured the flux taking place in psychoanalysis as it moved into its second century. Through the 1990s and the early 2000s, psychoanalysis would take a long, hard look at itself as practitioners tried to carve out a niche in the crowded therapeutic marketplace. They would, in retrospect, both succeed and fail in this venture, the field more secure than it was twenty years earlier yet in many respects still, as Michael J. Bader put it in 1997, "on the run."[2]

Dust Off the Couch

Although the fate of psychoanalysis would ultimately remain uncertain, at least one thing was sure: the opening up of psychoanalytic training to nonphysicians did, as expected, attract new blood to the field. About ten new training centers had started up by 1991, the demand too great for the American Psychoanalytic Association–approved institutes to handle. One of them, the Institute of Contemporary Psychoanalysis in Los Angeles, received far too many applicants than it could accept into its inaugural class of thirty-three. (By comparison, an American Psychoanalytic Association institute admitted about ten new students each year.) The influx of PhDs into the field also triggered a jump in articles, books, and conferences dedicated to psychoanalysis, with a new journal, *Psychoanalytic Dialogues*, shaking things up with its provocative views on the analyst-patient relationship. "As best I can tell, it's not simply a revival of interest but an explosion," said Jonathan Slavin of the American Psychological Association. Like many others, Slavin concluded that "no other perspective can compete with the way it informs your understanding and your capacity to deal with a whole range of people." There was also the feeling that psychoanalysis was becoming less rigid and authoritarian as more social workers and psychiatric nurses, not to mention women in general, entered the field (more than half of new analysts were women).[3]

Four years after the class-action lawsuit against the American Psychoanalytic Association was settled, in fact, everybody seemed quite happy about the way things had turned out. The arrival of psychologists seemed to be rejuvenating psychoanalysis, providing the field with a new pool of people at a time when it was much needed. Whether psychoanalysis would over time become completely free of a medical underpinning was uncertain, but it was clear that the good number of nonphysicians training to become psychoanalysts was helping reverse the slide that the field had experienced over the past couple of decades.[4] "Dust off the couch," *Psychology Today* announced in 1992, telling its readers that a new and improved version of psychoanalysis was gaining traction. "After two decades of decline, the therapeutic method that Sigmund Freud made famous is enjoying new popularity," the magazine reported in an article called "The Comeback Couch"—the leaner and meaner method now appealed to more Americans in search of answers. Most responsible for this turn of events was a renewed appreciation for the tremendous impact of trauma on personality development or, more brusquely, what a mind had to do to survive.[5]

With the couch back in vogue, having the right one seemed more important than ever. "This is not just furniture," Kerry Sulkowicz declared in 1992, the Manhattan shrink believing that one's couch was "central to your professional life and to your identity as an analyst." Sulkowicz went with a light gray wool while a colleague across town, David Gandler, opted for a Victorian oxblood red, both of these clearly of the as-neutral-as-possible school of psychoanalytic furniture. Other analysts, such as Sharon Messitte, thought style mattered; her earthy brown suede num-ber was designed to be so soothing that patients would look forward to lying down on it and unlocking their unconscious. Rather expectedly, the choice of a couch was heavily freighted with psychological overtones, the new analyst typically either buying the same one his or her shrink had or, conversely, rebelling against the parental figure by getting one completely different. Either way, the place for budding New York psy-choanalysts to get outfitted was Imperial Leather Furniture Company in Long Island City, which had been in the business for half a century. "Mostly, they buy black or maroon," said Fred Brafman, the sixty-one-year-old co-owner of Imperial, the notable exception being the time he sold a pair of matching hot pink and blue couches to a married couple who were both analysts.[6]

What made an analyst's couch different from your run-of-the-mill sofa readily available at any furniture store? No buttons, for one thing ("The patients are edgy," Brafman explained), and no fringe trim either ("The patients will just unravel it," he added). Most important, the couch should not be too much like a bed ("Enough erotic fantasies are going to come up anyhow," reasoned Wayne Myers, a psychoanalyst at New York Hospital–Cornell Medical Center) and it should have a built-in headrest. Prices generally ranged from seven hundred to three thousand dollars, although the king of all couches, the Mies van der Rohe Barcelona, cost a cool six thousand. Designed in 1929 and made in Italy, the black leather, sleek as a Ferrari beauty was the ultimate piece of psychoanalytic furniture despite the fact that its headrest felt not unlike a boulder. Every year, a few hundred American analysts were happy to fork out the six Gs and wait four months for a Barcelona, a symbol that one was playing in the Big Leagues. Some, feeling the Barcelona was too imposing and even threatening, chose a simpler one to make patients feel more at home than in a Knoll Studio showroom. Still others went with a custom-made, hiring a local craftsperson to create a couch that expressed their personal style.[7]

Given a long-overdue makeover, the psychoanalytic couch did indeed appear to be less tattered and worn than it had been. In his 1993 article for *Tikkun*, Michael J. Bader, a member of the San Francisco Psychoanalytic Institute, with a private practice in that city, acknowledged there were lots of good reasons to be critical and even cynical about psychoanalysis—its questionable relationships of authority and dark outlook, to name just a couple. But, like another psychoanalyst, Stephen Mitchell (who had, rather incongruously, recently written a book called *Hope and Dread in Psychoanalysis*), Bader believed that critics had largely ignored the major changes in the field that had taken place over the past twenty-five years. For one thing, Freud's desired state of a "rational ego" had evolved into the search for personal meaning and an authentic self. The quest to forge a purposeful and creative life within a community, with help from analysis, was very much in tune with the times. As well, the classic image of the analyst as Sherlock Holmes, in hot pursuit of his patient's elusive "Truth," had morphed into Columbo, Mitchell proposed, the contemporary shrink a lot more sensitive to and respectful of individuals' autonomy. Such changes reflected the distrust of authority and "experts" of all kinds that had invaded American society as a whole with a vengeance over the past couple of decades. In this sense, Bader explained, psychoanalysis was merely part of this much bigger cultural movement. Still, Bader insisted, psychoanalysis was no less effective. "Columbo, after all, in spite of his diffidence about his expertise and authority, does always get his man!" he exclaimed. The method remained as valuable as ever in helping people better understand the outside world through a better understanding of their inner world.[8]

And better late than never, perhaps, psychoanalysis was also starting to catch on in countries like Spain, Italy, and even the former Soviet Union—places in which the method had been unpopular if not taboo. The reason? Freud had "managed to create an intellectual edifice that feels closer to the experience of living . . . than any other system currently in play," Paul Gray of *Time* magazine argued in 1993. After nearly a century, he pointed out, psychoanalysis was still sprouting new leaves. Gray went even further, stating that Freud's theory of the unconscious was "this troubled century's dominant model for thinking and talking about human behavior," and his oeuvre was "something very close to common knowledge."[9]

Common knowledge or otherwise, Freud's theories remained a favorite intellectual punching bag. "Freud-bashing has gone from an argument to a movement," noted Jonathan Lear in 1995, and Richard Webster's new book, *Why Freud Was Wrong: Sin, Science, and Psychoanalysis*, was just the latest uppercut thrown at the man and his ideas. Lear believed there were three reasons for the most recent round of psychoanalytic pugilism that intensified with *Time*'s 1993 cover story asking the loaded question, "Is Freud Dead?" The first was the rise of Prozac Nation concomitant with brain research suggesting that talk therapy was, well, all talk. The second was the effect of health insurance policies favoring pharmacology over psychotherapy. The third represented the latest round of the collective, business-as-usual potshots taken at Freud and his methodology. Lear admitted that Freud's approach was occasionally shakier than one of his nervous patients but defended the man, locating him alongside other explorers of the human condition from Sophocles to Nietzsche. "Whatever valid criticisms can be aimed at him or at the psychoanalytic profession, it is nevertheless true that psychoanalysis is the most sustained and successful attempt to make . . . obscure meanings intelligible," Lear argued, Freud's theory of the unconscious "of great importance for human development." Underlying the gang-up on Freud was that Americans preferred to ignore the fact that life was complex and often dark, Lear suggested. A recognizable concept of happiness was much more palatable than dealing with the black hole that was the human soul. "We still need to account for the pervasive manifestations of human irratio-nality," he concluded. Freud's many critics had failed to see that few thinkers in history could be more helpful to this end than he.[10]

Freud's accounting for the pervasive manifestations of human irra-tionality notwithstanding, most Americans were looking elsewhere than psychoanalysis for fast-acting psychic relief. Roughly fifteen million Americans were in therapy in the mid-1990s, the vast majority opting for shorter, cheaper treatment. Behavioral-cognitive (or cognitive-behav-ioral) therapy and interpersonal therapy were especially popular choices, and sales of antidepressants like Prozac and Zoloft were booming. In 1985, the average psychoanalyst saw three patients three times a week but now, a dozen years later, the average practitioner had just one at three times a week. Some analysts' annual income had dropped from one hundred thousand dollars to fifteen thousand dollars as more patients chose, willingly or otherwise, managed care–friendly therapies.[11]

In fact, some analysts were thinking about retiring early, the paucity of clients a sign that their good run was over. Still, the answer to the question posed by *Time* in its cover story was an unequivocal no, as no other therapy or even drug could be definitively proven to work better than psychoanalysis or, in fact, work at all. On the ropes for decades, psychoanalysis just would not go down, mostly because no other theory or therapy could deliver a knockout blow. Few of the nation's forty thousand psychiatrists, sixty thousand psychologists, and seventy-five thousand social workers would call themselves psychoanalysts, but mem-bership in the American Psychoanalytic Association was holding steady at around three thousand. (A few thousand members also belonged to the American Psychological Association's Division 39—the division dedicated to psychoanalysis that had been founded in 1980.) As well, Freudian theory was proving, as it always had, how adaptable it was, used by a wide variety of mental health workers to explain the psycho-logical roots of hot issues like incest, alcoholism, obesity, and obsessive-compulsive disorder.[12]

Psychoanalysis had also found a role in the workplace, used by some human resources people to resolve personality conflicts between employ-ees. Psychologist and organization consultant Laura Huggler was one such HR professional treading the psychoanalytic waters in corporate

America in the late 1990s; her PIC methodology (psychoanalytically informed consultation) promised to solve particularly tough people problems in the office. By gaining "an in-depth understanding of the dynamics and underlying relationships among employees," Huggler explained in *HR Magazine*, she and her colleagues could diagnose snafus and figure out how to fix them. After a session with one CEO who was having trouble communicating with his board and management team, for example, Huggler determined that the man had been raised by an overcritical father, making him wary of authority figures as an adult. Huggler was able to help the CEO work though what sounded a lot like an Oedipal complex, a happy ending for all. PIC consultants were also working their Freudian magic in areas like crisis intervention, executive and managerial coaching, family-owned businesses, management-union relationships, and large-scale organizational changes, bringing companies' neuroses to the surface and trying to resolve them through psychoanalytic techniques. "Asking employees to lie down on the job (on the metaphorical couch, of course) may be just the prescription to restore harmony and enhance productivity," Huggler suggested. Her application of psychoanalysis was probably not something Freud imagined in Vienna a hundred years earlier.[13]

James Kaplan's dozen years in psychoanalysis was also something Freud would probably not have recognized or, at least, approved of. Kaplan's analytically trained psychologist was a far cry from a strict Freudian, he revealed in a 1997 article in *New York* magazine, the man not unlike the warm and fuzzy Judd Hirsch character in *Ordinary People*. Not only did Kaplan's analyst forego the couch and encourage his patients to use his first name—each departure from tradition anathema for hard-core Freudians—but he actually would serve refreshments (homemade cookies) to them; such hospitality crossed the line of familiarity and was thus strictly verboten. Kaplan, whose family was filled with therapists of various schools, was initially puzzled and a little disappointed that his analyst was not of the classical school, which would have demanded that the analyst remain remote and detached. "Analysis as an ordered, exhaustive excavation of the past—a one-sided outpouring of free association by me leading, by minute increments, to minor revelations—didn't seem to interest him," Kaplan recalled; the give and take of the sessions were not at all what he thought real psychoanalysis was about.[14]

Kaplan was careful to point out that his chatty analyst remained a Freudian at heart. "My therapist wasn't by any means rejecting Freud's monumental ideas but his austere tenet of analyst-as-mirror," he wrote. The self-importance, cultish nature, and monosyllabic ways of traditional psychoanalysis just did not fit his personality. Like many who rebelled against Freud in the belief that psychoanalysis had to be "humanized," Kaplan's analyst did not reject the method but rather forged a less rigid version of it that often worked better for both patient and therapist. The impossibility of the impossible profession also had not changed. "Melancholy, stress, and anxiety all still existed for me [but] I was somewhat better equipped to handle them," Kaplan remembered after deciding to call it quits. Precisely the same postanalysis audit typified the reports of others who went through classic Freudianism. Were the twelve years and one hundred thousand dollars' worth it, he reasonably asked? It was, he believed; the treatment served as a vehicle for him to "become more direct with [himself]." More than that, though, Kaplan perceptively recognized that he gained something much deeper, an outcome consistent with that of others who had spent years on the couch. "Another legacy [was] a heightened tendency to see all behavior in a psychoanalytic light, to feel that we're all driven by largely unconscious fantasies and desires, that our dreams define and rule us, and that every human presentation is only the tip of an iceberg," Kaplan eloquently explained. This altered way of seeing was perhaps the real and ultimate deliverable of psychoanalysis for those who knew it best.[15]

A Frenzy of Self-Examination

The desire by more people to become psychoanalysts was of course good news for training institutes specializing in the field. After some tough times in the early nineties, the William Alanson White Institute in New York was again thriving, with applications and admissions to the training center way up. Recognizing they needed more training, psychologists and psychiatrists in midcareer were coming to the institute, often blending their cognitive-behavioral backgrounds with a psychoanalytic approach. And with its new Center for the Study of Psychological Trauma, the institute offered training in treating issues related to HIV, eating disorders, substance abuse, and infertility, another way for practitioners to attract patients in the very competitive therapeutic marketplace of the late 1990s. Interestingly, when it came to patients, there seemed to be geographical differences in terms of choice of therapy, with the West Coast now more analytically inclined than the East. John Deri, a psychiatrist in analytic training in 1997, found that at least 80 percent of his patients in San Francisco chose psychoanalysis, their sessions (typically from two to four times a week) viewed as a wonderful means toward self-discovery. Now in New York, Deri's practice was mostly pharmacological, with Gothamites more interested in finding relief from depression and anxiety than cultivating the self. "In San Francisco, people worked on their character, their ability to have intimacy, and their ability to have curiosity and interest in the parts of themselves that thwarted their abilities to have those experiences," he nostalgically sighed, while New Yorkers' biggest issue seemed to be dealing with the feeling of not having enough time and money.[16]

On both coasts, there seemed to be a change in which way the therapeutic winds were blowing, if perhaps just a slight one. Edgar Levenson, a senior analyst with the William Alanson White Institute, was just one practitioner who sensed the makings of a backlash against psychotropics in the late nineties. More psychiatrists were recommending to their patients that they try to figure out why they had, say, agoraphobia or sexual impotency, rather than just medicate them for these conditions. Prozac or Zoloft did not help people get into or stay in relationships, after all, something that psychoanalysis often addressed head on. While certainly effective for most, drugs were a "blunt instrument," as one such psychiatrist put it, unable to deal with the subtleties of human internal experience or, more fundamentally, why people were unhappy.[17]

Even that most populist voice of the field *Psychology Today* took notice of the dusting off of the psychoanalytic couch. "Just when you thought psychoanalysis was dead, battered by managed care, Prozac, and neuroscience, word arrives that it is very much alive," wrote the editors of the magazine in 1998, with more patients in analysis and more analysts in training than in 1968. Interestingly, the detachment of psychoanalysis from medicine, which was heavily responsible for the surge in both training and as a therapy, seemed to also be giving it a boost in scholarly circles. Psychoanalytic theory was "positively thriving" in history and literature departments, the magazine found, with dozens of recent books and articles also raising the academic quotient of the field. "The idea of 'the story' and the idea of 'trauma' have leaped the bounds of psycho-analysis to become potent forces in the culture at large," said literature professor Judith Butler. She argued that the field's current focus on kinship and incest was particularly relevant. Arnold Cooper, a leading psychiatrist noted, "This is the headiest time in psychoanalysis since the early days of Freud's first discoveries." This was quite a claim given the field's salad days of the 1920s and 1950s.[18]

Journalists outside the field also found the overhaul of psychoanaly-sis a good story for general readers. "The threat of extinction has inspired a new vigor, a frenzy of self-examination and the urge to reach out and connect with the world at large," wrote Erica Goode for the *New York Times* in early 1999. Goode found the new and improved version of psychoanalysis "humbler, hipper, more communicative, and considerably more tolerant" than old-school Freudianism. No one knew of course whether the makeover would bring lots more patients into waiting rooms but, without making significant changes, it seemed certain that psychoanalysis as a therapy would eventually disappear. Just walking into an annual meeting of the American Psychoanalytic Association could tell you that the field had been transformed—the hundreds of men of a certain age wearing suits straight out of a funeral director's closet had been replaced by a decidedly younger, more female, and more ethnically diverse group of analysts. And rather than limit discussion to the intricacies of psychoanalytic technique, as in the old days, attendees were now discussing how issues such as race, adoption, homophobia, and sexual abuse related to their field. While the key fundamentals of psychoanalysis—the power of the unconscious and the importance of childhood experiences—remained the same, it was a much different story in terms of how they could be applied and by whom.[19]

Sandra Gail Hershberg of Bethesda, Maryland, was a good example of the fin de siècle psychoanalyst, believing her occupation was as rel-evant and valuable as ever. A graduate of Yale Medical School and the Washington Psychoanalytic Institute, Hershberg specialized in child and adolescent psychiatry and female development, tossing out the more clunky bits of Freudian theory (for example, penis envy) while retaining his ideas about the significance of the unconscious and existence of an inner life. "Freud frees us by enabling us to be aware of inner connections and see deeper motivations," she told *Washingtonian* magazine in 1998. Hershberg was convinced her techniques offered her patients relief from the conflicts that caused them suffering. "Once they've been able to peer into their innermost feelings, memories, and fantasies, they can make real choices," she explained, a blue-and-white pill or feel-good therapy (including now-all-the-rage yoga) simply unable to do that. Going further, Hershberg saw what took place between her and her patients as a "creative act" in which "something exceptional happens." The flurry of images and emotions that flew across the room in a typical session was every bit as interesting as a great work of art.[20]

Although psychoanalysis had unquestionably gone through a major transformation by the last summer of the twentieth century, at least one thing had remained relatively constant—shrinks' annual August pilgrimage to Cape Cod. Manhattan and Boston "psychs," as locals called them, had been coming to Wellfleet and nearby Touro, Massachusetts, for decades, drawn to the quaint towns on the Cape for their beauty and peacefulness (following in the tradition of Freud himself, who escaped Vienna in the summer for the country). In fact, in his 1981 novel *Free Association*, psychoanalyst Paul Buttenwieser located the chapter "Where Do Analysts Go in August?" in and around Wellfleet (describing his colleagues as "beached porpoises who could not stop talking shop even on vacation"). Almost twenty years later, the psychs seemed as chatty as ever. "Just go down the street and try to pass on the sidewalk—they block the sidewalk with their conversations!" remarked Elden Gray, an eighty-six-year-old who had summered in Wellfleet for fifty years, also taking note that "most all of them have chin whiskers."[21]

If some got their wish, the psychs—chin whiskers and all—would never come back to town after Labor Day. Psychoanalysis "utterly fails as a science," insisted Frederick Crews, the former true believer having come to the conclusion that Freud was, more than anything else, "an intellectual megalomaniac." Frank J. Sulloway, a neuroscientist and author of *Freud, Biologist of the Mind*, was even curter, feeling that psychoanalysis was, in a nutshell, "bad psychology."[22] Some of those who had not found happiness on the couch viewed the situation similarly but in more subtle terms. Adam Gopnik suggested in 1998 that the decline of psychoanalysis had much to do with our simply being "happier" and "busier," our patience for lengthy and mystical solutions to problems having worn thin. "Talking is out, taking is in," he felt. The routine taking of drugs had become the preferred treatment not just for anxiety and depression but for everything from hair loss to erectile dysfunction.[23]

Gopnik, a writer for the *New Yorker*, recalled his own six years on the couch with a traditional Park Avenue analyst, "Max Grosskurth," which began in 1990. Gopnik was a self-described "'creative' New York neurotic," suffering from "the usual mixture of hurt feelings, confusion, and incomprehension that comes to early-arriving writers when the thirties hit." Grosskurth's operative theory was that "creative" people often felt rage as a natural byproduct of their inherent narcissism. Grosskurth thus made no effort to cure his patients from their narcissism but rather helped them try to manage it, telling Gopnik and other intellectuals that "no one cared" about their petty resentments and jealousies because "people had troubles of their own." After initially resisting, Gopnik came to accept his analyst's view, but still felt he was getting the short end of the stick, therapeutically speaking. Late at night over bottles of red wine, he and his fellow "creative New York neurotics" would compare tales from the couch, finding that his friends had much more impressive stories to tell. One had discovered that his overprotectiveness stemmed from his mother's secret alcoholism, for example, while another had learned how his father's depression had shaped his own fears. A third had realized that his reluctance to publish his work was connected to his issues about having a child, this too way deeper than anything Gopnik took away. Despite feeling cheated by the experience ("Life has many worthwhile aspects" was the last thing Grosskurth had told him), Gopnik still felt his analyst was "inside me," his years of therapy leaving a definite and lasting impression.[24]

Hollywood on the Couch

As always, criticism of psychoanalysis did little or nothing to slow the public's fascination with it or its founder. Edward Dolnick's 1998 *Mad-*

ness on the Couch was a rather cruel attack on the field and Freud, with a number of other critics such as once-believer Crews making head-lines.[25] If anything, however, the public image of psychoanalysis was growing in the 1990s as more attention was given to the field's historical role within American popular culture. The intersection between psychoanalysis and another iconic national pastime, the movies, was an especially busy one as the twentieth century drew to a close. At the Anthology Film Archives in New York in 1990, for example, the National Psychological Association for Psychoanalysis sponsored a film and lecture series called "Camera on the Couch" in order to, as one of its members put it, "help demystify psychoanalysis and share our views of therapy." The event featured movies like the 1940 *His Girl Friday* (in which a psychoanalyst, complete with goatee, makes the lives of stars Cary Grant and Rosalind Russell more interesting), *The Snake Pit* (1948; starring Olivia de Havilland as a disturbed patient saved by analysis), *Whirlpool* (1949; with Gene Tierney as the kleptomaniac wife of a famous psychoanalyst), *The Three Faces of Eve* (1957; featuring Joanne Woodward as a woman with multiple personalities), and *Vertigo* (1958; starring James Stewart as a man who cures his fear of heights as only Alfred Hitchcock could have imagined it). (Mel Brooks's *High Anxiety*, with its "Institute for the Very, Very Nervous," was conspicuously absent, and unfortunately, the hilarious *What About Bob?*, in which Richard Dreyfus plays a psychiatrist who named his kids Sigmund and Anna, had not yet been released.)[26]

Some shrinks were more interested in psychoanalysis *of* movies than psychoanalysis *in* movies. The American Psychoanalytic Association had a film program, in fact, while the Washington DC–based Forum for the Psychoanalytic Study of Film was fully dedicated to reading movies through a Freudian lens. In 1986, Bruce H. Sklarew, a psychoanalyst from Chevy Chase, Maryland, teamed up with Gene Gordon, a teaching analyst at the Baltimore-Washington Institute of Psychoanalysis, to start the forum, with an impressive 350 members belonging to the group by 1991. Psychoanalysis-inspired directors Robert Altman, Ingmar Bergman, and Woody Allen were each adored by forum members, not surprisingly, but it was Bernardo Bertolucci who earned the top spot. "Psychoanalysis had added another lens to my camera," the Italian director once wrote,

his ten years in analysis infusing his films with a heavy dollop of Freudian themes. (Bertolucci even served on the forum board and had invited
Sklarew to the set of his film *The Sheltering Sky*.[27])

The connection between psychoanalysis and film was hardly random,
as those applying Lacanian theory (from French psychoanalyst Jacques
Lacan) to cinematic studies well knew. Movies were a lot like dreams,
Sklarew, like others, held, each often nonlinear and filled with odd imagery. The dreamer and filmgoer also had a lot in common, each entering
a passive, immobile, and often erotic state in which it was difficult to
tell what was real and what was fantasy. Constructing alternative narra-
tives of popular films was thus right up the alley of your typical movie-
loving psychoanalyst. Sklarew's reading of *Casablanca* was a tour de force
of cinematic psychoanalysis, for example, in which the co-chairman of
the forum argued that Rick was really bidding farewell to his parents
when telling Ilsa and Victor to get on the plane at the end of the film.
Victor was an idealized father figure but Rick decides not to pursue his
Oedipal yearning for Ilsa, Sklarew suggested, allowing him to begin
what could be a "beautiful friendship" with Captain Renault (Louie).
Sklarew actually had an even more Freudian take on the film but refused
to discuss it after being booed off of a stage in front of some diehard
Casablanca fans.[28]

The reason psychoanalysis was such a big part of films was also due
to the fact that psychoanalysis was frequently a big part of filmmakers'
real lives. The method had always gotten along well with Hollywood,
of course, with nearby Beverly Hills accounting for what was perhaps
the highest per capita ratio of psychoanalysts in the world. In their 1993
Hollywood on the Couch, Stephen Farber and Marc Green told the amazing story of Milton Wexler, the shrink to the stars for more than thirty
years. After training with the legendary Theodore Reik at Columbia and
serving in World War II, Wexler went to work at the Menninger Clinic,
specializing in treating schizophrenia. In 1951, Wexler set up shop in
Beverly Hills, rubbing (patched) elbows with Ralph Greenson, head of
the Los Angeles Psychoanalytic Institute. With patients including Marilyn Monroe, Frank Sinatra, and Vivien Leigh, Greenson's list of clients
read like a who's who of Hollywood, as did Wexler's after filling in for
him. (Wexler treated Monroe not long before she died in 1962.) Soon

Wexler was treating the likes of architect Frank Gehry and actress Jennifer Jones (introducing the latter to billionaire art collector and husband-to-be Norton Simon), his twice-a-week group therapy sessions *the* place for top industry types to see and be seen. At any given session in the 1970s, Farber and Green wrote, A-listers like Blake Edwards, Julie Andrews, Dudley Moore, and Sally Kellerman could be found trading confessions and, naturally, making deals on the side.[29]

No other filmmaker instantly brought psychoanalysis to mind more than Woody Allen. Because he often referenced psychoanalysis in his films, in fact, Allen's oeuvre could serve as a sort of barometer of the field. In his 1997 article for *New York* (cleverly titled "The Final Analysis"), Kaplan tracked the decades-long decline of psychoanalysis by how it was portrayed in Allen's films, an interesting measuring stick. In Allen's 1977 *Annie Hall*, "being analyzed was as integral to being a smart Manhattanite as martinis and evening clothes were in the movies of the thirties," Kaplan felt. In this period, the psychoanalyst was "a remote, godlike, intellectually overpowering figure, a direct avatar of Freud himself." (Alvy Singer, Allen's doppelganger in that film, had fifteen years and counting of analysis.) But two years later in *Manhattan*, Allen introduced a new and different kind of shrink, much like the cognitive variety currently in vogue, to contrast with his clearly orthodox Freudian analyst. Even if this sort of therapist was hardly godlike (at one point in that film, "Donny" called his client, Diane Keaton's character, at three in the morning weeping and, later, ends up in the hospital after a bad acid trip), it was clear that a new sheriff had come to town. By his 1996 *Everyone Says I Love You*, Allen had downgraded psychoanalysis to a minor plot point, used as a vehicle for the protagonist to discover what got Julia Roberts's character turned on.[30]

Woody Allen may no longer have been celebrating psychoanalysis but the biggest party for Freud in history was waiting in the wings. After three years of massaging, the controversial "Freud: Conflict and Culture"—the most comprehensive gathering of Freudiana ever brought together—finally opened at the Library of Congress in October 1998. Fifty anti-Freudians (Peter Swales and forty-nine others) had protested the exhibit when it was announced a few years earlier, forcing the library to focus more on the role of psychoanalysis in popular culture rather than whether or not it worked as a therapy. Just as in the beginning of the twentieth century, Freud was causing a major row, his theories no less incendiary than when they were first published. (One hundred and eighty pro-Freudian intellectuals from around the world signed a counter petition.) Manuscripts, photographs, and artifacts were also there to see, from his office doorplate ("Prof. Dr. Freud") to a prescription for cocaine. A stone's throw from Freud's desk chair and some of his handwritten notes were video monitors showing clips ranging from Homer Simpson's discourse on repression ("Doh"!) to a Woody Woodpecker cartoon to scenes from *Get Smart* and *The Bob Newhart Show*.[31]

The Library of Congress exhibit was truly a tour de force of psychoanalysis as portrayed in American popular culture. Visitors took in Freud's cinematic and televisual greatest hits, from Laurence Olivier's kiss on his "mother's" lips in the 1948 film *Hamlet* to Joanne Woodward's only-in-Hollywood epiphany ("I can remember, I can remember, I can remember!" she exclaims as a series of doors open in a long corridor) in the 1957 film *The Three Faces of Eve*. Despite having lived an epoch or two before Freud was born, Fred Flintstone also made an appearance, hypnotizing Wilma so she could bark like a dog. Candice Bergen too was there, her Murphy Brown character uttering the most famous thing Freud may or may not have ever said: "Sometimes a cigar is just a cigar." A film and video series accompanied the exhibit, the fifty-two works ranging from *How Old Is Ann?* (a one-minute movie from 1903 in which a man is driven mad by a puzzle in a newspaper) to a 1996 episode of *Frazier* (in which the Seattle radio host gets a dose of his own psychiatric medicine).[32]

Ironically, Woody Allen was conspicuously absent from the Library of Congress exhibit (he would not allow his work to be used), but a whole wall of *New Yorker* cartoons featuring the foibles of psychoanalysis seemed to make up for it. For those who wanted, literally, to read more about it, there was a companion book edited by the curator, Michael Roth; its eighteen essays ranged from the decidedly anti-Freudian to what were essentially intellectual fan letters. Coffee mugs (inscribed with "Freudian Sip") and pillowcases (inscribed with "Interpretation of Dreams") were sold in the library's gift shop, proof positive that psychoanalysis had gone pop. The show moved to the Jewish

Museum in New York, the Field Museum in Chicago, and the Skirball Cultural Center in Los Angeles. Apparently, Freud's tour of America on this occasion was much more successful than the one he had made ninety years previously.[33]

Despite the ruckus during its planning stages, critical response to the Library of Congress exhibition was favorable, nearly everyone agreeing that the show was about as fair a portrayal of the man and his ideas as possible. It "is timely and fascinating, rich in classical allusions and postmodern controversies that should spark an illuminating debate on the impact of Freud today, from Oedipus onward," enthused freelance journalist Suzanne Fields after a visit. Fields even thought that women in particular would like the exhibition. She proclaimed it a good example of the "double-edged sword of psychological determinism" that was now part of psychoanalytic theory when it came to issues of gender.[34]

Woody Allen may not have wanted his work shown at the Library of Congress but he was perfectly willing to be interviewed by a psychoanalyst before a live audience in 2002 (which was broadcast to ten Jewish community centers and two psychoanalytic societies across the country). "Have you ever actually been chased across a meadow by a breast in one of your dreams?" Gail Saltz asked Allen at the Ninety-second Street Y, referring to the funny, very loosely Freudian scene in *Sleeper*. Consistent with the frustration with analysis he often expressed in his films, Allen told Saltz, "I feel I have wasted a lot of time talking about dreams." He added, "On balance, I would say it has been helpful, but not as helpful as I had hoped and helpful in a way they didn't intend." Allen felt it had offered "no dramatic moments," "no insights," and "no tears." Allen also thought of himself as a disappointing patient, "like being in there with, like, a lawyer," as only he could describe it.[35] Six years later in an interview with *New York* magazine, Allen showed a deeper appreciation for psychoanalysis, crediting it for at least part of his success:

> People always tease me. The say, look at you, you went for so much psychoanalysis and you're so neurotic.... But I could also say to them, I've had a very productive life. I've worked very hard, I've never fallen prey to depression. I'm not sure I could have done all that without

being in psychoanalysis. People would say to me, oh, it's just a crutch. And I would say, yes. It's a crutch, and exactly what I need at this point in my life is a crutch.[36]

Other diehard New Yorkers recognized the value of psychoanalysis, one of them doing everything he could to ensure it would not become a historical relic. Michael Moskowitz, owner of Other Books and publisher of Other Press, was a man on a mission; his New York City bookstore and press were dedicated to keeping the field a going concern in the twenty-first century. Besides using his bookstore in a Chelsea brownstone as a gathering place for readings, lectures, and book parties ("Everybody knows how many psychoanalysts there are in New York City," he said), Moskowitz had published thirty titles in less than two years, hoping to get analysts and nonanalysts to talk to each other.[37] "We want to get scientists talking to humanists, clinicians to theorists, Lacanians to Freudians, and Americans to analysts all over the world," he told the *New York Times* in 2000. Moskowitz was upset at how psychoanalysts had historically cut themselves off from those who did not share their point of view.[38]

The forty-nine-year-old Moskowitz, who was an analyst himself, had also recently purchased *Psychoanalytic Quarterly*, the oldest independent journal on the subject, as well as the biggest British publisher of books about psychoanalysis. A group of European investment bankers who were interested in psychoanalysis were backing Moskowitz's operation. It was a curious situation given that the field was hardly what one would call an attractive business opportunity. However, Moskowitz and his angel investors were convinced that the rejuvenation the field was enjoying would continue and that its base would broaden along race, gender, and class lines. Opportunity knocked in South America as well, he thought, a journal for that market just the thing given how fast psychoanalysis seemed to be growing there. "Every hill town in Argentina has an analyst," he said only half-jokingly, the world his oyster when it came to psychoanalysis.[39] Psychoanalysis happened to also be thriving in France, Germany, Finland, and Canada (especially Quebec), in part because national health insurance covered the cost. With plentiful patients and psychoanalysts held in high regard, these countries seemed to be about a half-century behind the United States when it came to the talking cure, apparently resistant to the scientific and economic pressures within the American psychiatric community.[40]

Psychoanalysts may have felt a lot of pressure from the American psychiatric community but it would be a television show—*The Sopranos*—that brought them all together like one big happy family. Just about every member of the mental health community with premium cable watched the hit Sunday night HBO show with keen interest since it began airing in 1998. By the end of the third season, in May 2001, the show had become must-see-TV for psychologists and psychiatrists, especially the psychoanalytically inclined. "It's the best representation of the work we do that has ever been in film or on television," declared Philip Ringstrom, an analyst at the Institute of Contemporary Psychoanalysis in Los Angeles. Like his colleagues, Ringstrom was impressed and rather amazed that a television show could accurately (more or less) capture the therapeutic experience. In 2000, in fact, two of the show's writers received an award from the Western Regional Psychoanalytic Association for their depiction of Tony Soprano's therapy sessions, a rare case in which practitioners acknowledged an artistic representation of their field. Lorraine Braco, the actress who played Dr. Melfi, was also given an award at a special session of the American Psychoanalytic Association the following year. ("What, are they crazy?" she reportedly asked when she learned of the honor, later telling the audience, "I am *so* not Dr. Melfi."[41]) As well, Ringstrom had recently given a presentation on some of the therapeutic aspects of *The Sopranos* before a packed house of analysts at the American Psychological Association and was one of four shrinks regularly swapping insights after each episode of the show on *Slate*, the online magazine.[42]

Why were real-life psychoanalysts so obsessed with and compulsive about watching and discussing *The Sopranos*? "It's like a gift," explained Emmanuel Kaftal, a supervisor in the postdoctoral program in psychoanalysis at NYU. Kaftal was grateful for the show's portrayal of a psychologically complex character with a neurosis stemming from childhood trauma. Besides the opportunity to engage in "armchair analysis," the show was a public relations dream come true for the field, helping revive interest in talk therapy. That Melfi was a woman and Tony Soprano not exactly the hysterical female patient of mythology was icing on the cake, a sixty-minute-a-week advertisement for the more modern version of psychoanalysis that leaders of the field desperately wanted Americans to see. In a rather odd instance of life imitating art, Glenn Gabbard was using tapes of the show to teach psychiatry residents at the Menninger Clinic, considering Melfi's handling of Soprano's "erotic transference" to be "masterful." Patients too were watching the show, of course, often referencing the mob boss's fictional therapy sessions in their own real ones (and wondering why their analyst did not volunteer the same kind of direct, sharp-as-a-tack advice).[43]

Lifting the Veil

Perhaps inspired by Dr. Melfi's success with a particularly tough case, American psychoanalysts were determined to continue reinventing themselves. If only to survive, analysts were catching up to the rest of the mental health world, adopting a far more flexible attitude and approach. Some psychoanalysts were holding sessions by videophone and by e-mail, for example, while others were consulting to corporations and—the horror!—pursuing sports psychology, all things that a decade earlier someone in their field would not and could not have thought of doing. The public relations campaign the American Psychoanalytic Association had begun in 1998 also seemed to be paying off; the field continued to get more press coverage or, at least, more positive press coverage. The outside public relations consultant brought in also gave analysts media training so that answers to journalists' questions were "on message," a wise move given many shrinks' taciturn ways. ("We're very good at listening and terrible about talking about these processes," admitted Glenn Good, chairman of the organization's Subcommittee on Strategic Marketing.) Figuring out exactly what that message should be remained an issue, leading the American Psychoanalytic Association to bring in a marketing research consultant. Who was the typical patient in 2000? Why did he or she choose psychoanalysis? Members of the association were asked to provide answers to these critical questions via focus groups and surveys in order to better package psychoanalysis to the American consumer.[44]

Not surprisingly, just mentioning the word "marketing" to a fair share of psychoanalysts would elicit groans (if not primal screams). The idea of aggressively selling the method to the masses like breakfast cereal or soap was entirely contrary to the traditional restraint and dignity of the field. (This despite the fact that Freud often gave public lectures to disseminate his theories beyond his Viennese psychiatric circle.) The American Psychoanalytic Association was determined to promote psychoanalysis to the public, however, even putting an advice column, "Ask a Psychoanalyst," on its website (www.apsa.org). As with almost all businesses, the Internet was proving to be a revolutionary way to communicate with consumers. Interestingly, those analysts choosing to hold sessions via e-mail were finding the experience to be not that different from those in the real world; in fact, because patient and analyst were not in the same room, virtual analysis was even more anonymous than talk therapy, allowing some people to open up in a way they otherwise could not. "Patients have sent me thoughts that they haven't been able to convey in a session," said Kerry Sulkowicz, a Manhattan analyst. Sulkowicz was a fan of the new technology but still believed that there was no substitute for the nonverbal insights to be gleaned from observing a patient on the couch or in a chair.[45]

Some patients were no doubt also using e-mail to tell their analysts they had decided to end their treatment. "Termination," as it was generally known, was a particularly thorny subject, as emotional an issue as any that would come up during a session. Termination was the planned ending of analysis, something quite different from a patient suddenly quitting or an analyst stopping therapy because he or she believed it was unsuccessful. If and when their analysis should end was something every patient had to ask himself or herself at some point, and the answer was typically not as clear-cut as one would like. In her 2001 article, "Sorry, Your Time Is Not Up," in *New York*, Jennifer Senior explored the contentious issue of termination, wondering why analysts inevitably seemed to become "our jailers." A host of issues—progress, analyzability, efficacy, limitations, and, of course, time and money—came into play, the most maddening of all perhaps "commitment." Throughout the twentieth century, the median length of psychoanalytic treatment had gotten longer and longer, making the decision to terminate or not to terminate (yes, that is the question) that much more weighty. After ignoring the elephant in the room for decades, practitioners were now taking the matter seriously, with literature in the field and coursework at training institutes addressing its when, why, and how. Discussing the issue with one's analyst, sometimes over the course of years, was not unusual, though he or she often labeled a patient's decision to terminate "resistance," "passive aggression," or some other psychoanalytic form of acting out. Some patients never returned to the couch after their shrinks' August vacation while others simply went out for a smoke and never came back—a clear breach of the unofficial analytic contract.[46]

Stephen K. Firestein, professor of clinical psychiatry at New York University, even wrote a book on the subject, *Termination in Psychoanalysis*, believing analysis to be a nonstop "contest between the couch and the door." "Obviously, you'll only continue if the couch wins out," he thought. This became a raging battle for many if not most patients unsure whether they should invest more of themselves in the process. Logically, termination made sense when the patient felt physically and/ or emotionally "better," but it was rarely this neat and clean. Firestein suggested that patients who were considering terminating analysis ask themselves, "Can I accept, for the balance of my life, to feel, act, and be the way I am this afternoon?" with an answer of no cause enough to head back toward the couch rather than through the door. If the answer was maybe, some analysts recommended that their patient see another analyst (a "meta-analyst") who would help evaluate the relationship and then made a recommendation.[47]

Whether making the decision on their own or on advice from an expert in such things, there was no doubt that patients had terminated in droves over the last few decades. Perhaps most telling of the decline of psychoanalysis as a therapy over the past half-century was the fact that there were about as many Americans in full treatment in 2003 (five thousand) as there were cognitive therapists. Freud was now "a poor, eccentric cousin on the fringes of psychotherapeutic practice," wrote Lev Grossman that year in *Time*. There was more likely to be a patient on a couch in a *New Yorker* cartoon than in real life. Taking an "If you can't beat 'em, join 'em" approach, many shrinks were continuing to adapt cognitive techniques to their psychoanalytic model, sitting face-to-face with their patients and, if the situation called for such, actually talking with them. Some were prescribing psychotropics to their patients to go along with analysis, others offering psychodynamic treatment to cut sessions down to one or two a week. For the relatively few remaining believers in old-school analysis, however, there was, as the Porsche slogan went, no substitute. "It's allowed me to figure out some pretty basic things about myself and why certain situations keep coming up," said a thirtysomething woman from Brooklyn. She described her four years and counting in classical analysis as "one of the best decisions I ever made."[48]

Grossman too recognized the value psychoanalysis had and would continue to have for those willing to invest the time and money required. "Whatever else may have changed, the intellectual adventure of psycho-analysis, the delving into the depths, is still part of the Freudian tradition, and that's not going to disappear," he thought. No magic pill or cognitive coach could match the sheer intensity of the method.[49] In her *Why Psychoanalysis?*, Elisabeth Roudinesco, a French psychoanalyst, also made a strong case for the talking cure. She argued that the wholesale prescrib-ing of psychotropics without finding the cause of psychic distress was a big part of why the West had become, in her words, a "Depressive Society." Reducing emotions (and even creativity) to biology was a big mistake, she felt. The subjectivity of psychoanalysis was something that science could never match, even if the latter was clearly winning the day.[50]

Patients recognized this better than anyone. Like the patient from Brooklyn, Rachel H., another thirtysomething New Yorker, was not about to give up the couch despite all the obvious reasons to do so. "Don't you think that's *so* last century?" asked one of Rachel's friends, urging her to join the Prozac club, do yoga, or just get the hell out of the city to heal whatever ailed her. After spending six years in, and sixty thousand dollars on, psychoanalysis, however, Rachel was pleased with how her personality had evolved, considering herself a more responsible and compassionate person than before she entered treatment. "It's about lifting the veil, seeing relationships and seeing yourself, so that you can begin to make choices that will not lock you into an unhappy future and an unhappy life," she explained to a reporter in 2003 in the *New York Times*. For Rachel, the vision to be gained through analysis was simply unavailable anywhere else. Like Rachel, Patrick Cody, a forty-year-old, ten-year veteran of psychoanalysis from Washington DC, consciously chose the couch over chemistry: "I had this really strong conviction that my problems were psychological, and I wanted to deal with them psychologically." Cody believed, in true Freudian fashion, that his emotional difficulties were rooted in his unconscious. Some cognitive therapy and pill-popping dropouts also were finding that only psychoanalysis was able to help them establish intimate relationships or avoid destructive behavior patterns, reason enough to buck the psychiatric trend.[51]

Even those with many years of cognitive therapy found the need to "upgrade" to psychoanalysis after the top layers of emotions were peeled away. Following a dozen years of weekly cognitive sessions, for example, a Miami woman found herself still shackled with self-doubt, guilt, and remorse. Her analytically trained psychologist shifted the treatment modality to psychoanalysis after determining that these feelings were rooted in childhood, a wise move given the ultimate outcome. "Psychoanalysis is rigorous and tedious work; I was on the couch four times a week for five years," she later explained to me, but was happy to say that it was all worth it. "At the age of fifty-three I was finally able to step into my full potential; that has brought me much happiness," the woman beamed, going on to earn a doctorate and become a healing arts professional.[52]

With a single session with a Park Avenue analyst now costing more than two hundred dollars, one better have had a darn good reason to choose classic psychoanalysis over cheaper and faster alternatives. (Many patients with health insurance in once-a-week psychoanalytic therapy had a much more affordable copayment of anywhere from ten to forty dollars.) In a survey of 342 analysts, Norman Doidge of the University of Toronto found that was precisely the case, with most of their patients suffering from chronic anxiety, depression, or some other significant psychiatric disorder. The general public, however, was now basically clueless when it came to the potential benefits of psychoanalysis. Focus groups conducted by the American Psychoanalytic Association in 2000 revealed that most Americans had heard of Sigmund Freud and psychoanalysis but, when asked to describe the latter, answered that it "took a long time" and "involved a couch," as the *New York Times* reported. Membership in the association was now 3,500 (up five hundred in seven years) but 20 percent of them were in New York, skewing the field decidedly toward Gotham (despite San Franciscans' leanings toward psychoanalysis). Much more concerning, the average age of a member was sixty-two, not boding well at all for what was still the largest and most prestigious organization in the field.[53] Raising the average somewhat was Richard E. Cheney (not the ex–vice president), who became a psychoanalyst after a long career as head of Hill and Knowlton, one of the country's biggest public relations firms. Cheney started his second career at age seventy-one in 1994 and, a decade later, was still pursuing his real passion. "You live 150 years because you live through other people's lives, and you can really help," he said in 2003, believing that he had grown far more personally as an analyst than he had as a business executive.[54]

Thankfully, others long excluded from having that opportunity were finally having it. Throughout its history in the United States, the field had considered homosexuality an illness (a "developmental arrest" of the Oedipal complex), and homosexuals unfit to be psychoanalysts. (Freud's basic idea was that people start out as bisexual but homosexuals did not develop beyond a certain point, remaining attracted to the same sex.) The American Psychiatric Association removed homosexuality from its list of mental disorders in 1973, though some psychoanalysts continued to view it as a "perversion" or "character disorder" that could be cured. But in 1991, the American Psychoanalytic Association stopped its training institutes from keeping gays out, a clear sign of the changing attitude within the field (and in American culture as a whole). And in 2004, acknowledging the field's long history of homophobia, that association presented a forum called "Homophobia: Analysis of a 'Permissible' Prejudice" at its annual meeting. (Barney Frank, the gay congressman from Massachusetts, was invited to speak on the matter.) The organization was now also officially in favor of same-sex marriage, asking states not to interfere with gay couples' wishes. While a small portion of the nation's 3,200 American Psychoanalytic Association members disapproved of the direction their organization had taken (one considered it a "gay political agenda"), most no longer viewed homosexuality as a pathology that could be helped by therapy. Freud, ironically, was tolerant of homosexuality (It "is assuredly no advantage but ... it cannot be classified as an illness," he wrote in 1921), but American psychoanalysts were convinced it was a neurosis, a second opinion almost a century in the making.[55]

Isn't It Obvious?

A more diverse group of practitioners was certainly great news but one more thing was needed for the reformation of psychoanalysis to be complete: the long awaited transformation of the field from an art into a science. Finally, after many false starts, research was providing some evidence that there was some objectivity to the field's famous subjectivity. "Psychoanalysis is having a very good day today," wrote Norman Doidge for *Maclean's* in 2006, citing a recent German study showing that 80 percent of patients in analysis had improved significantly. Not only that, but these patients made more progress than those in shorter-term treatments, rebutting those who claimed that ten sessions was more than enough to get someone back on track. A different study from Sweden showed similar results, another victory for psychoanalysis.[56] Interestingly, a study conducted by Peter Fonagy of University College in London showed that patients with borderline personality disorder not only improved significantly while in analysis but continued to make progress over the next eighteen months after their treatment ended. The ability to deal with new problems as they arose pointed to the in-depth nature of psychoanalysis, one could argue, something that perhaps could not be matched by more quick-fix approaches.[57]

Such evidence suggesting that psychoanalysis did indeed work was obviously wonderful news for practitioners, but something even more exciting was emerging. Freud's theory of the unconscious, on the 150th anniversary of his birth, was turning out to be more than just a theory, with some neuroscientists supporting his assertion that much of our thinking is beyond our awareness. Freud was, after all, a neuroscientist before turning to psychology, correctly believing that the science of the brain was not yet advanced enough to explain the workings of the mind. But now, brain-scanning techniques were showing that many of Freud's ideas could very well be correct, with a whole new discipline—neuro-psychoanalysis—springing up to show just that. The brain was much more than a chemistry set, folks like Nobel Prize winner Eric Kandel and Oliver Sacks maintained, leading them and other top neuroscientists to put psychoanalysis to the test. Kandel and his colleagues at Columbia found that emotions can indeed register in the unconscious but not the conscious, just what Freud had argued in the 1890s.[58] Kandel's 2005 *Psychiatry, Psychoanalysis, and the New Biology of Mind* and *In Search of Memory* of the following year were each attempts to bring together the distant lands of neuroscience and psychology, with psychoanalysis serving as a useful bridge. That much of what we did was unconscious, that dreams had psychological meaning, that infants were thinking individuals, and that important insights could come from talking (and listening) were not just theories for Kandel but keys to unlocking the workings of the human mind and, thus, vital links between psychoanalysis and neuroscience.[59]

As well, PET scans done by researchers at the National Institutes of Health were revealing that lots of activity occurred in the id-like limbic part of the brain but not very much in the ego-like prefrontal cortex while one dreamt; these results too suggesting the presence (and power) of unconscious thought. Christopher Badcock, a teacher at the London School of Economics (and pupil of Anna Freud), also suggested there may be a biological underpinning to Freudian psychoanalysis, specifically that the very structure of the human brain might be the result of a conflict between paternal and maternal genes.[60] Finally, recent research was showing that early childhood trauma could negatively impact the development of the brain, meaning that events of the distant past could play an important cognitive role even if we did not remember them. With the wind behind the sails of the biology of psychoanalysis, major grant money was going toward determining whether new techniques, such as functional magnetic resonance imaging (fMRI) scans, could reveal the results of psychotherapy. Thus technology continued to supply other ways of finding connections between the brain and mind, just as Freud had imagined.[61]

Ironically, just as the scientific quotient of psychoanalysis was being raised, its philosophical and spiritual dimensions were also increasingly recognized. Psychoanalysis has played a role in the most recent "self-discovery" trend, in which those on some kind of spiritual quest (most visibly celebrities like Richard Gere and Madonna) have looked to "exotic" belief systems like Buddhism or the Kabbalah for answers to the big questions of life. Despite famously presenting God as an "illusion," Freud embedded ideas and language from Jewish texts into his own works, making psychoanalysis a lot more spiritual than one might think. The Kabbalah shares much with psychoanalysis, in fact, each focused on the existence and relationship between an inner world and outer world and the nature of reality. Kabbalah's "convoluted, spiralic way of looking at the inner workings of the mystical influence upon man's psyche, emotions, and actions is parallel in the psychoanalytic philosophical understanding," argued Stanley Schneider and Joseph H. Berke in a 2005 article in the journal *Midstream*. This could not be a coincidence given Freud's religious background. "Kabbalah and psychoanalysis intersect and parallel one another in the innermost reaches of the soul," these two psychoanalysts concluded. Freud's tired old theories are considerably more current (and cool) than many realize.[62]

The "very good days" that psychoanalysis has enjoyed in recent years can be seen in other ways than its greater status in both science and spirituality. There were forty or so psychoanalytic training institutes in America in 2006, not too shabby a number for a field many thought was being put out to pasture. There were 3,400 members of the American Psychoanalytic Association, 1,500 members of the National Association for the Advancement of Psychoanalysis, and more than 4,000 members of the American Psychological Association's Division 39, small change compared to the number of psychiatrists and psychologists, but more than there used to be. More telling than these numbers is that Freud's essential idea of repression—that we lead conflicted lives, as Jonathan Lear, has described it—lives on. K. Lynne Moritz, president of the American Psychoanalytic Association in 2006, insisted that Freud continues to "help us find deep meanings and motivations," something brief therapies and medications will never be able to provide. Referring to yet another "unique selling proposition" that the psychoanalytic brand has to offer, Glen Gabbard, now professor of psychiatry at Baylor College of Medicine, explained that some people "want the experience of being listened to and understood, to search for a truth about themselves." Most important is how patients describe the value of still time-consuming and expensive psychoanalysis. "It makes you examine your life, retell your life, to understand where your attitudes, your beliefs and behaviors come from," said one such patient, a married woman in her forties. This woman attested that she had found more happiness by answering the tough questions asked by her analyst.[63]

Many of these same benefits are being realized through psychoanalytic therapy (or psychology), the newer version of psychoanalysis that requires less of an investment in both time and money. Psychoanalytic therapy is "not your parents' psychoanalysis," declared Jamie Chamberlin of the American Psychological Association's *Monitor* in 2005. Its practitioners are doing a lot to broaden the reach of psychoanalytic thought and counter the decades-long criticism that the field is elitist. Psychoanalytic therapists, the majority of them members of Division 39, are now offering their services (often pro bono) to the poor and homeless, not something that most psychoanalysts of the past would have done. Deborah Luepnitz, a Philadelphia psychoanalytic psychologist and member of Division 39, is helping people who would otherwise have no access to psychoanalysis. "To be human is to struggle with unconscious conflicts, and that includes people who live on the corner by the convenience store," she said. Other members had worked with firefighters and families involved in 9/11 as well as Iraq war veterans. Through such efforts, the field was gradually losing its image as an austere and formal therapy exclusively for the upper class, and gaining respect for its social consciousness. Because of the influx of psychologists that had begun in the 1980s, psychoanalysis itself was changing, adopting more of a two-person, dynamic process that midcentury analysts might not recognize.[64]

Due largely to psychoanalytic therapy, psychoanalysis appears to have more very good days ahead, something that would have been difficult to predict twenty-five years ago. There were about a dozen psychoanalytic training schools in New York City alone in 2007, a new generation of shrinks-to-be eager to carry on (and challenge) the traditions of the talking cure. Andrew Gerber, a neuroscientist and analyst in training at Columbia University College of Physicians and Surgeons, was a great example of the state of the field in the early twenty-first century, working with his mentor to prove Freud's theories were more than interesting philosophy or great literature. Gerber was particularly interested in the biological component of transference (which he defined as the patient's assignment of feelings about important people in his or her life to the analyst), trying to capture on brain scans where that process took place. "Cognitive neuroscientists and psychoanalysts are ready to talk," said the thirty-four-year-old Gerber, sharing his preliminary findings at the annual meeting of the American Psychoanalytic Association. Validating psychoanalysis through science remains as important as ever, the only real way to respond to skeptics and remake the field into a competitive therapy.[65]

Meanwhile, at the oldest and most traditional of all training centers in the United States, the New York Psychoanalytic Society and Institute, classes are being filled again, another sign of the rebirth of the field. Through new programs, an expanded curriculum, and free discussions for the public by the likes of musician Laurie Anderson and writer Rick Moody, the institute is generating fresh interest in the field and, as it had done for almost a century, demonstrating that Freud was about much more than sex. With one 185 members and 31 analysts in training, the institute is a shadow of what it had been in its prime but it has survived and is growing—a feat many critics said would never happen.[66] The case of Gary Shteyngart, one of America's most popular and successful young writers, nicely illustrates why psychoanalysis is "the idea that wouldn't die," as Molly Knight Raskin of *Psychology Today* put it in 2011. Often depressed, Shteyngart, who came to the United States from Russia with his parents as a child, sought out psychoanalysis after concluding that his personality needed a thorough reexamination and perhaps overhaul. "Other forms of therapy do not explore and rewire the personality to the same extent," he told Raskin. The method's depth and complexity may explain its staying power. "Exploring our personal narrative—the modus operandi of psychoanalysis, the therapy—helps us to understand why we do what we do," Raskin agreed, finding meaning in certain behaviors the best way to change them, if necessary.[67]

Patients like Matthew von Unwerth were also good illustrations of why people still wanted to become psychoanalysts fifty or so years after the field peaked in popularity. Four times a week for the past ten years, the thirty-six-year-old von Unwerth had spent forty-five minutes on the couch, spilling his feelings, dreams, and stories to his analyst as part of what could perhaps be a lifelong intellectual journey. Von Unwerth was so smitten with analysis, in fact, that he decided to go to the other side of the couch, enrolling at the Institute for Psychoanalytic Training and Research in Manhattan. "Analysis becomes the center of a patient's life, a way of building profound relationships," he told *Newsday*. Von Unwerth believed that by learning an alternative telling of one's life story one gained "a do-over childhood." With no graduate degree, von Unwerth was also pursuing a master's degree in social work in order to meet the state's licensing requirement for therapists. But, as he made clear, it was all worth it. "In time, whatever you want to be, you become more of it," he said of analysis; the realization of self—something so many before him had similarly sought—is the main path to a better life.[68]

Psychoanalysis is also very much alive and well in university humanities and social science departments like literature, film, and history although, ironically, psychology departments consider it more like an archeological artifact. Rather than view psychoanalysis as "an ongoing movement and a living, evolving process," as the American Psychoanalytic Association reported in the *American Journal of Psychiatry* in 2008, psychology departments and textbooks present it as "desiccated and dead," the subject deemed no longer relevant for today's students. Of the 1,175 courses at 150 universities that referenced psychoanalysis, the association was understandably disturbed to find that 86 percent were outside of psychology departments. Because of the usual criticism—not enough scientific grounding, the wonders of neuroscience, and the misfit with managed care policies—most academics in psychology feel psychoanalysis is a marginalized field well outside mainstream thought. In some other departments, Freud and his theories are being welcomed with open arms, a useful platform for examining issues in everything from gender studies to postmodernism to queer theory. "American clinical psychoanalysis, and analysis as represented in academe, are at risk to become two ships that pass in the night," the American Psychoanalytic Association report read. The organization was not at all pleased at how the field was being treated by its own kind.[69]

Maybe one reason why university psychology departments do not teach psychoanalysis to students is that they (correctly) assume they already know the material. In his "Intellectual Heritage" course, Noah Shusterman, a lecturer at Temple University, found to his surprise that his undergraduate students not only easily grasped Freud's model of psychoanalytical therapy but assumed it was valid. Born in the late 1980s, the students were more familiar with the concept of making unconscious desires conscious in order to treat neuroses than they were with, say, the television show *M*A*S*H*. Freud's view of the way the human mind worked was considered as accurate as any, his Generation Y students felt. "In some ways they think that even spending time on the matter is somewhat odd because, well, isn't it obvious?" he wrote in the *Chronicle of Higher Education* in 2007. It was a profound sign of how entrenched psychoanalysis remains in society, and an indication that the method will continue to be an integral part of the American experience.[70]

What is the future of psychoanalysis in America? How will it continue to evolve? What will the next paradigm be like? Good questions all. But the larger, more important question is whether Americans will ever get over their need for psychoanalysis and other forms of therapy. Will we ever become happy, self-actualized human beings, eliminating the need for shrinks (or religion, one might ask)? Any history of psychotherapy begs the question of why many Americans have been less than happy, if not miserable, in their land of milk and honey (and despite having access to a billion-dollar mental health system). On the surface, at least, it appears that the "cult of the self" has proved to be an unsatisfying, spiritually bankrupt belief system, with even the best psychoanalyst in town unable to fully resolve that elephant in the room. A way of life predicated on consumer capitalism just does not offer what some of us need in order to become "complete," it seems, with even the most intensive "voyage of inward discovery" not addressing this more fundamental issue. In fact, while it has no doubt helped many people in serious distress, psychoanalysis and other forms of psychiatry have served to amplify the focus on ourselves, possibly doing a disservice to individuals and to American society as a whole.

Until we deal with this meta-issue, we are left with how best to heal our psychic wounds. Red flags definitely appear on the horizon of psychoanalysis in this regard. Today's more-competitive-than-ever therapeutic marketplace does not favor what was once considered the "golden craft," the head start it enjoyed more of a liability than an advantage. Once a true cultural phenomenon, a shock to our system, the "voodoo religion" is now more like a comfortable pair of shoes, part of the establishment rather than the avant-garde. Its celebrity aura and postwar glamour as dated as the Rat Pack, psychoanalysis has to survive on its wits. "America's leading hobby" is now more or less just another option in the tsunami of health care choices. Forged during a much different time and place, psychoanalysis remains, as critics have said for years, increasingly irrelevant and anachronistic as attitudes and values have changed. Robert Coles, a practicing psychologist and professor of psychology at Harvard, for example, has observed that Freud's patients were reluctant to share their secret thoughts about sexuality, the mores of the day making it nearly impossible for them to confront such taboo feelings on a conscious level. Today, many if not most Americans have no problem whatsoever revealing the most intimate details, having been exposed to, if not immersed in, our sexualized media landscape and kiss-and-tell culture. Does this fundamental distinction take a good part of the wind out of the sails of psychoanalysis? Or do we simply repress other things (Coles suggests we do, especially envy), making psychoanalysis sort of a whack-a-mole theory in which a new neurosis will pop up if another disappears.[1]

Despite the ongoing debate over the relevance of psychoanalysis, and given the ubiquity of the practice within American and, increasingly, global culture, it seems clear that there will be a future for psychiatry's "poor, eccentric cousin," something that was not always so clear. A Google search on "Freud" in December 2012 delivered about fifty-one million hits, a crude but compelling measure of the man's sheer presence across the cultural landscape. As well, the Freud archive at the Library of Congress, as impenetrable as Fort Knox for decades, has been opened up to scholars, this too boding well for the future of the field. And as neuroscientists continue to find links between the brain and psychoanalysis, the field is gaining some legitimacy among its many skeptics and critics. "New advances in neuroscience and technology are revealing the neurobiology of the dynamic unconscious that Freud, Janet, and others envisioned," wrote Heather A. Berlin and Christof Koch in *Scientific American Mind* in 2009. Berlin, assistant professor of psychiatry at the Mount Sinai School of Medicine, and Koch, a professor of cognitive and behavioral biology at Cal Tech, suggested that the psychoanalytic defense mechanisms of suppression and dissociation were being revived and reconceptualized as fMRI scans were used to measure brain activity. This kind of research would appear to be a very good thing for the field.[2]

In a 2010 article for *American Psychologist*, Jonathan Shedler offered empirical evidence that supported the efficacy of psychodynamic therapy (or psychoanalytic psychotherapy, the less "intense" form of psychoanalysis). Psychodynamic therapy has suffered from a belief that it lacks scientific evidence or is less effective than other forms of treatment, this due in large part to the past sins of psychoanalysis (condescension towards nonphysicians, most notably). "The scientific evidence tells a different story," Shedler, a psychologist at the University of Colorado School of Medicine, claimed. Shedler produced findings from a variety of sources indicating that psychodynamic therapy does indeed work. Patients who received this type of therapy tended not only to maintain their gains but continued to improve over time, contradicting popular expectations of the method. Shedler went even further, citing evidence showing that other effective therapies have been borrowing from psychodynamic theory and practice, lending more support for psychoanalytic-based thought.[3] Ironically, although it has strived for scientific legitimacy to this very day, psychoanalysis in some respects undermined the discourse of science through its populist appeal and portrayal in the mass media. Did it matter that something so powerful be accepted as genuine science? one could reasonably ask at any point in the field's history. Freud's almost godlike status in the no man's land between philosophy and medicine is in fact a retort to our cultural obsession with "hard evidence" and "solid proof."

There is no doubt that notices of the passing of prominent psychoanalysts can frequently be found in the obituary section of the *New York Times*; the generation of postwar practitioners, after all, is literally a dying breed. But in the decade since Michael Gazzaniga pronounced, "Psychology itself is dead" in his 1998 book *The Mind's Past*—the mind sciences allegedly taken over by evolutionary biology, cognitive science, neuroscience, psychophysics, and other disciplines—psychoanalysis has shown definite signs of life.[4] In 2008, for example, *Business Week* ran a semi-regular "Analyze This" column written by Kerry Sulkowicz, a psychoanalyst who advises CEOs on psychological aspects of business.[5] Psychoanalysts like Sulkowicz were strongly committed to the field, the findings of a 2009 survey showed. Most of the 138 alumni of the Chicago Institute for Psychoanalysis surveyed were still practicing, teaching, and writing fifteen years after graduating, according to the study reported in *Clinical Psychiatry News*, with analysts averaging two patients each of four-times-per-week analysis.[6] That the *New York Times* that year chose to publish a set of photos of psychoanalysts in their offices (also under the title "Analyze This," a reference to the 1999 movie starring Billy Crystal and Robert DeNiro) suggested that the field remained of some curiosity to readers, even if the images were not unlike watching paint dry.[7]

Much more dramatic has been *In Treatment*, the HBO series starring Gabriel Byrne as psychoanalyst Paul Weston. Adapted from a popular Israeli series, *In Treatment* was a hit as soon as it first aired in 2008, with viewers sucked into the individual therapy session featured in every show. That Weston has some demons of his own adds to the drama, the sessions with his own shrink, played by Dianne Wiest, rivaling those between the two analysts in *The Sopranos* in intensity (and making one wonder about HBO's apparent fixation with therapy). "Stepping inside the tangled mind of a man who counsels others for a living, *In Treatment* renders an intricate portrayal of the experts we rely on for perspective," the show's website tells fans, the series "bring[ing] dynamic focus to a staple of modern society—the psychotherapy session." Hype for sure, but the success of the show illustrates that two people talking in a room can be compelling entertainment, pretty incredible given that anything is now possible on the screen via computer-generated imagery.[8] And like *The Sopranos*, *In Treatment* has been embraced by the psychoanalytic community, used by shrinks (and patients) to discuss everything from professional practices to countertransference.[9]

While pop culture is breathing new life into psychoanalysis, real-life practitioners are actively energizing the field through partnerships and collaborations, helping to keep it relevant and reach audiences it otherwise would not. For decades now, practitioners of Zen Buddhism and psychoanalysis have been comparing notes: the fifth-century Chinese spiritual technique for realizing enlightenment has been bringing light to the darkness of the theory and therapy forged in late nineteenth-century Vienna. The relational school of psychoanalysis that emerged in the 1980s fit especially well with Zen Buddhism (each positing that suffering comes from isolation), with the unlikely couple's relationship getting closer at a conference in 1994 at the Harvard Club in New York.

Since then, quite a few analysts have incorporated meditation and other Buddhist ideas and practices into their work, this blending of East and West offering patients a potent existential combination of understanding the past while focusing on the present.[10] "These two radically different approaches to wellness have begun to intersect with new levels of respect and curiosity," noted Pilar Jennings in her *Mixing Minds: The Power of Relationship in Psychoanalysis and Buddhism*. In Jennings's view, Zen Buddhism's more universal view of human struggle nicely complements the self-centric process of psychoanalysis.[11]

Not surprisingly, psychoanalysis and psychodynamic psychotherapy are slowly but steadily building a following in China as the taboo of discussing personal worries and feelings gradually breaks down and as a new affluent class rapidly expands. Elise Snyder, one of a number of American analysts introducing the method to the Chinese, declares, "They're in love with psychoanalysis the way people my age were in love with it in New York in the fifties and sixties." (Many Chinese are also receiving analysis through Skype, the free video calling service.) Unlike in the United States, analysts in China, almost all foreigners, are treated like rock stars, encouraging a growing number of Chinese to enroll in psychoanalytic training. "Freud and Asia," the first conference organized by the International Psychoanalytic Association on that continent, was held in Beijing in 2010, a sure sign of the field's shift toward the east.[12]

As well, in their 2008 book *Centers of Power*, London-based Joseph H. Berke and Jerusalem-based Stanley Schneider, both psychoanalysts, found parallels between their field and Kabbalah, the Jewish mystical tradition. Both are ways to help people understand their relationships and spiritual purpose in life, they pointed out. Thus, Kabbalah's core principle of tikkun (restoration and renewal) is seen as analogous to the making whole of a patient's fragmented personality in psychoanalytic therapy.[13] Salman Akhtar's *The Crescent and the Couch* published the same year, meanwhile, explored the crosscurrents between psychoanalysis and Islam; the book was not just about educating therapists who treat Muslims but sought to propel the field into an entirely new orbit.[14] Fethi Benslama's 2009 *Psychoanalysis and the Challenge of Islam* examined the Muslim world's conflict with the West through a psychoanalytic lens, offering an interesting explanation for Islamist fundamentalism. Legitimately blamed in the past for being too rigid and isolated, psychoanalysis is clearly now a flexible field, willing if not eager to find common ground with other belief systems and add to our understanding of important global issues.

Besides the crosspollination of psychoanalysis with other fields, leading scholars in a variety of disciplines continue to find principles of the field useful in their work. Lacanian theory, for example—based on French psychoanalyst Jacques Lacan's thought concerning the relations among language, subjectivity, and society—is still produced in great quantities, year after year, helping to keep Freud's ideas in circulation. In fact, the best-known living philosopher, Slavoj Zizek, is a Freudian, his *How to Read Lacan* a classic on the subject almost as soon as it was published in 2007. In his own re-reading of Freud, based on Lacan's work—especially the latter's 1992 *The Ethics of Psychoanalysis*—Zizek observed how the hundredth anniversary of the publication of *The Interpretation of Dreams* in 2000 was a convenient occasion for critics to pronounce psychoanalysis deader than ever, if that were possible. Books like Todd Dufresne's 2004 *Killing Freud: Twentieth-Century Culture and the Death of Psychoanalysis* declared that neuroscience and psychotropic drugs were the final nails in the coffin, with Freud now lumped together with Marx as the biggest frauds of the last century. Rather than the radical, subversive idea we once thought it was, the notion that our ego was not a master in its own house was tame stuff compared to some of the recent revolutionary findings in neuroscience. Not just theory and therapy but society itself suggested that psychoanalysis was outdated, our tolerance (if not encouragement) of hedonistic pleasures, especially sex, making the entire field not just irrelevant but invalid.[15]

Zizek thought just the opposite. "In the case of psychoanalysis, the memorial service is perhaps a little bit too hasty," he proposed. "It is only today that the time of psychoanalysis has arrived." Lacan's "return to Freud" had inspired his own, each man seeing the unconscious not as the domain of irrational drives (the popular view) but rather, as Zizek put it, "the site where a traumatic truth speaks." Zizek shared Lacan's philosophical approach to psychoanalysis, the existential nature of Freud's theories more important and profound than their clinical applications. Both men believed that even Freud was not aware of the implications of his theories. His ideas could be taken to an entirely new level by applying knowledge from other disciplines as disparate as linguistics, structural anthropology, and mathematical set theory, and from philosophies ranging from Plato to Heidegger. Zizek was sure that Lacan had "unlock[ed] the secret treasures of Freud" and that the possibilities of psychoanalysis were just now being realized.[16]

Since the 1970s, film theorists have also been looking to Lacanian theory for inspiration, demonstrating yet another area where psychoanalysis continues to thrive. In his 2007 *The Real Gaze*, for example, Todd McGowan explained how Lacan's work was so widely recognized in cinema studies by the 1990s that it became simply known as "The Theory." Although "The Theory" fell out of favor in the mid-nineties, McGowan argued it was more useful than ever, reviving Lacan's (and therefore Freud's) work much like Zizek was doing. As others had previously observed, films had much in common with dreams, McGowan suggested: the shared state of illusion, disengagement of critical thought, and the concession to follow rather than lead a narrative were all examples of the relevance of psychoanalytic thought. McGowan believed that Lacanian film theory could open a window into "the potentially radical dimension of the filmic experience," and he proceeded to apply it in his analysis of films by D. W. Griffith, Orson Welles, Steven Spielberg, and others.

Also helping the cause of psychoanalysis is that its full story has yet to be told, rather remarkably. Historians (myself included, of course) continue to pick over the bones of psychoanalysis, either covering ground that has somehow been overlooked or coming at the field from a different angle. George Makari's 2008 *Revolution in Mind*, for example, was a self-described "historical examination of the core questions at the heart of the most influential theory of human inner life"—that the core questions are still there to be asked amazing in itself. As part of their Guides for the Perplexed series, Continuum published a book on Freud in 2008, recognizing that the man's ideas were being applied by current students in many academic fields outside psychoanalysis. And with Celine Surprenant's *Freud: A Guide for the Perplexed*, those in the social sciences and humanities could gain a solid overview of Freud's work without getting lost in the many rabbit holes—quite the valuable resource.[17]

Even better news for the field is that books about contemporary applications of psychoanalysis, and not just its history, are being published. One book in Routledge's Psychoanalysis in a New Key series is Therese Ragen's 2008 *The Consulting Room and Beyond*, for example, a collection of essays examining the current state of the field from both the practitioner's and patient's perspectives.[18] Practitioners too are blazing new trails, proving that it is possible to teach an old dog some new tricks. In her 2008 book *The V-Spot*, for example, Joan Lachkar, an instructor at the New Center for Psychoanalysis, cobbled together theories from a handful of notable analysts to come up with her innovative concept of the V- (for "vulnerable") spot. Fortunately, healing one's V-spot ("a concentration of highly charged emotional sensitivities emanating from early childhood experiences") was possible, Lachkar argued in her book, carrying on the field's proud tradition of helping those who have suffered psychic trauma when they were young.[19]

While its future seems promising for all these reasons, it is more the past that suggests Freud's legacy will not become a footnote in history. Having already survived a litany of major obstacles, worthy contenders, and outright enemies—the Vatican, the counterculture, feminism, a pharmacological revolution, the American insurance industry, not to mention a Great Depression and a couple of world wars—chances are good that psychoanalysis will be around in some form in the twenty-second century. The secret weapon or "killer app" of the talking cure—the recognition and exploration of the unconscious—is something other therapies or pills simply cannot match, this the thing that will keep it alive for generations to come. The darkness of psychoanalysis, typically viewed as a negative, is actually a strong positive, I believe, tempting us to discover what may lie within. Our inherent desire to investigate our inner or other self, to acknowledge what a journalist in the 1920s called "the monkey in the man," ensures that Freud's theories will remain part of our cultural vocabulary. As well, people will no doubt keep dreaming, the interpretation of dreams underscoring another key asset of psychoanalysis as we try to understand our unconscious selves. Attempting to explain the workings of the human mind—by far the most interesting thing in the world, in my opinion—is an unbeatable hand, the pursuit to know why people do the things they do universal to the human experience.

NOTES

Introduction

1. Patricia Cohen, "Freud Is Widely Taught at Universities, Except in the Psychology Department," *New York Times*, November 25, 2007. Classical psychoanalysis requiring sessions four times a week is rare, but psychoanalytic therapy of one to two times per week is currently quite common.
2. Cushman *Constructing the Self, Constructing America*, 149.
3. Cushman, *Constructing the Self, Constructing America*, 148.
4. Zaretsky, *Secrets of the Soul*, 66–67, 76.
5. Cushman, *Constructing the Self, Constructing America*, 187.
6. Hale, *Rise and Crisis of Psychoanalysis*, 234, 360.
7. Zaretsky, *Secrets of the Soul*, 76–77. Freud was not critical of ego psychology per se, but rather suspicious of psychoanalysis in the United States in general.
8. Zaretsky, *Secrets of the Soul*, 3.
9. Zaretsky, *Secrets of the Soul*, 76–77, 79. See Lunbeck's *Psychiatric Persuasion* for more on the transformation of psychiatry from nineteenth-century superstition to twentieth-century science.
10. Cushman, *Constructing the Self, Constructing America*.
11. Susan Cheever, "Mending the Mind," *Harper's Bazaar*, October 1995, 116.
12. Schnog, "On Inventing the Psychological," 3–5.
13. Lasch, *Culture of Narcissism*, 4, 31, 212.
14. Twenge and Campbell, *Narcissism Epidemic*, 1–2.
15. Eric Levin, "Putting Freud on the Couch: Historian Peter Gay Finds a Genius Whose Stature Time Cannot Shrink," *People Weekly*, June 6, 1988, 101.
16. Philip Chandler, "The Psychodynamic Approach," *Psychology Review*, September 2008, 8.
17. These refugees were the only ones permitted to practice psychoanalysis after 1938 in the United States without a medical degree in psychiatry. (According to the "1938 rule" of the American Psychoanalytic Association, only psychiatric physicians could study psychoanalysis at the American

institutes and become members of the association, with the exception of a small number of immigrant analysts who were extremely well known, e.g., Ernst Kris, Theodor Reik, Erik Erikson, and Bruno Bettelheim). After the war, the International Psychoanalytic Association ratified most of the American Psychoanalytic Association's 1938 demands. Freudian psychoanalysis likewise had no place in the American Psychological Association until the 1980s when a number of analysts successfully sued the organization and forced it to create the American Psychological Association's Division of Psychoanalysis, commonly called Division 39.

18. Gellner, *Psychoanalytic Movement*, xiii. For more on Freud's religious beliefs (or lack thereof), see Peter Gay's *A Godless Jew*.

19. Hale, *Rise and Crisis of Psychoanalysis*, 8–9.

20. Burnham, "Influence of Psychoanalysis upon American Culture," 52–72.

21. Burnham, "From Avant-Garde to Specialism," 128.

22. Aron and Henik, eds., *Answering a Question with a Question*; Aron and Henik argue that the historiography of psychoanalytic scholarship is a "Jewish wisdom tradition."

23. Burnham, "From Avant-garde to Specialism." The medicalization of psychoanalysis in the United States has a long and storied history in itself. According to Sandor Ferenczi, A. A. Brill's anger at being replaced as the chief translator of Freud's work into English (after Freud considered his translation of the 1913 *Totem and Taboo* less than satisfactory) led him to urge the New York State Legislature to ban licensing any psychoanalysts (and physicians) not trained in psychiatry to practice. Brill's success resulted in the medicalization of psychoanalysis in America for decades. See Librett, "Interpretation of Medicine or Medicine of Interpretation?," 55–67.

24. Herman, *Romance of American Psychology*, 5–6.

25. Burnham, "Influence of Psychoanalysis upon American Culture."

26. Stepansky, *Psychoanalysis at the Margins*, xi.

27. For a good overview of the contemporary Freud wars, see Librett, "Is Psychoanalysis a Science?," 525–33.

28. Gail A. Hornstein, "The Return of the Repressed: Psychology's Problematic Relations With Psychoanalysis, 1909–1960," *American Psychologist*, February 1992, 254–63.

29. Hornstein, "Return of the Repressed"; Boring, "Was This Analysis a Success?," 4–10. See also Murray, "What Should Psychologists Do About Psychoanalysis?," 150–75.

30. Hornstein, "Return of the Repressed."

31. Hornstein, "Return of the Repressed."

32. Levin, "Putting Freud on the Couch."

33. Suzanne Fields, "What Do We Want? Don't Ask Freud," *Insight on the News*, November 16, 1998, 48.

34. Jerry Adler, "Freud in Our Midst," *Newsweek*, March 27, 2006, 42–49.

35. Dolnick, *Madness on the Couch*.

36. Gellner, *Psychoanalytic Movement*, xi, xix, xxii, xxv.

37. Mark Solms, "Freud Returns," *Scientific American*, May 2004, 82–88. In their *The Freud Files*, Mikkel Borch-Jacobsen and Sonu Shamdasani take issue with comparisons between Freud and "rational scientists" such as Darwin and Copernicus. For a more supportive view, see Gunnar Karlsson's *Psychoanalysis in a New Light*.

38. Engel, *American Therapy*, xi.

39. Jonathan Shedler, "Getting to Know Me: What's Behind Psychoanalysis," *Scientific American Mind*, November–December 2010, 52–56; Avigail Gordon, "Total Treatment: The Benefits of Psychoanalysis Endure," *Psychology Today*, May–June 2010, 18.

1. The New Psychology

1. "Gives $5,000 to Aid Freud," *New York Times*, May 18, 1927.

2. Thomas L. Masson, "Psychoanalysis Rampant," *New York Times*, February 4, 1923.

3. S. T., "A Modern's Search in Science," *Century*, May 1929, 90–95.

4. George Sylvester Viereck, "Is Psycho-analysis a Science?," *Forum*, March 1925, 302–13.

5. "Is Freudianism Destined to Live?," *Current Opinion*, September 1920, 355–58.

6. James S. Van Teslaar, "Freud and Our Frailties," *Forum*, November 1921, 406–11.

7. Joseph Wood Krutch, "Freud Reaches Seventy Still Hard at Work," *New York Times*, May 9, 1926.

8. George Matheson Cullen, "Psycho-Analysis Attacked," *Living Age*, July 9, 1921, 103–8.

9. Raymond Recouly, "A Visit to Freud," *Outlook*, September 5, 1923; Freud, *General Introduction to Psychoanalysis*. In his *The Interpretation of Dreams*, Freud described himself as a "conquistador—an adventurer, if you want to translate the word."

10. Woodbridge Riley, "Freud's Origin," *Outlook*, June 3, 1925, 192–93.

11. Riley, "Freud's Origin"; Janet, *Principles of Psychotherapy*.

12. Cullen, "Psycho-Analysis Attacked."

13. Cullen, "Psycho-Analysis Attacked."

14. Smith Ely Jelliffe, "Unkinking the Mind," *Hygeia*, January 1929, 33–35.

15. Charles Baudouin, "Educating the Will," *Century*, July 1929, 335–43.

16. J. W. Bridges, "Psychoanalysis and Mental Health," *Hygeia*, April 1928, 185–88.

17. Ruth Hale, "Explaining Freud," *The Bookman: A Review of Books and Life*, May 1922, 302–4.

18. E. N. Merrington, "The Limitations of the New Psychology," *Contemporary Review*, April 1926, 500–508.

19. "Is Freudianism Destined to Live?," *Current Opinion*.

20. B. G., "Stravinsky and Psychoanalysis," letter to the editor, *New York Times*, April 27, 1924.

21. Masson, "Psychoanalysis Rampant."

22. "Ransom Note Fails as Smith Girl Clue," *New York Times*, January 27, 1928.

23. "Fashions Have a Clinical Test," *New York Times*, April 25, 1926.

24. Joseph Wood Krutch, "Freud Reaches Seventy Still Hard at Work," *New York Times*, May 9, 1926.

25. Maxwell Bodenheim, "Psychoanalysis and American Fiction," *Nation*, June 7, 1922, 683–84.

26. Viola Paradise, "The Sex Simplex," *Forum*, July 1925, 108–11.

27. Harvey O'Higgins, "Your Other Self," *Outlook and Independent*, November 28, 1928. Even within the Freudian community there was, of course, significant straying from his original theories. Many of Freud's disciples had serious reservations about the Oedipal complex, for example, and Freud himself ultimately modified his views about it.

28. Viereck, "Is Psycho-analysis a Science?"

29. Smith Ely Jelliffe, "Physician, Heal Thyself!," *Forum*, December 1927, 872–78.

30. "Meet Yourself," *New Republic*, December 22, 1926, 129–33.

31. Van Buren Thorne, "Psychoanalysis for International Understanding," *New York Times*, January 13, 1924.

32. "Washington and Wilson Were 'Schizoids,' Roosevelt a 'Syntonic,' Psychoanalyst Says," *New York Times*, June 6, 1924.

33. Harvey Carson Grumbine, "Reaction of a Layman to Psychoanalysis," *Scribner's Magazine*, November 1920, 602–6.

34. "Explaining Psychoanalysis to the Lay Mind," *Current Opinion*, December 1921, 770–72; Brill, *Fundamental Conceptions of Psychoanalysis*.

35. "Warns of Danger in American Life," *New York Times*, June 5, 1927.

36. Charles Baudouin, "Educating the Will," *Century*, July 1929, 335–43.

37. "Presses the Value of Psychoanalysis," *New York Times*, May 22, 1927.

38. L. S. London, "Instruction in Psychoanalysis," letter to the editor, *New York Times*, September 17, 1927.

39. Viereck, "Is Psycho-analysis a Science?"

40. Lucian Cary, "How It Feels to Be Psychoanalyzed," *American Magazine*, May 1925, 29.

41. William Brown, "Psychotherapy," *Century*, May 1929, 1–12.

42. Arthur Clutton-Brock, "Evil and the New Psychology," *Atlantic Monthly*, March 1923, 298–308.

43. Brown, "Psychotherapy."

44. Virginia Therhune Van de Water, "I Am Psychoanalyzed," *Century*, December 1926, 224–229.

45. Cary, "How It Feels to Be Psychoanalyzed."

46. "Confessions of an Ex-Psycho-Analyst," *New Republic*, March 24, 1926, 139–41.

47. S. T., "A Modern's Search in Science"; A. Clutton-Brock, "Psychology and Mysticism," *New Republic*, January 18, 1922, 201–3.

48. Keene Sumner, "What a Psychoanalyst Knows About You and Your Troubles," *American Magazine*, July 1925, 44–45.

49. Sumner, "What a Psychoanalyst Knows About You and Your Troubles."

50. "Can a Man Be His Own Psycho-analyst in Sickness?," *Current Opinion*, May 1922, 659–61; Hingley, *Psycho-analysis*, 659, 660.

51. George Jean Nathan, "Clinical Notes, *American Mercury*, July 1927, 369–71.

52. Nathan, "Clinical Notes."

53. S. T., "A Modern's Search in Science."

54. Jelliffe, "Unkinking the Mind."

55. "Dr. Freud to Head World Foundation," *New York Times*, July 24, 1925.

56. Ewen, PR!, 159–74.

57. Lisa Held, "Psychoanalysis Shapes Consumer Culture," *Monitor on Psychology*, December 2009, 32–34.

58. "Pastor Rakes Quacks in Psychoanalysis," *New York Times*, March 30, 1925.

59. "Declares Freud Devotees Can't Spell Psychoanalysis," *New York Times*, August 27, 1926.

60. "Wife Asks Arrest of Psychoanalyst," *New York Times*, April 8, 1926.

61. "Her Suicide Is Laid to Study of Freud," *New York Times*, January 4, 1922.

62. Masson, "Psychoanalysis Rampant."

63. "Religion Doomed, Freud Asserts," *New York Times*, December 27, 1927.

64. O'Higgins, "Your Other Self," *Outlook and Independent*, November 28, 1928. By the late twenties, Freud's major opponents were not the rationalists but rather the behaviorists, led by John B. Watson, who argued that humans not only did not have a subconscious but no conscious as well, with behavior purely a function of physical reactions.

65. Cornelia Stratton Parker, "The Capital of Psychology," *Survey*, September 1, 1925, 551–55.

66. "Freud Rebuffs Goldwyn," *New York Times*, January 24, 1925.

67. "Freudism Passing from Romance to Reality," *Current Opinion*, December 1920, 839–40.
68. Parker, "The Capital of Psychology."
69. Parker, "The Capital of Psychology."
70. "Freud Aids Opera Singer," *New York Times*, March 30, 1927.
71. "American Loses Suit Against Freud," *New York Times*, May 25, 1927.
72. Cullen, "Psycho-Analysis Attacked."
73. Harvey O'Higgins, "Natural Religion," *Outlook*, March 21, 1928.
74. Merrington, "Limitations of the New Psychology."
75. Merrington, "Limitations of the New Psychology"; Freud, *Psychopathology of Everyday Life*.
76. Merrington, "Limitations of the New Psychology."
77. C. A. Bennett, "Dilemma for Moralists," *Harper's Monthly Magazine*, July 1922, 267–68.
78. "Criticizes Freud as Poor Theologian," *New York Times*, January 23, 1928.
79. "Religion Doomed, Freud Asserts," *New York Times*, December 27, 1927.
80. "Turns Against Freud," *New York Times*, March 19, 1922.
81. "Is Freudianism Destined to Live?," *Current Opinion*, September 1920, 355–58.
82. Van Buren Thorne, "Fact and Fancy in the Science of Psychoanalysis," *New York Times*, October 7, 1923.
83. S. T., "A Modern's Search in Science."
84. Gilbert K. Chesterton, "Game of Psychoanalysis," *Century*, May 1923, 34–43.
85. "Psychoanalysis Fails to Account for the Artist," *Literary Digest*, October 4, 1924, 32.
86. Edna Yost, "Psychoparalysis," *Forum*, July 1928, 112–20.
87. Yost, "Psychoparalysis."
88. Mary Day Winn, "The Gentlemen with the Lamp," *North American Review*, February 1928, 221–25.
89. S. T., "A Modern's Search in Science."
90. Joseph Jastrow, "The Freudian Temper," *Century*, October 1929, 29–38.
91. Jastrow, "Freudian Temper."

2. The Voodoo Religion

1. "Psychoanalysis of Clients Architects Designing Trick," *Washington Post*, August 16, 1949.
2. "Maladies and Malingering," *New York Times*, February 22, 1931.
3. "Down With the Unconscious," *New York Times*, April 28, 1932.
4. Frederick W. Brown, "Leading Scientific Influences," *New York Times*, April 10, 1932.

5. "Psychiatry Stimulates McCormick," *Los Angeles Times*, October 16, 1930.

6. "Would Limit Field of Psychoanalysis," *New York Times*, April 16, 1932.

7. "Would Limit Field of Psychoanalysis," *New York Times*.

8. "Physicians Warned on Intangible Ills," *New York Times*, May 30, 1934.

9. "Psychiatry Not a Parlor Toy, Says Dr. Kirby," *Washington Post*, May 30, 1934.

10. "Lays Mental Quirks to Ills of the Body," *New York Times*, June 3, 1932. Founded in 1911, the American Psychoanalytic Association is the oldest national psychoanalytical organization in the United States and has been part of the International Psychoanalytic Association, the largest worldwide psychoanalytic organization, since its very beginnings. Reflecting mainstream psychiatric theory and treatment (psychodynamic in the past but now biomedical), the American Psychiatric Association was founded in 1921 but its roots could be traced all the way back to 1844.

11. "Dr. Brill Describes Lincoln as 'Manic,'" *New York Times*, June 6, 1931.

12. "Dr. Brill Describes Lincoln as 'Manic,'" *New York Times*.

13. "Asks Psychoanalysis Ban," *New York Times*, June 10, 1931; "Hits Quack Psychiatrists," *New York Times*, November 29, 1931.

14. "Mind Analysis Perils Hinted," *Los Angeles Times*, March 27, 1932.

15. Kathleen McLaughlin, "Calls Hunting for Complexes Perilous Sport," *Chicago Daily Tribune*, August 7, 1931.

16. Lillian G. Genn, "Quit Dissecting Romance," *Washington Post*, October 16, 1932.

17. "Woman Accused as Fake Healer," *New York Times*, December 19, 1933.

18. "Psychoanalysis Institute Opens Here Monday," *Chicago Daily Tribune*, September 30, 1932.

19. "Blame Mental Ills on Trials of Machine Age," *Chicago Daily Tribune*, December 8, 1932.

20. "Psychoanalysis Urged to Test Drivers' Fitness," *Washington Post*, January 29, 1933.

21. "Never Crush Pride, Chief Marital Rule," *Washington Post*, August 11, 1934.

22. "Sees Psychoanalysis No Marital Mediator," *New York Times*, June 12, 1930.

23. W. Beran Wolfe, "The Twilight of Psychoanalysis," *American Mercury*, August 1935, 385–94.

24. Wolfe, "Twilight of Psychoanalysis."

25. "Sees Machine Doom of 'Feeble-Minded,'" *New York Times*, May 8, 1936.

26. "Freud vs. Results," *New York Times*, August 9, 1936.

27. "Freudian Fiascos," *New York Times*, January 14, 1934.

28. "'Silly' Dreams Often Warn Against Disaster—Let This Home Institute Book Tell You How," *Los Angeles Times*, May 7, 1936.

29. Alma Whitaker, "Stars' Queer Complexes Bow to Psychoanalysis," *Los Angeles Times*, February 7, 1932.

30. Frank S. Nugent, "The Screen," *New York Times*, January 13, 1937.

31. B. R. C., "The Screen," *New York Times*, May 22, 1939.

32. "Psychoanalysis to Music," *New York Times*, January 26, 1941. A farce about fraudulent psychoanalysis, *Lady, Behave* had less luck on the Great White Way two years later. The show opened November 16, 1943, at the Cort Theater, moved to the Ambassador after just a week, and closed a couple weeks later, having given a total of twenty-three performances. "A. L. Golden Farce to Close on Dec. 4," *New York Times*, November 27, 1943.

33. Donald Ogden Stewart, "Watch Out for a Trend," *New York Times*, May 4, 1941.

34. Nelson B. Bell, "'Lady in the Dark' Brings Magnificence to Palace Screen," *Washington Post*, April 13, 1944.

35. Nelson B. Bell, "Hitchcock-Bergman Magic Masters New Field in *Spellbound*," *Washington Post*, February 8, 1946.

36. Mae Tinee, "Movies," *Chicago Daily Tribune*, March 3, 1946.

37. Farber and Green, *Hollywood on the Couch*, 70.

38. Gabbard and Gabbard, *Psychiatrist in the Movies*, 60–61.

39. "Concerning Radio," *New York Times*, November 27, 1949.

40. Greer Williams, "The 'Ex-Insane' Revolt," *Forum and Century*, July 1939, 12–17.

41. Odette Pannetier, "Appointment in Vienna," *Living Age*, October 1936, 138–44.

42. Lorine Pruette, "Psycho-Analyzing Psycho-Analysis," *Washington Post*, July 14, 1940; Gontard, *In Defense of Love*.

43. Marcia Winn, "Finds America and Freud Just Can't Agree," *Chicago Daily Tribune*, September 4, 1941.

44. "Psychoanalysis Shows Why Girls Go Boy Crazy," *Los Angeles Times*, December 27, 1933.

45. Livingston Welch, "Freudian Theory," *New York Times*, May 7, 1939.

46. Lionel Trilling, "The Progressive Psyche," *Nation*, September 12, 1942, 215–17.

47. "Asks Substitute for Sex in New Psychoanalysis," *Chicago Daily Tribune*, December 5, 1942.

48. "Hypnoanalysis," *Time*, August 28, 1944, 54–56.

49. William C. Menninger, "An Analysis of Psychoanalysis," *New York Times*, May 18, 1947.

50. W. Menninger, "An Analysis of Psychoanalysis."

51. "Homesick Soldiers," *New York Times*, July 4, 1943.

52. "Hypnosis and Psychoanalysis Combined in New Treatment," *Washington Post*, September 12, 1943.

53. "Psychoanalytic Milestone," *New York Times*, September 19, 1944.

54. "$300,000 Fund Sought," *New York Times*, November 30, 1945.

55. "Group Aid is Urged for Mental Ills," *New York Times*, May 28, 1946.

56. "Freud and the Catholic Church," *Time*, August 4, 1947.

57. "The Couch and the Confessional," *Time*, August 2, 1948, 37–38.

58. Gregory Zilboorg, "Psychoanalysis and Religion," *Atlantic Monthly*, January 1949, 47–50.

59. "Sheen Denounces Psychoanalysis," *New York Times*, March 10, 1947.

60. Fanny Sedgwick Colby, "Monsignor Sheen and Mrs. Luce," *American Scholar*, January 1948, 35–44. Sheen had a history of taking shots at psychoanalysis in his Sunday sermons at St. Patrick's Cathedral. In 1940, for example, Sheen announced from his pulpit that psychoanalysis "keeps the wound of sin open," while confession offered forgiveness, the latter thus far superior to the former. "We do not want our sins explained away, we want our sins forgiven," he added, trying to keep his flock from defecting from his church's ranks. "Msgr. Sheen Says 'Sense of Guilt' Oppresses U.S.," *Washington Post*, March 11, 1940.

61. "Dr. Brill Replies to Msgr. Sheen," *New York Times*, July 6, 1947.

62. "Msgr. Sheen Lays Errors to Press," *New York Times*, July 21, 1947.

63. "Sheen Criticized by Psychoanalyst," *New York Times*, July 22, 1947.

64. "Freud Is Unfair . . . ," *Nation*, August 2, 1947, 115.

65. Colby, "Monsignor Sheen and Mrs. Luce."

66. "Psychiatry Study Urged for Rabbis," *New York Times*, April 1, 1947.

67. John Storck, "The Methods of the Mental Doctors," *New York Times*, December 15, 1946.

68. Lucy Greenbaum, "Dreams—Fantasies or Revelations?," *New York Times*, November 10, 1946.

69. "Psychiatric Testing Urged for Leaders To See if They Are Fit to Wield Power," *New York Times*, May 13, 1946.

70. George S. Stevenson, "Doctors of the Mind," *New York Times*, January 26, 1947.

71. Stevenson, "Doctors of the Mind."

72. Franz Alexander, "Wider Fields for Freud's Techniques," *New York Times*, May 15, 1949.

73. W. Menninger, "An Analysis of Psychoanalysis."

74. W. Menninger, "An Analysis of Psychoanalysis."

75. Mildred Edie Brady, "The Strange Case of Wilhelm Reich," *New Republic*, May 26, 1947, 20–24.

76. Zaretsky, *Secrets of the Soul*, 225; Makari, *Revolution in Mind*, 462. Reich died in prison in 1957.

77. See Christopher Turner's fascinating *Adventures in the Orgasmatron* for the full story.

78. Brady, "The Strange Case of Wilhelm Reich."

79. Norman and Amelia Lobsenz, "Beware of Psychoquacks," *Los Angeles Times*, October 19, 1947.

80. Frederic Wertham, "The Cult of Contentment," *New Republic*, March 29, 1948, 22–25.

81. "Leaders in Debate on Psychoanalysis," *New York Times*, December 11, 1948.

82. Lucy Freeman, "My Experience With Psychoanalysis," *American Mercury*, October 1949, 415–24.

83. Alexander, "Wider Fields for Freud's Techniques."

3. The Horizontal Hour

1. "Aid to Peace Seen in Psychoanalysis," *New York Times*, April 6, 1950.

2. Lucy Freeman, "Increase Is Shown in Psychoanalysts," *New York Times*, May 4, 1951.

3. Frank G. Slaughter, "Tensions That Make Men Sick—and What's to Be Done," *New York Times*, August 13, 1950.

4. Dorothy Ferman, "The Psychoanalytical Joy Ride," *Nation*, August 26, 1950, 183–85.

5. Ferman, "Psychoanalytical Joy Ride."

6. Patrick Mullahy, "On What Makes Man What He Is," *New York Times*, December 17, 1950.

7. Marguerite Clark, "Not Schizophrenic," *Saturday Review*, August 25, 1951, 17–18.

8. Karl Menninger, "What Psychoanalysts Do," *New York Times*, July 8, 1951.

9. Philip Wylie, "What It's Like to Be Psychoanalyzed," *Washington Post and Times-Herald*, October 21, 1956.

10. Wylie, "What It's Like to Be Psychoanalyzed."

11. Frederic Wertham, "Too Much Psychiatry?," *Science Digest*, December 1950, 67–72.

12. Nancy Lynch, "A Walk in a Dark Room," *Mademoiselle*, October 1957, 98–99.

13. "Celibacy Can Be Healthy, Doctor Says," *Los Angeles Times*, January 1, 1956.

14. William Barrett, "New Designs in Our Bohemia," *New York Times*, August 20, 1950.

15. Frederic Wertham, "The Ivory Couch," *Saturday Review*, January 13, 1953, 16–17.

16. Frederic Wertham, "What to Do Till the Doctor Goes," *Science Digest*, December 1950, 67–72.

17. Gregory Zilboorg, "Ignorance—Amateur and Professional," *Science Digest*, December 1950, 67–72.

18. Wertham, "The Ivory Couch."

19. "Patchwork for Psychoanalysis," *Science Digest*, January 1953, 36.

20. Dorothy Roe, "Aunt Hettie's Vapors May Have Been Best," *Washington Post*, April 17, 1952.

21. Helen M. Lynd, "An Undiscovered Language," *Nation*, May 31, 1952, 527– 29.

22. Rollo May, "The Target is Freud," *New York Times*, May 4, 1952.

23. Martin Gumpert, "From Vienna to Park Ave.," *New York Times*, December 27, 1953; Oberndorf, *A History of Psychoanalysis in America*.

24. "Personal Values Held Peace Base," *New York Times*, April 5, 1951.

25. Lynch, "Walk in a Dark Room."

26. "'Nondirective' Mental Treatments," *Science Digest*, November 1951, 38.

27. "Poor Man's Psychoanalysis," *Newsweek*, October 16, 1950, 58–59.

28. "Need of Laws for Mental Therapy Seen," *Los Angeles Times*, April 16, 1950.

29. Morton M. Hunt, "How the Analyst Stands the Pace," *New York Times*, November 24, 1957.

30. Richard L. Frank, "Practice of Psychoanalysis," *New York Times*, March 11, 1954. The "Greenberg Amendment" was ultimately defeated. See Stuart W. Cook and Herbert Zucker's "The Demise of the Greenberg Amendment," *American Psychologist*, September 1954, 549–52.

31. "Rome Clergy Told to Ban Indulgence in Psychoanalysis," *Chicago Daily Tribune*, April 9, 1952.

32. "Pius' View Defined on Psychoanalysis," *New York Times*, September 21, 1952, 31.

33. "Pope Sets Limits to Secrets in Psychoanalysis," *Washington Post*, April 16, 1953.

34. "Message From Pope Strikes at Psychoanalysis," *Los Angeles Times*, February 6, 1955.

35. "Healing of Mind Linked to Spirit," *New York Times*, March 14, 1955.

36. Norman Vincent Peale, "Tell All—and You May Gain Peace," *Washington Post and Times-Herald*, January 22, 195510. Peale's fluency in religion-informed psychiatry or psychiatry-informed religion had deep roots. In the 1930s, Peale and Smiley Blanton, a psychoanalyst, set up a religious-psychiatric clinic next door to the Marble Collegiate Church in Manhattan, where Peale served as pastor for many years. In 1951 the clinic became the American Foundation of Religion and Psychiatry, with Blanton handling the psychotherapy and Peale the spirituality side. The two men also coauthored a number of books, including the 1940 *Faith Is the Answer: A*

Psychiatrist and a Pastor Discuss Your Problems. See Donald Meyer's *The Positive Thinkers* for more on this fascinating collaboration.

37. Leonard Engel, "An Analysis of Sigmund Freud," October 4, 1953, *New York Times.*

38. "Russians Launch Drive Against Psychoanalysis," *Chicago Daily Tribune,* November 26, 1958.

39. "Break With Reds Told by Producer," *Los Angeles Times,* March 5, 1954; Seymour Korman, "He's Psychoanalyzed; Reds Kick Him Out," *Chicago Daily Tribune,* November 24, 1953.

40. Emma Harrison, "Clue to Reds Seen in Parent Hatred," *New York Times,* December 6, 1958.

41. "Racism Is Linked to Inner Conflict," *New York Times,* April 26, 1959.

42. "Cleveland Shops Drop Freud Book," *New York Times,* March 7, 1953.

43. "Cleveland Shops Drop Freud Book," *New York Times.*

44. "Cleveland Eases Censorship Drive," *New York Times,* March 15, 1953.

45. Rudolf Flesch, "Freudians Losers in Science Debate," *Los Angeles Times,* August 9, 1959.

46. "Psychiatrist Loses Out on Tax Cut," *Washington Post,* December 19, 1959.

47. Evan Esar, "It's Funny—and It's Freud," *New York Times,* November 19, 1950.

48. Esar, "It's Funny—and It's Freud."

49. Esar, "It's Funny—and It's Freud."

50. Wolcott Gibbs, "A Couch of My Own," *New Yorker,* February 19, 1955, 29–30.

51. Jules Feiffer, "Couch-as-Couch-Can School of Analysis," *New York Times,* May 18, 1958.

52. Feiffer, "Couch-as-Couch-Can School of Analysis."

53. Feiffer, "Couch-as-Couch-Can School of Analysis."

54. Philip K. Scheuer, "Bud Analyzes the Analysts!," *Los Angeles Times,* March 4, 1958. Another comedienne, Elaine May, married her psychoanalyst, causing quite a sensation in the field because of the taboo of getting involved with a patient.

55. Brooks Atkinson, "At the Theater," *New York Times,* October 19, 1951.

56. Brooks Atkinson, "At the Theater," *New York Times,* December 18, 1953.

57. Brooks Atkinson, "The Haunted Lady," *New York Times,* January 20, 1957.

58. Philip Weissman, "Author or Analyst?," *New York Times,* September 1, 1957.

59. Lawrence Laurent, "Psychoanalysis Applied to TV 'Adult Westerns,'" *Washington Post and Times-Herald,* September 18, 1958.

60. "The Cartoonists Analyze the Couch," *New York Times,* March 8, 1959.

61. Gerald Walker, "Psychoanalysis of the Couch," *New York Times,* April 13, 1958.

62. Walker, "Psychoanalysis of the Couch."

63. "Rapid Gains Seen in Psychoanalysis," *New York Times*, May 10, 1958.
64. "Psychoanalysts Meet," *New York Times*, April 27, 1959.
65. Morton M. Hunt, "How the Analyst Stands the Pace," *New York Times*, November 24, 1957.
66. Hunt, "How the Analyst Stands the Pace."
67. Hunt, "How the Analyst Stands the Pace."
68. Lynch, "Walk in a Dark Room."
69. Lynch, "Walk in a Dark Room."
70. "Mental 'Uprising' Is Linked to Freud," *New York Times*, May 7, 1952.
71. Bennett Cerf, "The Cerfboard," *Los Angeles Times*, July 26, 1953.
72. Emma Harrison, "Physician Urges No-Fee Analysis," *New York Times*, April 29, 1956.
73. Emma Harrison, "Clinic Broadens Mental Aid Base," *New York Times*, March 3, 1957.
74. "'Age of Anxiety' Blamed On Diminished Identity," *Washington Post and Times-Herald*, January 28, 1958.
75. Norma Lee Browning, "We're Not Losing Our Minds!," *Chicago Daily Tribune*, October 4, 1953.
76. Howard Whitman, "New Kind of Calmness Required for Jet Age," *Washington Post and Times-Herald*, March 12, 1957.
77. "Psychoanalysis for Elephant," *New York Times*, August 2, 1953.
78. Joanne Bourne, "We Turn, Nervously, to Canine Neuroses," *New York Times*, January 20, 1957.
79. Bourne, "We Turn, Nervously, to Canine Neuroses."
80. Alson J. Smith, "Be Happy if You're NEUROTIC!," *Chicago Daily Tribune*, March 25, 1956.
81. Jacob Arlow, "Theory, Vienna; Technique Kansas," *Saturday Review*, July 11, 1959, 30.
82. Maurice Zolotow, "The Mystery of Marilyn Monroe," *Washington Post and Times-Herald*, October 2, 1955.
83. Bennett Cerf, "The Late, Late Show-ups," *Los Angeles Times*, September 20, 1959.
84. "Body's Language Is Revealing," *Science Digest*, February 1950, 30.
85. "Wants to Film Psychoanalyst's Couch," *Science Digest*, December 1956, 21.
86. Harry Nelson, "These Psychoanalysts Analyze Other Analysts," *Los Angeles Times*, April 21, 1958.
87. "New Use of Film Cuts Psychoanalysis Time," *Los Angeles Times*, March 22, 1959.
88. Samuel, *Freud on Madison Avenue*, 88–120.

89. "Subliminal Flashes Aid Psychiatry," *Washington Post and Times-Herald*, April 28, 1959.

90. "New Drugs Give Mentally Ill Second Chance," *Chicago Daily Tribune*, August 2, 1956.

91. Morris Kaplan, "Analyst Hits Use of Calming Drugs," *New York Times*, March 11, 1956.

92. Emma Harrison, "Psychic Energy Reduced by Drug," *New York Times*, December 8, 1956.

93. Harry Nelson, "Fantastic Sensations Gained with New Drug," *Los Angeles Times*, March 13, 1958.

94. Joe Hyams, "How a New Shock Drug Unlocks Troubled Minds," *Los Angeles Times*, November 8, 1959.

4. The Pernicious Influence

1. Peter Grose, "African 'Head Shrinker' Mixes Freud, Voodoo," *Washington Post and Times-Herald*, May 5, 1962.

2. John R. Seeley, "The Americanization of the Unconscious," *Atlantic*, July 1961, 68–72.

3. Seeley, "Americanization of the Unconscious."

4. Ralph Schoenstein, "Merrily We Probe Along," *Saturday Evening Post*, August 25, 1962, 10.

5. Schoenstein, "Merrily We Probe Along."

6. Geoffrey Gorer, "Are We 'By Freud Obsessed,'" *New York Times*, July 30, 1961.

7. Joan Ormont, "Analysis of the Analyst's Wife," *New York Times*, November 12, 1961.

8. Ormont, "Analysis of the Analyst's Wife."

9. Ormont, "Analysis of the Analyst's Wife."

10. Rilyn Babcock, "Freud Frappe," *Atlantic*, October 1963, 134–35.

11. David Newman and Robert Benton, "Man Talk," *Mademoiselle*, November 1964, 106–8.

12. Newman and Benton, "Man Talk."

13. Emma Harrison, "Analysis Is Given Rank of Science," *New York Times*, May 5, 1963.

14. Harrison, "Analysis Is Given Rank of Science."

15. "Traffic Department To Use Psychiatry In Safety Program," *New York Times*, September 25, 1963.

16. Lisa Hammel, "Police Studying Human Relations," *New York Times*, February 20, 1966.

17. Harry Nelson, "Psychology of Future Spacemen Explored," *Los Angeles Times*, May 7, 1967.

18. Nelson, "Psychology of Future Spacemen Explored."

19. Norma Lee Browning, "The Case for Psychoanalysis," *Chicago Daily Tribune*, April 9, 1961; Lawrence Galton, "After Fifty Years—An Analysis of Analysis," *New York Times*, February 12, 1961.

20. Browning, "The Case for Psychoanalysis."

21. H. J. Eysenck, "What's the Truth About Psychoanalysis?," *Reader's Digest*, January 1960, 38–43.

22. "Bans Priests from Practice of Freud Plan," *Chicago Daily Tribune*, July 16, 1961.

23. Sister Michael Marie, "The Importance of Freud," *Catholic World*, January 1967, 212–18.

24. "Monks in Psychoanalysis," *Time*, December 2, 1966, 80.

25. Dan L. Thrapp, "Ex-Prior Sees End of Catholicism," *Los Angeles Times*, May 4, 1969.

26. Norma Lee Browning, "Is the Couch on Its Way Out?," *Chicago Daily Tribune*, April 2, 1961.

27. Browning, "Is the Couch on Its Way Out?"

28. Browning, "Is the Couch on Its Way Out?"

29. "Is the Couch on Its Way Out?"

30. Galton, "After Fifty Years—An Analysis of Analysis."

31. Morton Hunt and Rena Corman, "Analysis of Psychoanalysis," *New York Times*, November 11, 1962.

32. Harry Nelson, "New Therapy," *Los Angeles Times*, April 29, 1968.

33. Rasa Gustaitis, "New Treatment for Neurotics Explained," *Washington Post and Times-Herald*, April 15, 1962.

34. Robert Coles, "Doppelganger for Freud," *New York Times*, October 8, 1967.

35. "New Theory Urged to Replace Freud's," *New York Times*, April 7, 1962.

36. William Glasser, "The Research Frontier," *Saturday Review*, March 6, 1965, 54–56.

37. "Boston Debates Freudians' Role," *New York Times*, August 23, 1964.

38. "Boston Debates Freudians' Role," *New York Times*.

39. Willard Clopton Jr., "The Case For and Against the 'Talking Cure,'" *Washington Post*, October 10, 1965.

40. Natalie Jaffe, "Psychiatry Urged to Shift Emphasis," *New York Times*, April 14, 1966.

41. John Leo, "Psychoanalyst Calls Myths a Clue to Reality," *New York Times*, November 25, 1968.

42. John Leo, "Youth Said to See Analysis as Passé," *New York Times*, April 17, 1968.

43. Alan Watts, "The Mystic More Freudian than Freud," *New Republic*, May 1, 1965, 22.

44. Thomas S. Szasz, "How Sick Is Sick?," *New Republic*, May 6, 1967, 21–23.

45. John Leo, "Psychoanalysis Reaches a Crossroad," *New York Times*, August 4, 1968.

46. Leo, "Psychoanalysis Reaches a Crossroad."

47. Willard Clopton Jr., "Psychoanalysts Search for Image," *Washington Post and Times-Herald*, January 14, 1968.

48. "They Want to Be Understood," *Science News*, May 25, 1968, 495.

49. Mortimer Ostow, "Role of Psychoanalysis," *New York Times*, August 12, 1968.

50. Leo, "Psychoanalysis Reaches a Crossroad."

51. Bosley Crowther, "Fellini in a Psychic Wonderland," *New York Times*, November 7, 1965.

52. Josh Greenfeld, "Portnoy's Complaint," *New York Times*, February 23, 1969.

53. Walter Kerr, "Viewer Must Go Some To Reach 'Far Country,'" *Washington Post and Times-Herald*, May 14, 1961; Cecil Smith, "Far Country Puts Freud on Couch," *Los Angeles Times*, November 26, 1961. *A Far Country* actually first appeared on television (*The United States Steel Hour*) but was completely rewritten for the stage.

54. Charles Hamblett, "Film Analysis of Sigmund Freud, *New York Times*, October 29, 1961.

55. Philip K. Scheuer, "'Misfits' a Strange Study of Loneliness," *Los Angeles Times*, February 2, 1961.

56. John Huston, "Focus on 'Freud,'" *New York Times*, December 9, 1962. Klaus Kinski's 1984 *The Secret Diary of Sigmund Freud* was a much lighter depiction of the man and his work, while David Cronenberg's 2011 *A Dangerous Method* focused on the intense relationship between Freud and Jung and the birth of the method.

57. "Freud Family Protests Film," *Los Angeles Times*, August 29, 1963. To his credit, Huston did everything he could to get cooperation from Anna and Ernst Freud but failed.

58. Joe Hyams, "Acting's a Bum's Life in Marlon Brando's Opinion," *Washington Post and Times-Herald*, January 31, 1960.

59. Browning, "Case for Psychoanalysis."

60. Joseph A. Brandt, "Millionaire Found Purpose Late," *Los Angeles Times*, June 28, 1964.

61. Judy Klemesrud, "Dustin Hoffman: From 'Graduate' to Ratso Rizzo, Super Slob," *New York Times*, July 14, 1968.

62. "Sister Blames Ills on Psychoanalysis," *Los Angeles Times*, June 24, 1969.

63. Kitty Kallen, "My 'Lost' Years in Analysis," *Washington Post and Times-Herald*, March 6, 1960.

64. Kallen, "My 'Lost' Years in Analysis."

65. Joe Finnigan, "4 Years' Analysis and She's Ready," *Chicago Daily Tribune*, Match 6, 1960.

66. Clarence Petersen, "Trouble in Tinsel Town," *Chicago Tribune*, July 21, 1962.

67. Hedda Hopper, "Sellers Schedules Interviews Hourly," *Los Angeles Times*, May 15, 1962.

68. Peter Bart, "Natalie in Analysis," *New York Times*, July 3, 1966.

69. Joe Hyams, "Hollywood on the Couch," *Los Angeles Times*, November 19, 1961.

70. Hyams, "Hollywood on the Couch."

71. Hyams, "Hollywood on the Couch."

72. Hyams, "Hollywood on the Couch."

73. Hyams, "Hollywood on the Couch."

74. Aaron Karush, MD, as told to Walter S. Ross, "A Psychiatrist Talks About His Work," *Today's Health*, February 1968, 48–53.

75. Harold Rosenberg, "Psychoanalysis Americanized," *Commentary*, April 1965, 72–74.

76. Magoroh Maruyama, "The Computer that Psychoanalyzes You," *Science Digest*, January 1966, 70–75.

77. Maruyama, "Computer that Psychoanalyzes You."

78. Maruyama, "Computer that Psychoanalyzes You."

79. Flora Rheta Schreiber and Melvin Herman, "The Computer Age in Psychoanalysis," *Science Digest*, January 1965, 18–19.

80. "Grid Puts Executives on the Griddle," *Business Week*, October 18, 1969, 158–60.

81. Martin Tolchin, "Vacations Begun by Psychiatrists," *New York Times*, July 31, 1967.

82. "Psychoanalysis: In Search of Its Soul," *Time*, March 7, 1969, 68–69.

5. The Impossible Profession

1. Peter Osnos, "Analyzing the Analysts," *Washington Post and Times-Herald*, February 28, 1970.

2. Osnos, "Analyzing the Analysts."

3. May V. Seagoe, "Two Studies of Group Encounter Therapy," *Los Angeles Times*, May 17, 1970. The 1969 film *Bob & Ted & Carol & Alice* begins with a weekend self-discovery session designed to get participants to feel rather than think, a pretty realistic portrayal of the real thing.

4. Vivian Gornick, "Through Encounter Land," *Washington Post and Times-Herald*, June 24, 1970.

5. Gornick, "Through Encounter Land."

6. S. I. Hayakawa, "Here's Your Sunday Psychology Lesson," *Chicago Tribune*, December 20, 1970.

7. David Dempsey, "Love and Will and Rollo May," *New York Times*, March 28, 1971.

8. Dempsey, "Love and Will and Rollo May."

9. John L. Hess, "Piaget Sees Science Dooming Psychoanalysis," *New York Times*, October 19, 1972.

10. Jean Murphy, "Analysts Rapped by Libbers," *Los Angeles Times*, September 2, 1971.

11. Anne Roiphe, "What Women Psychoanalysts Say About Women's Liberation," *New York Times*, February 13, 1972; Kate Millett, *Sexual Politics*.

12. Elizabeth Mehren, "Conferences on 'Phases of Eve' Sets a Place at the Feminist Table for Freud," *Los Angeles Times*, March 2, 1984.

13. Nancy Baltad, "Emotional Illness Called Basic Fear," *Los Angeles Times*, March 11, 1973.

14. Anatole Broyard, "Neuroses Are Just No Fun Anymore," *New York Times*, November 30, 1978.

15. Donna Joy Newman, "Which Route Is Best Trip to Emotional Health?," *Chicago Tribune*, March 4, 1975; Yontef, *Awareness, Dialogue, and Process*.

16. Newman, "Which Route Is Best Trip?"

17. Newman, "Which Route Is Best Trip?"

18. "Ann Landers," *Washington Post*, January 26, 1977.

19. "Ann Landers," *Washington Post*.

20. "Amateur Psychoanalyst Is a Tough Nut to Crack," *Los Angeles Times*, May 9, 1971.

21. "Psychoanalysts Urged to Widen Role in Easing Urban Problems," *New York Times*, December 11, 1972.

22. "Acupuncture Tied to Psychoanalysis," *New York Times*, September 29, 1974.

23. "Acupuncture Tied to Psychoanalysis," *New York Times*.

24. Philip Nobile, "A Controversial Discipline," *New York Times*, October 10, 1976; Abrahamsen, *Nixon vs. Nixon*.

25. Israel Shenker, "When a Patient's Dreams Put Him to Sleep, He May Defy Analysis," *New York Times*, December 17, 1976.

26. Shenker, "When a Patient's Dreams Put Him to Sleep, He May Defy Analysis."

27. Suzanne Gordon, "A Freud in Every Pot," *New York Times*, June 7, 1978.

28. Arnold A. Rogow, "Shrink-Shrinking," *New York Times*, April 23, 1978; Szasz, *The Myth of Psychotherapy*; Gross, *Psychological Society*.

29. Judith Martin, "'Interiors': Hollow Voices, Empty Rooms," *Washington Post*, September 29, 1978.

30. Linda B. Martin, "The Psychiatrist in Today's Movies: He's Everywhere and in Deep Trouble," *New York Times*, January 25, 1981.

31. Virginia Adams, "Freud's Work Thrives as Theory, Not Therapy," *New York Times*, August 14, 1979.

32. Adams, "Freud's Work Thrives as Theory, Not Therapy."

33. Jane Shapiro, "Why I Chose Psychoanalysis," *Mademoiselle*, October 1979, 166–167.

34. Donna Joy Newman, "Psychoanalysis Aims to Retrace Path to Self-Esteem," *Chicago Tribune*, September 25, 1979.

35. Newman, "Psychoanalysis Aims to Retrace Path to Self-Esteem."

36. Lance Lee, "American Psychoanalysis: Looking Beyond the 'Ethical Disease,'" *Los Angeles Times*, March 23, 1980.

37. Lee, "American Psychoanalysis: Looking Beyond the 'Ethical Disease.'"

38. Stephanie Mansfield, "Social Worker's Psychoanalysis Ruled a Business Expense," *Washington Post*, May 23, 1980.

39. Larry Kart, "'Impossible Profession' Is Amusing in the Final Analysis," *Chicago Tribune*, October 7, 1981; Malcolm, *Psychoanalysis: The Impossible Profession*.

40. Kart, "'Impossible Profession' Is Amusing in the Final Analysis."

41. Kart, "'Impossible Profession' Is Amusing in the Final Analysis."

42. Bryce Nelson, "Demands of Intense Psychotherapy Take Their Toll on Patient's Spouse," *New York Times*, December 8, 1982.

43. Nelson, "Demands of Intense Psychotherapy Take Their Toll on Patient's Spouse."

44. Nelson, "Demands of Intense Psychotherapy Take Their Toll on Patient's Spouse."

45. Robert Cross, "Inside Chicago's Shrink Factory," *Chicago Tribune*, January 31, 1982.

46. Ralph Blumenthal, "Scholars Seek the Hidden Freud in Newly Emerging Letters," *New York Times*, August 18, 1981.

47. Joan Sweeney, "Is Psychoanalysis Flawed by Freud's Own Failing?," *Los Angeles Times*, February 14, 1984.

48. Ralph Blumenthal, "Freud Archives Research Chief Removed in Dispute Over Yale Talk," *New York Times*, November 9, 1981.

49. Sweeney, "Is Psychoanalysis Flawed by Freud's Own Failing?"

50. Daniel Goleman, "Psychoanalysis Appears Stung but Little Harmed," *New York Times*, January 24, 1984.

51. Robert Coe, "The Intellectual Odyssey of Peter Swales," *Rolling Stone*, September 27, 1984, 25–26.;

52. Goleman, "Psychoanalysis Appears Stung but Little Harmed."

53. Daniel Goleman, "Is Analysis Testable As Science, After All?," *New York Times*, January 22, 1985; Erdelyi, *Psychoanalysis*.

54. Daniel Goleman, "Pressure Mounts for Analysts to Prove Theory Is Scientific," *New York Times*, January 15, 1985.

55. Frederick Crews, "The Future of an Illusion," *New Republic*, January 21, 1985, 28–33; Edelson, *Hypothesis and Evidence in Psychoanalysis*; Grunbaum, *Foundations of Psychoanalysis*.

56. Beverly Beyette, "A Timely Conference on Sigmund Freud," *Los Angeles Times*, April 17, 1986.

57. "75 Years on the Couch," *Washington Post*, May 28, 1986.

58. Dan Wakefield, "My Six Years on the Couch," *New York Times*, December 20, 1987.

59. Wakefield, "My Six Years on the Couch."

60. Thea George, "I Hate Myself! Am I Crazy?," *Mademoiselle*, December 1988, 158–59.

61. Peter Freundlich, "Confessions of a Head Case," *Esquire*, September 1989, 231–34.

62. David Gelman, "Where Are the Patients?," *Newsweek*, June 27, 1988, 62–67.

63. Daniel Goleman, "Institutes to Admit Psychologists," *New York Times*, October 20, 1988.

64. Daniel Goleman, "New Approach Draws from Diverse Schools of Psychotherapy," *New York Times*, February 18, 1988.

65. "McFreud's," *Harper's*, August 1989, 32.

6. The Comeback Couch

1. Sarah Boxer, "Analysts Get Together for a Synthesis," *New York Times*, March 14, 1998.

2. Michael J. Bader, "Post-Modernism and Psychoanalysis: Fiddling While Rome Burns," *Tikkun*, March–April 1997, 15.

3. David Gelman, "Revival Sessions," *Newsweek*, November 25, 1991, 60–61.

4. Robert Pear, "MDS Make Room for Others in Ranks of Psychoanalysts," *New York Times*, August 19, 1992.

5. "The Comeback Couch," *Psychology Today*, July–August 1992, 14.

6. Meryl Gordon, "Analyzing the Analyst's Couch," *New York Times*, March 19, 1992.

7. Gordon, "Analyzing the Analyst's Couch."

8. Michael J. Bader, "That Old Psychoanalysis Just Ain't What It Used to Be," *Tikkun*, July–August 1993, 41.

9. Paul Gray, "The Assault on Freud," *Time*, November 29, 1993, 46.

10. Jonathan Lear, "The Shrink Is In," *New Republic*, December 25, 1995, 18.

11. James Kaplan, "The Final Analysis," *New York Magazine*, October 20, 1997, 26–33.

12. John Hogan, "Why Freud Isn't Dead," *Scientific American*, December 1996, 106.

13. Laura Huggler, "Companies on the Couch," *HR Magazine*, November 1997, 80.

14. Kaplan, "Final Analysis."

15. Kaplan, "Final Analysis."

16. Kaplan, "Final Analysis."

17. Kaplan, "Final Analysis."

18. "Psychoanalysis Scorecard," *Psychology Today*, July–August 1998, 88.

19. Erica Goode, "Return to the Couch: A Revival for Analysis," *New York Times*, January 12, 1999.

20. Ken Adelman, "What Freud Got Right," *Washingtonian*, October 1998, 35–38.

21. Carey Goldberg, "'The Psychs' of August Are Back for Summer Retreats on Cape Cod," *New York Times*, August 9, 1999.

22. "Psychoanalysis Scorecard," *Psychology Today*; Sulloway, *Freud: Biologist of the Mind*.

23. Adam Gopnik, "Man Goes to See a Doctor," August 24–31, 1998, *New Yorker*, 114–21.

24. Gopnik, "Man Goes to See a Doctor."

25. Marci McDonald, "Burying Freud and Praising Him," *U.S. News & World Report*, October 19, 1998, 60–61.

26. Alessandra Stanley, "Mental Images: Psychoanalysis on the Screen," *New York Times*, November 16, 1990. Some scholars argue that *The Snake Pit* may have had a greater influence in regard to psychoanalysis than *Spellbound*. Besides being one of the five top-grossing films of 1949, as Gabbard and Gabbard have pointed out, the movie "question[ed] the [psychiatric] profession's effectiveness from a more informed point of view." Society and institutions dealing with mental illness were often as much the problem as the solution, *The Snake Pit* suggested, anticipating a genre of films that would be made more than a decade later. Gabbard and Gabbard, *Psychiatrist in the Movies*, 60–61.

27. William Grimes, "Buried Themes: Psychoanalyzing Movies," *New York Times*, December 23, 1991.

28. Grimes, "Buried Themes."

29. Stephen Farber and Marc Green, "Star Shrink," *Los Angeles Magazine*, September 1993, 57–58; Farber and Green, *Hollywood on the Couch*.

30. Kaplan, "Final Analysis."

31. Robin Rauzi, "Conscious of His Impact," *Los Angeles Times*, April 6, 2000.

32. Richard Pollak, "Sigmund Freud Redux," *Nation*, December 7, 1998, 14.

33. Richard Brookhiser, "The Final Analysis," *National Review*, November 23, 1998, 41–44.

34. Suzanne Fields, "What Do We Want? Don't Ask Freud," *Insight on the News*, November 16, 1998, 48.

35. Sarah Boxer, "So, Woody, Do You Feel Like Talking About It?," *New York Times*, November 11, 2002.

36. Adam Moss, "New York's Hometown Auteur on Whether a Lifetime of Psychoanalysis Has Paid Off, and Why Kids from Yale No Longer Like Good Movies," *New York Magazine*, October 6, 2008, 172–78.

37. "An Analyst Creates, Well, a Kind of Head Shop," *New York Times*, July 18, 1999.

38. Robert S. Boynton, "Getting Alienated Freudians to Associate," *New York Times*, March 25, 2000.

39. Boynton, "Getting Alienated Freudians to Associate."

40. Erica Goode, "Even in the Age of Prozac, Some Still Prefer the Couch," *New York Times*, January 28, 2003.

41. Sarah Boxer, "Therapists Go Crazy for One in 'Sopranos,'" *New York Times*, December 29, 2001.

42. Deborah Stead, "Therapists Reveal Their New Obsession: 'The Sopranos,'" *New York Times*, May 29, 2001.

43. Stead, "Therapists Reveal Their New Obsession."

44. Dinitia Smith, "Analysts Turn to PR to Market Themselves," *New York Times*, December 9, 2000.

45. Smith, "Analysts Turn to PR."

46. Jennifer Senior, "Sorry, Your Time Is Not Up," *New York Magazine*, August 11, 2001, 24–29.

47. Senior, "Sorry, Your Time Is Not Up"; Firestein, *Termination in Psychoanalysis*.

48. Lev Grossman, "Can Freud Get His Job Back?," *Time*, January 20, 2003, 76–81.

49. Grossman, "Can Freud Get His Job Back?"

50. Mary Carroll, "Why Psychoanalysis?," *Booklist*, December 15, 2001, 685.

51. Goode, "Even in the Age of Prozac, Some Still Prefer the Couch."

52. Interview with anonymous, February 3, 2009.

53. Goode, "Even in the Age of Prozac, Some Still Prefer the Couch."

54. Geraldine Fabrikant, "Spin Doctor Finds a New Calling," *New York Times*, May 28, 2003.

55. Erica Goode, "On Gay Issue, Psychoanalysis Treats Itself," *New York Times*, December 12, 1998.

56. Norman Doidge, "The Doctor Is Totally In," *Maclean's*, May 8, 2006, 40–42.

57. Goode, "Even in the Age of Prozac, Some Still Prefer the Couch."

58. Doidge, "The Doctor Is Totally In."

59. Claudia Kalb, "Interview: Biology of the Mind; A Nobel Prize Winner on Psychiatry, Freud, and the Future of Neuroscience," *Newsweek*, March 27, 2006, 47.

60. Badcock, "Genetic Conflict and Freudian Psychology," 16–19.

61. Doidge, "The Doctor Is Totally In."

62. Stanley Schneider and Joseph H. Berke, "Discovering Oneself: Kabbalah and Psychoanalysis," *Midstream*, November–December 2005, 24–27.

63. Jerry Adler, "Freud in Our Midst," *Newsweek*, March 27, 2006, 42–49.

64. Jamie Chamberlin, "Not Your Parents' Psychoanalysis," *American Psychological Association Monitor*, October 2005, 70.

65. Jamie Talan, "Psychoanalysis Reinterpreted: To Help Keep Freudian Therapy Alive, Researchers are Using Modern Science to Measure the Process," *Newsday*, February 20, 2007.

66. Saki Knafo, "Patching Up the Frayed Couch," *New York Times*, September 9, 2007.

67. Molly Knight Raskin, "The Idea That Wouldn't Die," *Psychology Today*, May–June 2011, 78.

68. Talan, "Psychoanalysis Reinterpreted."

69. Patricia Cohen, "Freud Is Widely Taught at Universities, Except in the Psychology Department," *New York Times*, November 25, 2007.

70. Noah Shusterman, "We're Assigning the Wrong Freud," *Chronicle of Higher Education*, January 12, 2007.

Conclusion

1. Robert Coles, "The Hidden Power of Envy," *Harper's*, August 1995, 20–23.

2. Heather A. Berlin and Christof Koch, "Neuroscience Meets Psychoanalysis," *Scientific American Mind*, April–May 2009, 16–19.

3. Jonathan Shedler, "The Efficacy of Psychodynamic Psychotherapy," *American Psychologist*, February–March 2010, 98–109.

4. Gazzaniga, *Mind's Past*.

5. Kerry Sulkowicz, "Analyze This," *Business Week*, May 19, 2008, 15; Kerry Sulkowicz, "Analyze This," *Business Week*, November 17, 2008, 20.

6. "New Survey Shows Analysts Remain Committed to Work," *Clinical Psychiatry News*, September 2009, 15.

7. "Analyze This," *New York Times*, March 8, 2009, CY4.

8. The website of the HBO drama *In Treatment* is found at http://www.hbo.com/in-treatment/index.html#/in-treatment/about/index.html.

9. "Talk Therapy With Gabriel Byrne," CBS *Sunday Morning*, March 3, 2007.

10. Chip Brown, "How a Zen Master Found the Light (again) on the Analyst's Couch," *New York Times Magazine*, April 26, 2009, 34.

11. Jennings, *Mixing Minds*.

12. Evan Osnos, "Meet Dr. Freud," *New Yorker*, January 10, 2011, 54.

13. "Centers of Power: The Convergence of Centers of Psychoanalysis and Kabbalah," *Reference & Research Book News*, August 2008, 1330.

14. "The Crescent and the Couch: Cross-Currents between Islam and Psychoanalysis," *Reference & Research Book News*, May 2008, 1190.

15. See Zizek, *How to Read Lacan*. Freud's observation that humans were not masters of their own house was the last of three narcissistic "blows." (The first was Copernicus showing that the earth was not at the center of the universe, the second Darwin's revelation that humans and apes were descended from a common ancestor.)

16. Zizek, *How to Read Lacan*.

17. "Freud: A Guide for the Perplexed," *SciTech Book News*, June 2008, 1410.

18. "The Consulting Room and Beyond," *Internet Bookwatch*, December 2008.

19. "The V-spot: Healing Your "V"ulnerable Spot from Emotional Abuse," *SciTech Book News*, June 2008, 1460.

BIBLIOGRAPHY

Abrahamsen, David. *Nixon vs. Nixon: An Emotional Tragedy*. New York: Farrar, Straus and Giroux, 1977.

Akhtar, Salman. *The Crescent and the Couch: Cross-Currents Between Islam and Psychoanalysis*. Lanham MD: Jason Aronson, 2008.

Alexander, Franz, and Thomas Morton French. *Psychoanalytic Therapy: Principles and Application*. New York: Ronald Press, 1946.

Anders, John. *Prescription for Marriage*. New York: Julian Messner, 1933.

Aron, Lewis, and Libby Henik, eds. *Answering a Question with a Question: Contemporary Psychoanalysis and Jewish Thought*. Brighton MA: Academic Studies Press, 2009.

Badcock, Christopher. "Genetic Conflict and Freudian Psychology." *Psychology Review* 7, no. 3 (February 2001): 16–19.

Bakan, David. *Sigmund Freud and the Jewish Mystical Tradition*. Princeton NJ: D. Van Nostrand, 1958.

Beeding, Francis. *The House of Dr. Edwardes*. Boston: Little Brown, 1928.

Benslama, Fehti. *Psychoanalysis and the Challenge of Islam*. Minneapolis: University of Minnesota Press, 2009.

Berg, Charles. *Deep Analysis: A Clinical Study of an Individual Case*. London: George Allen & Unwin, 1946.

Berke, Joseph H., and Stanley Schneider. *Centers of Power: The Convergence of Centers of Psychoanalysis and Kabbalah*. Lanham MD: Jason Aronson, 2008.

Bernays, Edward L. *Propaganda*. New York: Liveright, 1928.

Berne, Eric. *Games People Play: The Psychology of Human Relationships*. New York: Grove Press, 1964.

———. *The Mind in Action: Being a Layman's Guide to Psychiatry*. New York: Simon & Schuster, 1947.

Blanton, Smiley, and Norman Vincent Peale. 1940. *Faith Is the Answer: A Psychiatrist and a Pastor Discuss Your Problems*. Facsimile of the first edition. Whitefish MT: Kessinger, 2007.

Borch-Jacobsen, Mikkel, and Sonu Shamdasani. *The Freud Files: An Inquiry into the History of Psychoanalysis*. Cambridge and New York: Cambridge University Press, 2012.

Boring, Edwin G. "Was This Analysis a Success?" *Journal of Abnormal and Social Psychology* 35, no. 1(January 1940): 4–10.

Brill, A. A. *Fundamental Conceptions of Psychoanalysis*. New York: Harcourt, Brace, 1921.

Brooks, Van Wyck. *The Ordeal of Mark Twain*. New York: E. P. Dutton, 1920.

Buhle, Mari Jo. *Feminism and Its Discontents: A Century of Struggle with Psychoanalysis*. Cambridge: Harvard University Press, 1997.

Burnham, John C. "From Avant-Garde to Specialism." *Journal of the History of the Behavioral Sciences* 15 (April 1979): 128–134.

———. "The Influence of Psychoanalysis upon American Culture." In *American Psychoanalysis: Origins and Development*, edited by J. M. Quen and E. T. Carlson. New York: Brunner/Mazel, 1978.

Buttenwieser, Paul. *Free Association: A Novel*. Boston: Little Brown, 1981.

Church, Archibald, and Frederick Peterson. *Nervous and Mental Diseases*. New York: W. B. Saunders, 1903.

Crews, Frederick C. *Out of My System: Psychoanalysis, Ideology, and Critical Method*. New York: Oxford University Press, 1975.

Cushman, Philip. *Constructing the Self, Constructing America: A Cultural History of Psychotherapy*. Indianapolis: Addison Wesley, 1995.

De Grazia, Sebastian. *Errors of Psychotherapy*. New York: Doubleday, 1952.

Deutsch, Helene. *The Psychology of Women: A Psychoanalytic Interpretation*. New York: Greene and Stratton, 1944–45.

Dolnick, Edward. *Madness on the Couch: Blaming the Victim in the Heyday of Psychoanalysis*. Darby PA: Diane, 1998.

Dufresne, Todd. *Killing Freud: Twentieth-Century Culture and the Death of Psychoanalysis*. London: Continuum Books, 2004.

Edelson, Marshall. *Hypothesis and Evidence in Psychoanalysis*. Chicago: University of Chicago Press, 1984.

Engel, Jonathan. *American Therapy: The Rise of Psychotherapy in the United States*. New York: Gotham, 2008.

Erdelyi, Matthew. *Psychoanalysis: Freud's Cognitive Psychology*. New York: W. H. Freeman, 1985.

Erikson, Erik H. *Gandhi's Truth: On the Origins of Militant Nonviolence*. New York: W. W. Norton, 1969.

———. *Young Man Luther: A Study in Psychoanalysis and History*. London: Faber and Faber, 1959.

Ewen, Stuart. *PR! A Social History of Spin*. New York: Basic Books, 1996.

Eysenck, H. J. *Sense and Nonsense in Psychology*. New York: Penguin, 1956.

———. *Uses and Abuses of Psychology*. New York: Penguin, 1953.

Farber, Stephen, and Marc Green. *Hollywood on the Couch: A Candid Look at the Overheated Love Affair between Psychiatrists and Moviemakers*. New York: William Morrow, 1993.

Fieve, Ronald R. *Moodswing: The Third Revolution in Psychiatry*. New York: Bantam, 1975.

Firestein, Stephen K. *Termination in Psychoanalysis*. Madison CT: International Universities Press, 1978.

Frank, Justin A. *Bush on the Couch: Inside the Mind of the President*. New York: Harper Paperbacks, 2007.

———. *Obama on the Couch: Inside the Mind of the President*. New York: Free Press, 2011.

Freeman, Lucy. *Fight Against Fears*. New York: Crown, 1951.

Freud, Sigmund. *Dream Psychology: Psychoanalysis for Beginners*. New York: James A. McCann, 1921.

———. *The Future of an Illusion*. New York: Horace Liveright and the Institute of Psycho-Analysis, 1928.

———. *A General Introduction to Psychoanalysis*. New York: Horace Liveright, 1920.

———. *Group Psychology and the Analysis of the Ego*. New York: Boni and Liveright, 1922.

———. *The History of the Psychoanalytic Movement*. New York: Nervous and Mental Disease, 1917.

———. *Introductory Lectures on Psycho-Analysis (translated)*. Leipzig-Vienna: Hugo Heller, 1915–17.

———. *Psychopathology of Everyday Life*. London: T. Fisher Unwin, 1901.

———. *Reflections on War and Death*. New York: Moffat, Yard, 1918.

Freud, Sigmund, and Joseph Breuer. *Studies in Hysteria*. Leipzig and Vienna: Deuticke, 1895.

Gabbard, Glen O., and Kim Gabbard. *The Psychiatrist in the Movies*. Washington DC and London: American Psychiatric Press, 1999.

———. *Psychiatry and the Cinema*. Chicago: University of Chicago Press, 1987.

Gay, Peter. *Freud: A Life for Our Time*. New York: W. W. Norton, 1988.

———. *Freud for Historians*. New York: Oxford University Press, 1985.

———. *A Godless Jew: Freud, Atheism, and the Making of Psychoanalysis*. New Haven: Yale University Press, 1987.

Gazzaniga, Michael. *The Mind's Past*. Berkeley: University of California Press, 1998.

Gellner, Ernest. *The Psychoanalytic Movement*. Malden MA: Blackwell, 2003.

Gontard, Gert V. *In Defense of Love: A Protest Against "Soul Surgery."* London: Longmans, Green, 1940.

Gorer, Geoffrey. *The American People.* New York: W. W. Norton, 1948.

Greer, Germaine. *The Female Eunuch.* New York: McGraw-Hill, 1971.

Gross, Martin L. *The Psychological Society: A Critical Analysis of Psychiatry, Psychotherapy, Psychoanalysis, and the Psychological Revolution.* New York: Random House, 1978.

Grunbaum, Adolf. *The Foundations of Psychoanalysis: A Philosophical Critique.* Berkeley: University of California Press, 1984.

Hale, Nathan G. *The Rise and Crisis of Psychoanalysis in the United States: Freud and the Americans, 1917–1985.* New York: Oxford University Press, 1995.

Hall, Calvin S. *The Meaning of Dreams.* New York: Harper, 1953.

Hartmann, Edward von. *Philosophy of the Unconscious.* Berlin: Duncker, 1869.

Herman, Ellen. *The Romance of American Psychology: Political Culture in the Age of Experts.* Berkeley: University of California Press, 1995.

Hingley, R. H. *Psycho-analysis.* New York: Dodd, Mead, 1922.

Hinkle, Beatrice. *The Re-Creating of the Individual: A Study of Psychological Types and Their Relation to Psychoanalysis.* New York: Harcourt, Brace, 1923.

Hook, Sidney, ed. *Psychoanalysis, Scientific Method, and Philosophy.* New York: New York University Press, 1959.

Horney, Karen, ed. *Are You Considering Psychoanalysis?* New York: W. W. Norton, 1946.

———. *New Ways in Psychoanalysis.* New York: W. W. Norton, 1939.

Howard, Jane. *Please Touch: A Guided Tour of the Human Potential Movement.* New York: McGraw-Hill, 1970.

Hubbard, L. Ron. *Dianetics: The Modern Science of Mental Health.* Victoria BC: Hermitage House, 1950.

Huxley, Aldous. *Brave New World.* London: Chatto & Windus, 1932.

Janet, Pierre. *Principles of Psychotherapy.* New York: Macmillan, 1924.

Jennings, Pilar. *Mixing Minds: The Power of Relationship in Psychoanalysis and Buddhism.* Somerville MA: Wisdom, 2010.

Kandel, Eric. *In Search of Memory: The Emergence of a New Science of Mind.* New York: W. W. Norton, 2006.

———. *Psychiatry, Psychoanalysis, and the New Biology of Mind.* New York: American Psychiatric Publishing, 2005.

Karlsson, Gunnar. *Psychoanalysis in a New Light.* Cambridge and New York: Cambridge University Press, 2010.

Katz, Sander (ed.). *Freud: On War, Sex, and Neurosis.* New York: Arts & Science Press, 1947.

Knight, John. *The Story of My Psychoanalysis*. New York: McGraw-Hill, 1950.

Kohut, Heinz. *The Analysis of Self*. Madison CT: International Universities Press, 1971.

Krafft-Ebing, Dr. R. von. *Psychopathia Sexualis*. Philadelphia: F. A. Davis, 1894.

Kugelmann, Robert. *Psychology and Catholicism: Contested Boundaries*. New York: Cambridge University Press, 2011.

Lacan, Jacques. *The Ethics of Psychoanalysis*. London: Routledge, 1992.

Lackhar, Joan. *The V-Spot: Healing Your "V"ulnerable Spot from Emotional Abuse*. Lanham MD: Jason Aronson, 2008.

La Piere, Richard. *The Freudian Ethic: An Analysis of the Subversion of American Character*. New York: Duell, Sloan and Pearce, 1959.

Lasch, Christopher. *The Culture of Narcissism: American Life in an Age of Diminishing Expectations*. New York: W. W. Norton, 1979.

Librett, Jeffrey. "Interpretation of Medicine or Medicine of Interpretation? Some Remarks on State, Religion, and the Question of Lay Analysis." *Journal of Culture and the Unconscious* 1, no. 2 (2001): 55–67.

———. "Is Psychoanalysis a Science?" *Science as Culture* 8, no. 4 (1999): 525–33.

Liebman, Joshua Loth. *Peace of Mind*. New York: Simon & Schuster, 1946.

Lindner, Robert. *Prescription for Rebellion*. New York: Rinehart, 1952.

———. *Rebel Without a Cause: The Story of a Criminal Psychopath*. New York: Grove Press, 1944.

Ludwig, Emil. *Doctor Freud: An Analysis and a Warning*. New York: Hellman, Williams, 1947.

Lunbeck, Elizabeth. *The Psychiatric Persuasion: Knowledge, Gender, and Power in Modern America*. Princeton NJ: Princeton University Press, 1994.

MacIver, Joyce. *The Frog Pond*. New York: George Braziller, 1961.

Makari, George. *Revolution in Mind: The Creation of Psychoanalysis*. New York: HarperCollins, 2008.

Malcolm, Janet. *In the Freud Archives*. New York: Alfred A. Knopf, 1983.

———. *Psychoanalysis: The Impossible Profession*. Northvale NJ: Jason Aronson, 1977.

Mann, John. *Encounter: A Weekend With Intimate Strangers*. Northvale NJ: Jason Aronson, 1970.

Mark, Robert W. *The Horizontal Hour*. New York: David McKay, 1957.

Masson, Jeffrey Moussaieff. *The Assault on Truth: Freud's Suppression of the Seduction Theory*. New York: Farrar Straus & Giroux, 1984.

May, Rollo. *Love and Will*. New York: W. W. Norton, 1966.

McGowan, Todd. *The Real Gaze: Film Theory after Lacan*. Albany: SUNY Press, 2007.

Meyer, Donald. *The Positive Thinkers*. New York: Pantheon Books, 1965.

Millett, Kate. *Sexual Politics*. New York: Doubleday, 1970.

Mitchell, Stephen. *Hope and Dread in Psychoanalysis*. New York: Basic Books, 1993.

Mowrer, O. Hobart. *The Crisis in Psychiatry and Religion*. Princeton NJ: D. Van Nostrand, 1961.

Murray, H. A. "What Should Psychologists Do About Psychoanalysis?" *Journal of Abnormal and Social Psychology* 35, no. 2 (April 1940}: 150–75.

Oberndorf, C. P. *A History of Psychoanalysis in America*. New York: Grune & Stratton, 1953.

Pfister, Joel, and Nancy Schnog, eds. *Inventing the Psychological: Toward a Cultural History of Emotional Life in America*. New Haven: Yale University Press, 1997.

Pfister, Louise. *I Married a Psychiatrist*. New York: Dell, 1961.

Puner, Walker. *Freud: His Life and His Mind*. New York: Grosset & Dunlap, 1947.

Quen, J. M., and E. T. Carlson, eds. *American Psychoanalysis: Origins and Development*. New York: Brunner/Mazel, 1978.

Ragen, Therese. *The Consulting Room and Beyond: Psychoanalytic Work and Its Reverberations in the Analyst's Life*. New York: Routledge, 2008.

Rieff, Philip. *Freud: The Mind of the Moralist*. New York: Viking, 1959.

———. *The Triumph of the Therapeutic: Uses of Faith after Freud*. New York: Harper & Row, 1966.

Roazen, Paul. *The Historiography of Psychoanalysis*. Edison NJ: Transaction, 2000.

———. *The Trauma of Freud: Controversies in Psychoanalysis*. Edison NJ: Transaction, 2002.

Rogow, Arnold A. *The Psychiatrists*. New York: G. P. Putnam's Sons, 1970.

Roth, Philip. *Portnoy's Complaint*. New York: Random House, 1969.

Roudinesco, Elisabeth. *Jacques Lacan & Co.: A History of Psychoanalysis in France, 1925–1985*. Chicago: University of Chicago Press, 1990.

———. *Why Psychoanalysis?*. New York: Columbia University Press, 2001.

Ruitenbeek, Hendrik M., ed. *Psychoanalysis and Contemporary American Culture*. New York: Delta, 1964.

Rycroft, Charles. *Psychoanalysis Observed*. New York: Coward McCann, 1967.

Salter, Andrew. *The Case Against Psychoanalysis*. New York: Henry Holt, 1952.

———. *Conditioned Reflex Therapy: The Direct Approach to the Reconstruction of Personality*. New York: Creative Age Press, 1949.

Samuel, Lawrence R. *Freud on Madison Avenue: Motivation Research and Subliminal Advertising in America*. Philadelphia: University of Pennsylvania Press, 2010.

Schnog, Nancy. "On Inventing the Psychological." In *Inventing the Psychological: Toward A Cultural History of Emotional Life in America*, edited by Joel Pfister and Nancy Schnog. New Haven: Yale University Press, 1997.

Shepard, Martin, and Marjorie Lee. *Marathon 16: New Concept in Therapy*. New York: G. P. Putnam's Sons, 1970.

Skinner, B. F. *Science and Human Behavior*. New York: Macmillan, 1953.

Stepansky, Paul E. *Psychoanalysis at the Margins*. New York: Other Press, 2009.

Sullivan, Harry Stack. *Conceptions of Modern Psychiatry*. Washington DC: William Alanson White Psychiatric Foundation, 1940.

Sulloway, Frank J. *Freud, Biologist of the Mind: Beyond the Psychoanalytic Legend*. New York: Basic Books, 1979.

Surprenant, Celine. *Freud: A Guide for the Perplexed*. London and New York: Continuum, 2008.

Szasz, Thomas S. *The Myth of Mental Illness: Foundations of a Theory of Personal Conduct*. New York: Dell Publishing, 1961.

———. *The Myth of Psychotherapy: Mental Healing as Religion, Rhetoric, and Repression*. New York: Anchor Press, 1978.

Thigpen, Corbett H., and Harvey M. Cleckley. *The Three Faces of Eve*. New York: McGraw Hill, 1957.

Turkle, Sherry. *Psychoanalytic Politics: Freud's French Revolution*. New York: Basic Books, 1978.

Turner, Christopher. *Adventures in the Orgasmatron: How the Sexual Revolution Came to America*. New York: Farrar, Straus and Giroux, 2011.

Twenge, Jean M., and W. Keith Campbell. *The Narcissism Epidemic: Living in the Age of Entitlement*. New York: Free Press, 2009.

Webster, Richard. *Why Freud Was Wrong: Sin, Science, and Psychoanalysis*. New York: Basic Books, 1995.

Winson, Jonathan. *Brain and Psyche: The Biology of the Unconscious*. New York: Doubleday, 1985.

Wortis, Joseph. *Fragments of an Analysis with Freud*. New York: Simon & Schuster, 1954.

Yontef, Gary M. *Awareness, Dialogue, and Process: Essays on Gestalt Therapy*. Gouldsboro ME: Gestalt Journal Press, 1993.

Zaretsky, Eli. *Secrets of the Soul: A Social and Cultural History of Psychoanalysis*. New York: Alfred A. Knopf, 2004.

Zizek, Slavoj. *How to Read Lacan*. New York: W. W. Norton, 2007.